Margarethe von Trotta

Renate Hehr

Margarethe von Trotta

Filmmaking as Liberation

Edition Axel Menges

ISBN 3-930698-76-5

Reproductions: Gábor Mocsonoky, Budapest
Printing and binding: Szegedi Kossuth Nyomda KFT, Szeged

Translation into English: Ilze Klavina
Design: Axel Menges
Editorial supervision: Dorothea Duwe

Jacket photo: Ute Karen Seggelke

6 **Preface**

8 **1. Historical and cultural background**
8 Echoes of childhood and adolescence
9 Early influences and driving forces
10 The great awakening – the movement of '68
12 The New German Cinema
14 *Die verlorene Ehre der Katharina Blum* (*The Lost Honor of Katharina Blum*)
16 The independent women's movement in the '70

19 **2. The filmmaker as a chronicler of her time**
19 The personal is political
21 The objective dimension of the subjective point of view
23 Films for the cinema
Das zweite Erwachen der Christa Klages (*The Second Awakening of Christa Klages*) 23 – *Schwestern oder Die Balance des Glücks* (*Sisters or The Balance of Happiness*) 25 – *Die bleierne Zeit* (*Marianne and Juliane*) 28 – *Heller Wahn* (*Sheer Madness*) 31 – *Rosa Luxemburg* 34 – *Felix* 38 – *Paura e amore* (*Love and Fear)* 38 – *L'Africaine* (*The African Woman*) 41 – *Il lungo silenzio* (*The Long Silence*) 44 – *Das Versprechen* (*The Promise*) 47
51 Films for television
Winterkind (»Winter Child«) 52 – *Mit fünfzig küssen Männer anders* (»At Fifty Men Kiss Differently«) 55 – *Dunkle Tage* (»Dark Days«) 59

62 **3. Characteristic features of Margarethe von Trotta's artistic direction**
62 The dialectics of contemporary events versus state of mind as a formal principle
65 The symbolism of the world of objects – colors and shapes, worlds of light and shadow
69 The mise en scène of the inward story
77 Images that convey mood
78 Cinema as a Gesamtkunstwerk – music, literature, painting
81 Actors

85 **4. Elements of Margarethe von Trotta's individual cinematic language**
85 The destruction of the traditional image of women
86 The search for a new female identity
87 Couples in relationship
90 The other woman as a threat
92 The doppelgänger motif – mirrors and mirror images
96 Switching roles
101 The world inside versus the world outside
The house as a feminine living space 101 – The house as a cave: retreat and inner prison 105 – Imprisoned in the labyrinth of one's own self 108 – Into an unknown, menacing world 111 – The public sphere as prison 114
117 Filmmaking as liberation
Memory: mourning and elixir of life 117 – Speech and feminine language 119 – Filmmaking: conquest of public space and inner liberation 120

123 **Appendix**
123 Notes
124 List of works
127 Films about Margarethe von Trotta and her work
127 Bibliography

Preface

Film interpretation, by its very nature, is always subjective, regardless whether we are talking about a cinemagoer's intuitive approach to understanding a film, or systematic analysis by a film studies scholar. This is because, unlike spoken language, the language of film is not a more or less closed system of symbols, but consists of an infinite number of individual visual and acoustic elements: Dialogues, frames, movements form a plot; a setting establishes the locale and tells its own story; light, colors, music, noises convey additional information, and moods; the perspective and the camera's angle of vision give the position of the spectator in relation to what is happening; the camera's movement gives rise to certain dynamics; the montage of image and sound can bring about leaps in time and space; it creates a rhythm and produces connections and associations.

There is no standard and unambiguous cinematic language, for in theory an unlimited number of modes of expression are available to filmmakers. It is up to the filmmakers to make a choice. That is, they reinvent the language of film every time, so to speak. The more opportunities they have to influence the process of filmmaking, the more distinctive will be the artistic impact they have on the film. Whether and how cinemagoers understand the language of a film depends on how well they recognize its symbols and know how to assign a meaning to them. However, since the language of film cannot be learned like spoken language, but must be decoded anew every time in order for a story to form in the minds of the viewers, the reception of a film involves a large number of factors that vary from individual to individual. Personal and social experiences and interests, background information about the story and the filmmaker's intentions, habitual ways of seeing, familiarity with cinematic conventions and the symbols used, or knowledge of the creative possibilities of the medium can lead to totally different ways of understanding a film. Thus in the reception of films the filmmaker's subjective way of seeing overlaps with that of the cinemagoer. Ideally, the two ways of seeing coincide.

Some time ago, when Dorothea Duwe, the co-owner and editor of Edition Axel Menges, proposed that I should write a book about the films of Margarethe von Trotta, nothing could have been further from my mind. After returning from South America, where I had lived for 11 years – from 1982 until 1993 – and had hardly come into contact with German films, which are almost never shown there, I was in the middle of a process of adjustment. I really had other things to think about, and writing a book was not one of them. Besides, the name Margarethe von Trotta held only vague associations for me: films I had seen a long time ago, in what seemed a different, bygone life with which I had no connection at the time. Nevertheless I began – somewhat offhand – to look into the subject.

As it happened, the first film I saw, ironically, was *Das Versprechen* (*The Promise*), this film about 30 years of German history and their consequences – which I myself encountered with bewilderment in this unfamiliar, incomprehensible, different Wall-less Berlin to which I had returned. And suddenly I began to get a clearer sense of what was going on around me. After that I watched the films in chronological sequence, and as I did so, buried memories stirred within me, memories of long-ago events, of ideas, problems, desires that had once been an important part of my life, an expression of a bygone period characterized by a desperate search for a meaningful life and a better world. My interest was now aroused, and I decided to tackle the project.

At first I saw my preoccupation with Margarethe von Trotta's films as a rediscovery of the past that would help me to overcome the lack of continuity caused by my absence from Germany. I planned both to reappraise the past I had experienced myself – including my personal knowledge and my factual knowledge – and to fill the gap of more than ten years during which I had had no personal experience of developments that had taken place in the European cultural scene. Margarethe von Trotta's films are admirably suited for this undertaking, for they are all subtly nuanced portrayals of the society of their time. It is not so much about telling the story – although the filmmaker frequently takes up contemporary issues of the period – but that she conveys social trends, moods, ideas, and contradictions that mirror the way people experienced life at the time, and that tell a great deal more about the epoch than would the historical events. On the other hand, many elements of the films cannot be understood until they are placed in the context of their time. That is why it was important and necessary to include in the interpretation of the films the historical and cultural background of the period when they were made. It goes without saying that because of the distance in time, and the personal and social changes related to this, certain facets are revealed in retrospect that influence one's understanding.

Moreover, the films convey a subliminal, ambivalent level of meaning which, at the first viewing, often leaves one thoughtful, sometimes perplexed, but also arouses one's curiosity. The late Agnes Fink, who died in 1994, one of the most renowned German actresses of the postwar period, once said of the films of Margarethe von Trotta that they are like an iceberg, only a minute part of which is visible, while the rest is concealed and must be explored. Take the plot, for a start: Hidden behind the individual stories in Trotta's films, which, looked at superficially, seem to be circumstance-related, closer analysis reveals the great existential questions as to identity, the meaning of life, striving for happiness, social responsibility, and individual guilt. The development of the inner conflict and the emotional flow determine the course of the action and the artistic form, in which intuition plays an important part. The structural elements – particularly a system of metaphorical images, antagonisms, symmetries and parallels, and a narrative structure that includes flashbacks, dream sequences, and visions – all serve to condense inner processes and to lend an added dimension to events. Thus even after a comprehensive study of a film each new examination reveals new facets of meaning that give added depth to the intrinsic meaning of the film. It is this complexity that constitutes the artistic quality of Trotta's films which has brought the filmmaker countless awards, and caused Ingmar Bergman to include the film *Die bleierne Zeit* (*Marianne and Juliane*) in his list of the ten films that have influenced him the most.

However, the fact that Margarethe von Trotta's films are so multilayered makes their analysis extraordinarily difficult, and herein lie the limits of this work. If, as here, one is interested in examining the artist's work as a whole, one must inevitably focus on the thematic and structural constants that are the filmmaker's unique artistic trademark, which means that a whole series of specific elements cannot be taken into consideration. Also, the more complex the intrinsic meaning of the film is, the greater is the space given to the subjective aspect of the interpretation, and the more the meaning is condensed metaphorically and symbolically. What is more, to a very large degree, the auteur/filmmaker's subjective worldview and her own artistic concepts find their way into the work of someone like Margarethe von Trotta, and one cannot avoid considering her personality. To do so, I read countless interviews with Margarethe von Trotta published during her more than 20 years of filmmaking; especially helpful were my personal meetings with her, for which she found the time and patience in spite of her many activities. I am sure that my interpretation of her films has been influenced by the mutual affection that developed during our conversations, but also by the additional information Margarethe von Trotta gave me. Aware of this, I stuck close to the films in my interpretation, and not only made them the point of departure of this work, but also constantly went back to them to verify my ideas.

This book would not have been possible without all those who supported it, wittingly or unwittingly. My special thanks to Mr. Thau, the manager of the video archive of the Institut für Theaterwissenschaften of the Freie Universität Berlin, who was inestimably helpful to me in letting me use copies of almost all of Trotta's films; to the press department of WDR, Regina-Ziegler-Film-Produktionen, and Bioskop-Film, who placed film copies and photographic material at my disposal; to the staff of the archives of the Akademie der Künste in Berlin and the Hochschule für Film und Fernsehen Konrad Wolf in Potsdam-Babelsberg, from whom I received a wealth of journalistic material; to Frau Schwinger and Herr Koch of the Staatsoper Stuttgart press office, who supplied photographs of the opera *Lulu* and above all to Margarethe von Trotta herself, who supported this book at all times and in many different ways, as well as to Dorothea Duwe and Axel Menges, without whose encouragement, advice, and generous support this book would never have been written.

Renate Hehr

1. Historical and cultural background

Echoes of childhood and adolescence

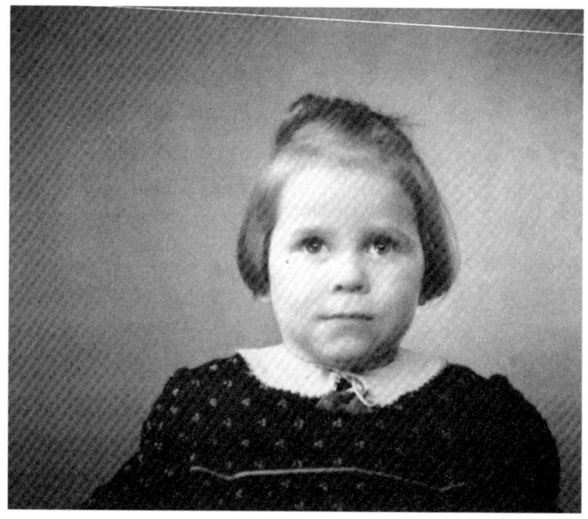

Margarethe von Trotta was born on February 21, 1942, in Berlin, where she spent the first years of her life with her mother. Her experiences during the war and the destruction of the city made lasting impressions on her which she later used in her film *Die bleierne Zeit* (*Marianne and Juliane*) memories of nightly air-raid warnings, of terrified people hurrying downstairs, sitting side by side crowded in the darkness of an air-raid shelter, and listening panic-stricken as the bombs fell.

At the end of the war, she and her mother moved to the Rhineland. There she spent most of her childhood and adolescence. At first she went to a Protestant boarding school, where Christian spiritual exercises dominated the daily schedule. The rigor of the school's rules of behavior, and the inwardly oriented asceticism and antagonism toward pleasure expressed in Protestant ritual, which she experienced as repressive, were the reason for her critical attitude toward the Church as an institution. Catholicism, on the other hand, fascinated her because of the magnificent way the Church portrayed itself, and above all she felt that confession as an act of freeing oneself from sins offered a tempting opportunity for self-purification.

When it became apparent that boarding-school life and the separation from her mother were more than she could take, her mother brought her back home for good, and from then on Margarethe stayed at home alone all day while Frau von Trotta was at work. They had very little money and moved frequently, renting rooms in homes where the only privacy they had was the corner in which they slept. She remembers years of solitude while she was cared for by mostly elderly people in whose homes she and her mother lived. Later, in her films, Trotta features petit-bourgeois elderly women, often prison guards, authoritarian and hostile, who make sure the rules are observed: a type of woman characteristic of the rigid authoritarian structures of post-war German society.

It was in the fantasy world of the countless books she devoured that she found consolation and distraction. On the other hand, she was also an outgoing child and never had trouble finding friends. The time she and her mother spent in an old Godesberg villa seemed like paradise to her: The room they inhabited had a view of the Siebengebirge, and she could play with other children in the garden or go on bike rides to the Rhine after her mother bought her a bicycle at considerable financial sacrifice. Ever since, the river and nature have been synonymous for her with breaking away from the daily round, with peace and quiet.

At that time, the only fixed point in Margarethe von Trotta's life was her mother. The daughter of Baltic aristocrats, Frau von Trotta had emigrated from Russia after the Revolution, but felt like a stranger in Germany all her life and never allowed herself to be Germanized. This sense of alienation and of critical distance from a German identity was passed on to her daughter, who did not become a German citizen until the 1960s on the occasion of her first marriage.

At 42, her mother had made a decision that was very courageous for those times: She intended to raise her daughter single-handedly. Having received the education of an upper-class girl, but no professional training, she supported herself and her daughter by taking temporary jobs. Margarethe von Trotta's close ties to her mother had a decisive influence on her personality: Her mother was her best friend, and Margarethe trusted her implicitly. She could always count on her support – for instance, whenever her mother was summoned to school, which happened frequently, since Margarethe, while intelligent, was a very rebellious child. Her mother taught her that it was not material values that mattered, but personality: She gave Margarethe self-confidence and encouraged her to learn by her own experience, to approach people fearlessly, and to have the courage of her own convictions.

Men had hardly any importance in her childhood. She barely developed a relationship with her father, the painter Alfred Roloff. In Berlin, he would come and visit her once a week in order to take her to the zoo. Later, in the Rhineland, she saw him only during school holidays. He was much older than her mother and had no idea what to do with a small child. All he cared about was painting, and he tried to teach her how to paint and draw. However, since he set her tasks that were too difficult for someone her age, he soon decided she was totally without talent. He died when she was ten, and all she had left were vague memories and warm-hearted, loving letters that she would not be able to appreciate until later. As for her male relatives on her mother's side of the family, she felt they were authoritarian and aggressive. Her mother's brother, who was ill as a result of a war injury, was very irritable and therefore often in a bad mood, while the hus-

1. Margarethe von Trotta, 1944.
2. With a friend, 1953.
3. Villa in Bad Godesberg, where she spent her childhood.
4. The filmmaker's mother, Elisabeth von Trotta gen. Treyden.
5. Margarethe von Trotta with her father Alfred Roloff, 1951

band of her mother's sister, an officer of the old guard, molded by Prussian military ethics, struck her with a whip whenever she disobeyed.

These experiences shaped her world view during her childhood: Her mother was the one who was good, while all the others, particularly men, were evil. The important role she assigned to her mother later found expression in her films. There is hardly one Trotta film where the figure of the mother does not appear, while fathers occur only rarely.

Early influences and driving forces

After she finished school, Margarethe von Trotta, like many young people of her generation, felt the urge to break out of the narrow, claustrophobic atmosphere of Germany, a wish linked in her mind with America as the promised land of freedom and happiness. However, America was far away, and so, after receiving her lesser leaving certificate, spending two years at a commercial school, and a few months working in a Düsseldorf office, she accepted an au-pair job in Paris, the city of light and bohemianism. Half a year later she returned to Düsseldorf, less willing than ever to spend the rest of her life in an office as a secretary. She decided to get a secondary-school diploma, and then began to study art, a move that soon brought her back to Paris for a semester as a visiting student at the Sorbonne. It was this period that was very influential for her personal and artistic development. After she met a group of students who were cinema enthusiasts, she began to take more interest in film than in her studies. Together, she and the students made a few initial short films with an 8 mm camera, followed by the feature *Morte la Mort*, which they financed with donations from relatives and friends.

Even more important, however, was her discovery of the films of the Nouvelle Vague, and especially the films of Ingmar Bergman and the Italian filmmakers, which left deep impressions on her and made her aware of the potential for artistic expression inherent in the medium. Traces of this first encounter with European art film can be recognized in her later works. Like Bergman, she wants to make visible the inner world of her film characters; concentrates on people and faces; makes use of the dynamics between the actors to produce tensions and resolve them; deliberately includes dreams, visions, and fantasies; condenses events considerably. Influences by Michelangelo Antonioni, of whose films *El grido* (*The Cry*) particularly impressed her, can be found in the way she frames her scenes: creating characteristic living spaces for her protagonists by careful, detailed staging of the scene; structuring the frame in clear lines; using colors intentionally; stringently stylizing architectural elements and landscapes to convey moods and atmosphere; visual motifs with constantly recurring symbolism like windows, iron bars, water, mirrors and mirror images, and the use of visual analogies. Another director whose work was to have special importance for her was Alfred Hitchcock. Of course, she was already familiar with his films from German movie houses, but as she began to get involved in the artistic creation of films she gained an increasingly better understanding of his work. What she and Hitchcock have in common particularly, beside the ability to create an atmosphere of unabating, subliminal menace, is the split in the personality of their film characters, in whom good and evil, love and hatred are interdependent and one can be explained by the other.

Paris was also the place where Margarethe von Trotta first became politically aware as a result of meeting communist students who opposed military service in the Algerian War. At the same time she was constantly confronted with questions about the German past, and began to look closely at the problem of the repression of guilt for the crimes of the Nazi period. Also important in her development were the writings of Sigmund Freud, which forced her to deal with the question of how we overcome the past, and how the past is submerged in our subconscious.

It was during this period that Margarethe von Trotta first realized that she wanted to be a filmmaker. In the early 1960s, however, this seemed inconceivable for a woman, and so, for the time being, she continued to study art history. Back in Germany, she soon realized that as a woman she had hardly any job prospects in this profession, whereupon she gave it up and began taking German studies and Romance languages and literatures in Munich. At the same time she studied at a drama school in order to get a step closer to her dream of being a movie director. In 1963 she got her first engagement in Dinkelsbühl, followed by another during the 1964/65 season at the Theater der Altstadt in Stuttgart. In 1964 she married the editor and journalist Jürgen Moeller. She gave birth to their son Felix in 1965. While her son was young, she worked part-time at home as a translator and also played nonrepertory parts, including some at the Theater am Zoo in Frankfurt/Main. Her first husband was a left-winger who was involved in the movement

against rearmament and atomic weapons, and who influenced her own political ideas. He was very supportive of her work in the theater, but when, in 1968, she accepted her first movie role, in Gustav Ehmck's *Schräge Vögel*, he disapproved, for he could not identify with this passion for the cinema. Besides, he was not familiar with the milieu: It frightened him because he realized she was becoming estranged from him. Since she in turn believed that her chances for artistic expression in the theater were decidedly limited, and she was primarily interested in the cinema, she felt that her marriage hindered her in her development. In 1969, she separated from her husband. A divorce followed in 1970 – a step she saw as an act of emancipation, and for which she had found the courage by exploring the new world view of the movement of '68.

The great awakening – the movement of '68

In Germany, the movement of '68 was the social and political background for the rise of a new indigenous film culture that was to have a lasting influence on the personal and artistic development of Margarethe von Trotta and of many other politically committed filmmakers. The expression of a societal change in the 1960s, this movement was supported by the first postwar generation, whose experiences Margarethe von Trotta shares. The rebellion of the movement of '68 was rooted in the »emotionless, dreary '50s« of the Adenauer era, when the work ethic, doing one's duty, and competitiveness were considered to be the highest human values, and everyone was trying to attain prosperity as quickly as possible. The perpetrators of the National Socialist crimes and their fellow travelers were in the saddle once again, and anyone who asked critical questions regarding the past was suspected of Communism, the declared archenemy of a much-invoked freedom and democracy. It was in the years of the German economic miracle (»Wirtschaftswunder«) that the glorification of consumption first began. Advertising created the need for love, tenderness, acceptance, sexuality, freedom, and adventure, while in the schools, the press, and the speeches of soapbox politicians the values of Western democracy were extolled. This was how young people developed ideas about life that were in sharp contrast with social reality, for reality was shaped by pressures to do well, to compete; by authoritarian structures at home, at school, and on the job; and by petit-bourgeois moral precepts. It was this breeding ground that fostered the wish to break out of rigid constraints, and the demand that consumer society should finally make good on its promises of happiness. The early 1960s saw the development of a countercultural protest that was still largely apolitical in its opposition to order, petit-bourgeois values, and authority. Direct and visible expressions of this mood were rock 'n' roll with the new music of Elvis Presley, the Beatles, or the Rolling Stones, and the beatniks, whose outward appearance and attitude provocatively deviated from bourgeois norms.

6. Margarethe von Trotta and Volker Schlöndorff with Alfred Hitchcock, 1972. (Photo: R. H. Binder.)
7. With friends during filming in Morocco, 1961.
8. Volker Schlöndorff, Margarethe von Trotta, Alexander Kluge in 1972 at the Venice Film Festival.
9. Jürgen Draeger, Margarethe von Trotta and Horst Janson in Gustav Ehmck's *Schräge Vögel*, 1968.

In the mid-'60s, the counterculture assumed a more radical character. Within the tradition of protest against rearmament and the atomic weapons of the '50s arose a movement whose criticism was directed against, and called into question, the »practical constraints« and power interests of a capitalist industrial and achievement-oriented society. As a result of the civil rights movement by blacks and Latinos and protests against the Vietnam War in the United States, the younger generation in the Federal Republic of Germany became conscious of racial discrimination, imperialist interventions, and the problems of the third world, and the idealized image of democracy and America lost its glamor. Illusions about democratic freedom were also shattered when the government intensified its actions against the opposition's criticism, and also passed the Notstandsgesetze (»Emergency Powers Act«). The 1966/67 economic crisis called into question the postwar era's formulas for prosperity, safety, and a free market economy and aroused interest in a different social system, such as that propagated by communism. The interest in social change was favored by a general climate of renewal brought about by the fact that official policy was trying, through innovations and reforms, to control a looming economic slowdown and structural crisis. This process of change found its political expression in the great coalition of the SPD (German Social Democratic Party) and the CDU (Christian Democratic Union), which was in keeping with a motto coined by CDU Chancellor Erhard that society should be »brought into alignment« around the Constitution. Against this background sensitivity to political contradictions grew, adding new depth to the protest movement. The younger generation lost its faith in a functioning civil democracy. Only extraparliamentary strategies still promised the chance of radical social change. The APO (»Extraparliamentary Opposition«) was created. Its driving force and organizational sponsors were the Kampagne für Abrüstung (»Campaign for Disarmament«) that had emerged from the Ostermarsch (»Easter Peace March«) movement, and the Sozialistischer Deutscher Studentenbund, or SDS (»Socialist German Students' Association«), around both of which a broad protest movement had formed beginning in 1965. This protest movement contrasted the rigidified power structures in the family, at the university, on the job, and in public life with the utopia of an antiauthoritarian, antihierarchical world order and system of values without oppression and wars. Moved by their horror at the mass slaughter in the Vietnam War, thousands went out in the streets to protest against the United States, and raised the question as to the political and economic causes of wars. The protesters were struck by parallels to the German past, and confronted the generation of their fathers, blaming them for the atrocities of mass murder in the Nazi death camps and in World War II.

Along with this went an intensive scrutiny of art, culture, and the media. The role of the mass media as a means of manipulation was unmasked, and the ultraconservative Springer Press was declared to be the chief enemy. One of the high points of the student revolt was the 1968 attack on the Springer building in Berlin. Cultural orientation underwent a change, expressed as a desire for alternative information, continuing education, the exchange of challenging ideas, and collective experience. A left counterculture was established, giving rise to theater projects like the Berliner Schaubühne or the Grips-Theater, leftist publishing houses, and political bookstores. Radical changes also took place in the private and interpersonal sphere. Conventional bourgeois mores in the marriage or nuclear family were suddenly considered to be outdated. Many young people followed the example of Communes I and II in Berlin and founded their own communes in order to try out new forms of living together. Alternative concepts of education were discussed, and antiauthoritarian education was proposed in lieu of the authoritarian education prevalent in the '50s and '60s. A left-wing pub subculture developed. Gathering places like the »Republikanischer Club« in Berlin provided venues for political discussion and self-assertion, and going to the pub became a political act, a way for people to declare their support for left-wing goals and to express their feeling of solidarity. Even the clothes people wore and the way they addressed each other were a deliberate departure from bourgeois conventions.

Against this background a new public of cinemagoers evolved. Their expectations were radically different from those of traditional moviegoers, who consumed films as entertainment and diversion from day-to-day problems, in the style of the Hollywood dream factory. This new public, influenced by the student movement, expected a visit to the cinema to be a group experience – a collective adventure and an act of self-affirmation. It was of secondary importance whether the communal experience and self-affirmation were provided by a communal sensual experience and shared perception of the world, or by a problem-oriented cinema that offered thought-provoking ideas and a rather rational scrutiny of societal problems. At all events it was crucial that the cinema audience should be offered the correct ideological and political viewpoint and recognize their own experiences.

During this period, opportunities for financing films improved: there was a system of public sponsorship, film prizes were established, and there was now a legally backed framework for co-productions with television, accomplished largely through the efforts of the«Syndikat der Filmemacher« (»Filmmakers' Syndicate«), which was founded in the early 1970s. This way, German film production was at least partially freed from the constraints of competing in the marketplace, and even young, unknown directors were given the opportunity to try out their ideas. At the same time, new marketing opportunities arose, for example, through the »Filmverlag der Autoren« (»Auteurs' Film Distribution Agency«), founded in 1971, and the »Berliner Basis-Film-Verleih« (»Berlin Grass Roots Film Distributors«), founded in 1974. Moreover, beginning in 1970, a group of community movie theaters that screened alternative films were created in several of the larger cities, and in 1972 the commercial art cinema houses formed the »Arbeitsgemeinschaft Kino e.V.« (»Associated Cinemas Inc.«), whose membership rose to over sixty in the years that followed.

The New German Cinema

These conditions encouraged the emergence of a culturally motivated and artistically ambitious cinema – one that was critical of society and supported by a huge number of young engaged filmmakers. This movement, later referred to abroad as the New German Cinema, had one of its strongholds in Munich. Of the many directors who worked there in the late 1960s, some of the best-known included Rainer Werner Faßbinder, Volker Schlöndorff, Werner Herzog, Wim Wenders, Reinhard Hauff, Herbert Achternbusch, and Alexander Kluge. Margarethe von Trotta came into contact with this group when Volker Schlöndorff hired her and Faßbinder for the film *Baal*. From this time on she and the Munich filmmakers were closely associated. She gave up working in the theater, and from 1969 she regularly worked as an actress with Faßbinder, Hauff, Achternbusch, and particularly with Schlöndorff, whom she married in 1971. Influenced by the spirit of the movement of '68, she joined the protesters in the streets and took part in the violent and radical debate around social alternatives. When the first arrests took place in the early '70s, she became a member of the »Rote Hilfe« (»Red Aid«) and supported the struggle against solitary confinement by visiting political prisoners in the Crailsheim prison.

At the time it seemed possible that the world could be changed from the ground up, and the young filmmakers placed cinema at the service of the movement at large. Discussing film projects together, exchanging experiences, collaborating on many different projects, and engaging in joint activities to push through demands relating to cinema politics provided a very fruitful climate for the artistic work of all those involved; in this climate Margarethe von Trotta developed

10. Margarethe von Trotta and Rainer Werner Faßbinder in Volker Schlöndorff's *Baal*, 1969.
11. Margarethe von Trotta in Franz Josef Spieker's *Drücker*, 1969. (Photo: Ingeborg Mutschler.)
12. Margarethe von Trotta with Rainer Werner Faßbinder, 1970.
13. In *Strohfeuer* (*Summer Lightning*), 1972.
14. In *Der Fangschuß* (*Coup de Grâce*), 1976.
15. With Volker Schlöndorff in Morocco, 1974.

her own view of filmmaking and learned her craft. Never losing sight of her goal – to be a film director – she took advantage of her work as an actress to familiarize herself with the process of production and directing, and to gather experience. Starting in 1970, she also began writing scripts for Volker Schlöndorff, and worked with him as an assistant director. In addition to her apprenticeship with Schlöndorff, she was particularly impressed by the working methods of Faßbinder, who always approached shooting with a clear idea of a particular scene, and was thus able to work extremely quickly and economically. She, too, lets her films run in her head countless times even as she is writing the script, and always knows exactly what she wants as soon as she starts shooting. Fundamental to the way the New German Cinema filmmakers saw themselves was their conception of cinema as counterculture, as distinguished, first and foremost, from commercial American cinema. Films were regarded as an instrument that could be used to point out existing needs and problems, provide food for thought, provoke the audience – ideas that Margarethe von Trotta adopted. In the '70s, this requirement led to an ongoing debate on the pros and cons of realism, the point of which was to determine how a complex social reality could best be recorded in the film medium so as to make the audience aware of certain social problems and move them to political action. The results ranged from Berlin working-class films, whose goal was direct politicization, to the semidocumentary forms of Alexander Kluge, to the mise-en-scène of pathos and the perverse identification of someone like Faßbinder. Margarethe von Trotta and Volker Schlöndorff gave some thought to this question as well and finally decided to go back to »something that film has done best since its early days: the description of individuals, by means of which reality can be portrayed without much interpretation or theory«,[1] as Volker Schlöndorff stated.

Margarethe von Trotta kept to this approach in her later films, but combined it with a very characteristic, individual standpoint. Many of the issues preferred by the New German Cinema also appear in Trotta's work, especially her early films, at least as peripheral aspects – the predilection for romantic subjects and motifs; the ambivalence between aggression against others and against oneself; the way she scrutinizes the boundaries of the scope of the action and the consequences of crossing those boundaries; or the analysis of the family and of the German past. But her artistic program included an additional aspect, one that is not encountered in the work of male directors: the influence of the women's movement of the '70s. For the central themes and problems that Margarethe von Trotta continues to examine in her films have to do with the history of that generation of women.

Her influence on Schlöndorff's work during this period becomes apparent particularly in the films *Strohfeuer* (*Summer Lightning*), 1972, and *Der Fangschuß* (*Coup de Grâce*), 1976, whose scripts she co-authored. In both films, the central figure is a woman. The film *Strohfeuer*, based on Margarethe von Trotta's personal experiences, is about a woman who initially regards her escape from her marriage as an act of liberation, but eventually takes refuge in a new relationship that promises to follow the same pattern as the first. The film contains a critical examination not only of the society in which the woman protagonist's every attempt at emancipation turns against her, but also of her own inability to get out of the rut of old behavior patterns. In *Fangschuß* (*Coup de Grâce*), the central figure is the daughter of an impoverished Baltic aristocratic family shortly after the Russian Revolution, who lives alone in a mansion with her aunt. When an international volunteer corps takes up its quarters there in order to suppress the revolt of the Communists, she falls in love with a Prussian officer. At the same time, however, she supports the revolutionaries, and is eventually captured together with a group of partisans. She knows that the anticommunist mercenaries take no prisoners, and although her lover offers to save her, she forces him to execute her himself. In the foreground of the action is the woman's rebellion against the world of the aristocratic landowners and its ossified, outdated norms – a world represented by the protagonist's family and lover. As far as cinematic structure goes, both films bear the stamp of Schlöndorff. On the other hand, Margarethe von Trotta must be credited with the subject matter and its dramatic treatment, and particularly with the personal, emotional, less distant way the subject is approached, characteristics that do not appear in later Schlöndorff films. These films show women who live alone and isolated in a world of men and who are defeated by it. The analysis of relationships between women, a central thematic motif in Trotta's films, is not yet touched upon here.

Die verlorene Ehre der Katharina Blum (*The Lost Honor of Katharina Blum*)

In 1975, together with Volker Schlöndorff, Margarethe von Trotta co-directed *Die verlorene Ehre der Katharina Blum* (*The Lost Honor of Katharina Blum*). The script and the conception of the scenes were a collaborative effort. On location, however, they practiced division of labor: he was in charge of camera work, while she worked with the actors. This film must be seen as an outgrowth of the changed political climate of the early '70s. After peaking in the summer of 1968, the momentum of the student movement had soon diminished. The failure of the campaign against the Notstandsgesetze (»Emergency Powers Act«), and the invasion of Czechoslovakia by the Warsaw Pact states dampened the combative mood and intensified the contradictions within the APO (»Extraparliamentary Opposition«). When the DKP (German Communist Party), the West German offspring of the GDR regime, was founded in September 1968, the »Kampagne für Abrüstung« (»Campaign for Disarmament«) lost its character of a coalition movement and ceased to be viable after 1970. The last delegates' conference of the SDS (»Socialist German Students' Association«) took place in the fall of 1968. What was left were a multitude of political splinter groups, some of whom concentrated on industrial workers as a revolutionary subject and organized themselves in so-called K-groups (»communist groups«), while others relied on a fringe group strategy and got involved in local politics, house occupations, projects to help the homeless and prisoners, or independent youth work. Others again pinned their hopes on »working within institutions«, especially since, in 1969, the great coalition had been replaced by the social-liberal government of Willy Brandt, which promised far-reaching social reforms. The most radical segment pursued the strategy of revolutionary guerrilla warfare and formed the Rote Armee Fraktion (RAF, or »Red Army Fraction«) in order to fight the existing system by violent means from the underground. The actions of this group triggered a hysterical persecution campaign by the state and the conservative press that did not limit itself to those who were directly involved, but included all left-wing groups. Events reached a turning point when Helmut Schmidt took the place of Chancellor Willy Brandt. Pragmatism replaced the planning euphoria that had characterized the first two years of social-liberal government, and the demand for reforms was withdrawn. The 1972 Berufsverbot (ban on the employment of radical teachers and civil servants), as a result of which members of left-wing groups could be excluded from the civil service, aggravated the political climate and provoked resistance. The 1972/73 oil crisis clearly showed how dependent the economy was on petroleum imports, and pushed forward plans involving intensive use of atomic energy, as a result of which the debate about energy policies and criticism of an ideology that advocated growth increased sharply. The result was the rise of a new protest movement that covered a broad spectrum, from citizens' initiative groups, the youth subculture and the squatter scene, communist groups and other left-wing organizations to liberal groups. At the same time the state extended its security and surveillance system in order to stem political resistance.

The hate campaign against so-called »sympathizers« increased to such proportions that even liberal intellectuals were not immune from attack. This was the experience of Heinrich Böll, who subsequently described in a story how a young woman, respectable, full of integrity, is caught in the maze of the police and the judicial system, and is branded as a terrorist by the press. He sent the book to Volker Schlöndorff and Margarethe von Trotta, who saw in it the appropriate subject for a film about how protest had been criminalized.

In their hands the story became a fable with a clear line of conflict: on the one side, an exaggerated caricature of the machine of government oppression and the cynicism of the tabloid press, represented by »Die Zeitung«, its style based on that of the Springer company's *Bild-Zeitung*; on the other side, the domestic servant Katharina Blum as an innocent victim of a hysterical fear of anarchists. Katharina Blum gets in the clutches of the judicial system when she meets Ludwig Götten at a carnival party. Götten has deserted from the army, where he stole the regimental coffers, and is subsequently declared to be an »anarchist« by the police and the press. Katharina falls in love with him and takes him home with her for the night, not knowing that he is being observed by the police. The next morning a police commando, armed to the teeth, force their way into her apartment, but shortly before this Ludwig manages to escape through the ventilation shaft with Katharina's help. She is arrested, which marks the beginning of the systematic destruction of her life. The police, the prosecuting attorney's office, and the press drag the intimate details of her life into the limelight and interpret trivial and mundane facts as circumstantial evidence proving supposedly subversive machinations. The fact that Katharina, a domestic servant, can afford to buy her own apartment and car, her habit of going for long drives on her days

16. Inspector Beizmenne (Mario Adorf) and Katharina Blum (Angela Winkler) during the interrogation. (Photo: Bioskop-Film.)
17. Katharina with Ludwig Götten (Jürgen Prochnow) the morning after they first met. (Photo: Bioskop-Film.)
18. Katharina waiting for the journalist Werner Tötges. (Photo: Bioskop-Film.)

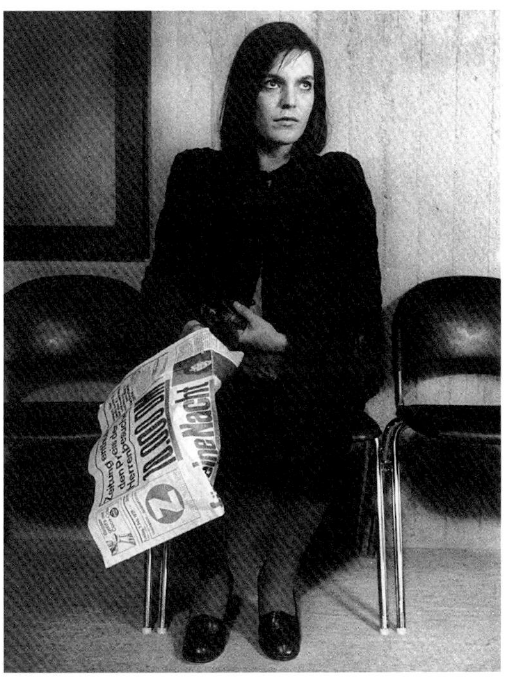

off, and even her customary reserve toward men are enough to convince the police that she is Götten's accomplice, and that her apartment is a meeting place for conspirators. Because of the »Zeitung« report, she is bombarded with obscene calls and letters after her release. What is more, the police have tapped her telephone, and observe her every movement until finally, in a fit of rage, she smashes the furniture of her apartment and flees to her aunt's house. The reporter Tötges questions the inhabitants of the village where she was born as well as Katharina's ex-husband, and distorts their statements so much that they fit in with the image of the anarchist's moll he has been disseminating about Katharina in the »Zeitung«. Suspicion is cast on the aunt who has been defending Katharina to the police: she is accused of being a »sympathizer«, because in the 1930s her father was a Communist. Tötges makes even the positive opinion of Katharina given by her employer, the attorney Blorna, when questioned while on vacation by a »Zeitung« correspondent, mean the opposite. All further attempts by Blorna and his wife to protect Katharina also fail. The prosecuting attorney who is working on the case, Hach, a friend of Blorna's, rejects the latter's intercession on Katharina's behalf, arguing that he is merely doing his job and does not wish to be bothered with it in his free time. The industrialist and professor Stäubleder, a client of Blorna's who once forced his attentions on Katharina, is worried above all that his name might be linked with hers, and refuses to use his good connections with the owner of the »Zeitung« to intervene on her behalf. Tötges does not even shy away from questioning Katharina's critically ill mother in the hospital, causing her to have a relapse and to die. Finally Götten is arrested by a huge number of police, yet the terror against Katharina goes on. The next day, the headline of the »Zeitung« reads, »Götten Arrested, Mother Dies! Anarchist's Moll Claims First Victim!« After this, Katharina makes an appointment with Tötges, allegedly to give him an interview, and shoots him. The film ends with the journalist's funeral, at which his publisher, in his funeral oration, describes the death as an attack on the freedom of the press. The inserted text that follows underlines the cynicism of his words and emphasizes how it relates to reality: »Similarities with certain journalistic practices are neither intentional nor acccidental, but unavoidable.«

The film takes an unambiguous stand: It condemns the methods of the police, the judicial system, and the press, and denounces the misanthropic alliance between the state, the economy, and science. It brings this about by clearly differentiating between good and evil characters. The figure embodied by Katharina is positive through and through: hardworking, thrifty, orderly, trusting, naïve, vulnerable, and loyal to the point of martyrdom. Her aunt is portrayed as someone who has the courage to stand up for her beliefs and stick to her principles, who tries to protect her niece despite all adversities and without fear of possible consequences to herself, and resolutely expresses her protest against the actions of the police. The Blornas champion Katharina's cause far beyond their obligation as her employers. They break off their vacation, try to use their connections in order to put a stop to the psychological terror against her, consider legal steps, and are prepared to lose an important client because his opportunism and egotism fills them with revulsion. All of the characters represent the left-wing liberal spectrum of society in the Federal German Republic of the mid-'70s, which feels helpless and powerless, at the mercy of the power structure of the state and the economy. On the opposing side are representatives of the establishment, who enforce the repressive policy of the state in the name of a fundamental order based on the principles of freedom and law: police commissioner Beizmenne, an affable cynic; prosecuting attorney Hach, an opportunistic social climber; and the unscrupulous reporter Tötges, who will stop at nothing to get a story that will boost sales. The film clearly shows that even the policemen who act friendly toward Katharina only do so, when all is said and done, in order to make her submissive. By stressing their thoughtless inhumanity, their slavish trust in authority, the way they destroy Katharina's identity as a matter of course, and their sordid sexism, their portrayal draws comparisons with the methods of the Nationalist Socialist state. Inner contradictions in the characters are not shown, and here lies an important difference to Margarethe von Trotta's later films.

On the other hand, many of the formal elements of this film do reappear in later Trotta films: memory in the form of flashbacks as an explanation for Katharina's motives; the use of visual metaphors such as glass panes, windows, and mirrors to express vulnerability, fragility, and loss of identity; or the crosshair of a video camera as the cameraman's sights are trained on Ludwig Götten in the beginning sequence; the visual symbolism of spatial relationships between people, and between people and objects, to illustrate closeness and distance or the balance of power; and the use of music, planned down to the last detail.

Die verlorene Ehre der Katharina Blum (*The Lost Honor of Katharina Blum*) was one of the first great successes of New German Cinema. But since the film was attributed primarily to Volker

Schlöndorff, it did not yet bring Margarethe von Trotta the recognition she deserved as a film director. Before she could make her own first film, three more years were to go by. In the meantime, women's opportunities for gaining a foothold as filmmakers had increased considerably. In the first place, since the mid-'60s schools for filmmakers had sprung up that allowed women as well as men access to professional training, and produced a whole series of women film directors. Secondly, public support made it easier to finance films, at least in theory. In practice, however, it was initially still extremely difficult for women filmmakers to get funding for full-length feature films, for funders did not trust their ability. Margarethe von Trotta, too, had to learn things the hard way: she received the money for her own first film only through the influence of her husband Volker Schlöndorff. What determined the emergence of a considerable number of women film directors, finally, was another factor: There was now a large female audience which, influenced by the women's movement, had come to feel the need for a revision of traditional images of women in the cinema.

19. Margarethe von Trotta with Christa Wolf, Akademie der Künste, Berlin (GDR), 1987. (Photo: Christian Kraushaar.)

20. At the 1979 Hamburg Film Festival with Werner Herzog and Norbert Kückelmann. (Photo: Lutz G. Lueen.)

21. At the Viareggio Film Festival 1990 with Lana Gogobaridze (first from left), Vera Chytilowa (next to her right) Martha Meszaros (extreme right), Maja Turowskaja (second from left below) and Agnezka Holland (second from right below).

The independent women's movement in the '70s

From the outset, the career of the feminist filmmakers was linked to the women's movement. It is significant that at the height of the student revolt in September 1968, at the 23d delegates' conference of the Socialist German Student Association (SDS) in Frankfurt, it was none other than the film director Helke Sander who gave a programmatic speech on behalf of the »Aktionsrat zur Befreiung der Frauen« (»Action Council for Women's Liberation«) considered to be the prelude to the independent women's movement. In it the SDS women dissociated themselves from the patriarchal behaviors of their male comrades. During the period that followed, a series of independent women's groups, consisting largely of university students, were formed. The most important result of their work was the Kinderladen (day-care) movement, which created grass-roots day-care centers for children in which alternative ideas on education were put into practice, and which gave the mothers the freedom to do political work. Meanwhile, the first impulses for joint film projects also came from these groups. The first films critically probed into the situation of women in the Federal Republic, and were still imbued with the revolutionary ideals of the student movement. It was during this phase that films like Erika Runge's *Warum ist Frau B. glücklich?* (»Why Is Mrs. B. Happy?«), 1968, Cristina Perincioli's, *Für Frauen, 1. Kapitel* (»For Women, Chapter 1«), 1971, Helma Sanders-Brahms's *Angelika Urban, Verkäuferin* (»Angelika Urban, Salesclerk«), 1969, and Helke Sander's *Eine Prämie für Irene* (»A Bonus for Irene«), 1971, were created. These films were analyses of particular situations that took the form of documentaries, features, and film essays whose goal was to sensitize especially working-class women to the radical political message of the student movement. However, the women directors' personal dismay at women's oppression was not directly recorded in these films.

In spring 1971, after a temporary lull in activities, the women's movement received new impetus when Alice Schwarzer brought the campaign of the Paris women's movement against the antiabortion law to Germany. In June of the same year, a declaration by 374 women appeared in *Stern* magazine under the title »Ich habe abgetrieben« (»I have had an abortion«), and the issue thus reached a broad public for the first time. In the subsequent campaign to abolish Paragraph 218, which prohibited abortions and made them a punishable offence, women from all walks of life expressed their solidarity, and new women's groups and self-help groups related to contraception were formed all over the Federal Republic. In the years that followed self-governing women's centers were created in many of the larger towns. These, in turn, organized a large number of women in so-called encounter groups where women told their stories and questioned female behavior patterns. As awareness of the oppression of women grew, the political focus changed. It was no longer capitalism, but the patriarchal system that was regarded as the main obstacle to the free development of the personality. Women began to protest against their status as objects, and against the female role model in a male-dominated society; they declared that they would use their own authentic experiences, feelings, and needs as the point of departure in their search for a new female identity. A second big campaign, begun in the mid-'70s under the motto »Violence against women«, was directed against violence and rape in marriage, in the field of medicine, in the media, and on the streets. The campaign included public demonstrations against cases of rape; women's self-defense groups, safe houses, and telephone hotlines for women who had been raped were organized; and traditional social institutions like marriage, the family, and the dominant role of men in the economy, politics, and science were called into ques-

tion. Out of the desire for new ways of life developed a large number of alternative women's projects such as bookstores, publishing houses, periodicals, seminars, pubs, and communal households for women. At the same time women felt the need for self-portrayal, for new figures with which they could identify in art, literature, and the media.

One factor favored the continuing development of women's cinema: It was soon possible to create an organizational basis for it, thus providing both an infrastructure and a lobby. In November 1973, Claudia von Alemann and Helke Sander organized the »First International Women's Film Seminar« in Berlin, at which only films by women filmmakers from various countries were shown. The main programmatic focus of this event was on providing »facts and analyses about discrimination against, and oppression of, women in various social spheres.« Further women's film seminars followed in other German cities such as Munich, Erlangen, Frankfurt, and Tutzing. In 1974 Helke Sander founded the journal *Frauen und Film* (»Women and Film«), which became an important discussion forum for the movement. At the 1979 Hamburg Film Festival, the »Verband der Filmarbeiterinnen« (»Association of Women Working in Cinema«) was founded. Margarethe von Trotta was one of those who joined this association, and she is still a member. The association's goal is to represent the interests of the filmmakers before the public. Women also became active in production and marketing: Regina Ziegler and Renée Gundelach founded production companies, and Clara Burckner was involved in the Basis Film Verleih (»Grassroots Film Distribution«). Women also found it easier to access public funding, especially with television companies, which had discovered the issue of women's rights as a new topic. A number of women filmmakers were finally given the opportunity to make their first full-length film. In 1977 not one, but several women film directors met with success. Helma Sanders-Brahms won the Bundesfilmpreis (»Federal German Film Award«) for her film *Heinrich*, Heidi Genée received the »Filmband in Silber« (»Filmstrip in Silver«) for *Grete Minde*, and several film projects by women were given financial awards and other public funding. That same year, Margarethe von Trotta succeeded in obtaining financing for the first feature film under her own direction – *Das zweite Erwachen der Christa Klages* (*The Second Awakening of Christa Klages*), which came out at the beginning of 1978.

The developmental process of the women's movement found expression in the work style and topics chosen by feminist filmmakers. They used film as a medium through which the women's movement could portray itself by taking up such problems as the bringing up of children, abortion, contraception, the situation of women at work, and spousal abuse. But even more important was the fact that cinema was increasingly being used as a means of gaining self-awareness, of questioning one's own existence, searching for a new identity, and presenting the subjective, specifically feminine point of view. Instead of putting the personal below the political, or in contrast to the political, as early feminist documentaries had tended to do, women filmmakers now saw the personal as an expression of political and social oppression, and hence as political. As before, the films portrayed social and private constriction, but now they also examined self-limiting behavior and deformations in lives that were determined by others; the films also pointed out new directions. The analysis of social and private subordinations and constraints, of relationships between men and women, and of women among themselves, became important themes. The filmmakers' own experiences as a form of the authentic expression of female existence increasingly found their way into the films. This reorientation exploded the boundaries of earlier documentaries, and the filmmakers turned to forms that made fictional representation possible. Hybrid forms were created, like the semiautobiographical films of Helke Sander, *Die allseitig reduzierte Persönlichkeit* (*All-Around Reduced Personality*), 1977, and *Der subjektive Faktor* (»The Subjective Factor«), 1981, and especially feature films, in which documentary elements were frequently used in order to stress the historical perspective and the connection between the personal and the political.

Out of the realization that identity is always derived from historical development and that official, male historiographers largely suppress the historical significance of women, feminist cinema discovered the revision of women's history as an important set of issues. The life histories of individual women were a way to get closer to a complex historical reality. One example of such revision was the rediscovery of nineteenth-century feminist activists, a topic chosen by Claudia von Alemann, for instance, in her film *Die Reise nach Lyon* (»Journey to Lyon«), 1980, where she examines Flora Tristan, as well as the historical role of women as keepers of secrets, of magic knowledge – witches, healers, and midwives. Especially significant was the preoccupation with more recent history, and particularly with the role of women in the Third Reich, frequently analyzed by probing traditional family structures and mother-daughter conflicts. The examination of the mother as a negative role model was one of the most important themes, which was linked to the repression of female sexuality and to personality disorders in women, as, for instance, in Jutta Brückner's *Hungerjahre* (»Years of Hunger«), 1980. Often the films took up extreme cases, in which the split in female existence leads to self-destruction and violence against others. The films thus made it possible for the »normal« woman to recognize her own contradictions in the other, the outsider. Some films used this rediscovery of oneself in the other woman as their central theme: Women protagonists who are seemingly well-integrated socially are confronted with women who are social outsiders, as in Ulrike Ottinger's *Bildnis einer Trinkerin* (*Portrait of a Woman Drinker*), 1979, or Helma Sanders-Brahms's *Die Berührte* (*No Mercy, No Future*), 1981.

It is specifically such motifs as the mirroring of differently delineated female figures and the doubling through role reversal, as well as the individual's break-out through self-destruction and violence against others that are central to most of Margarethe von Trotta's films. In addition, her entire opus, as regards both the starting point of her work and her choice of themes, has basically been molded by the development of women's cinema. From the start, she identified with feminist ideas and found in them the explanations for everything she disliked about the movement of '68: the top-heaviness and the unquestioning belief in theory; the crude political language in speeches, the press, and leaflets; and above all the supremacy of the men, who dismissed the demands of the women with the argument that these were a contradiction of secondary importance.

Also, among other things, she supported the campaign against Paragraph 218 by signing the pro-choice declaration in *Stern* and participating in demonstrations. At the same time, however, like the other feminist filmmakers, she regarded her films as her most important contribution to the movement and thought of them as a means of exploring the conditions of female life and as a search for a new image of women both in the literal and figurative sense. Thus the central figures of most of her stories are women whose personal development is linked to the women's movement of the '70s and through whom she introduces her own experiences and autobiographical elements into the films. A constant theme is the struggle for self-realization and the endeavor to transcend personal boundaries through liberation from social and private restraints and dependencies – though she relates this to both men and women. In this struggle, a central role is assigned to the critical scrutiny of private relationships, mainly between women, but also between men and women – relationships that frequently have a political component. The analysis of the role of women in the German past during this century is a theme she has used in several of her films. There are also many side references to the women's movement – for instance, the day-care movement of the early '70s and life in a women's communal household in *Das zweite Erwachen der Christa Klages* (*The Second Awakening of Christa Klages*), the pro-choice campaign and work at an alternative women's magazine in *Die bleierne Zeit* (*Marianne and Juliane*), or the exploration of women's literature from past centuries in *Heller Wahn* (*Sheer Madness*) and *Paura e amore* (*Love and Fear*).

2. The filmmaker as a chronicler of her time

The personal is political

In the course of her artistic career, Margarethe von Trotta has remained true to her roots. For her, as a matter of principle, filmmaking is about the critical exposition of social reality. All her films have a political dimension, which, however, does not arise from a political sense of mission, but from the endeavor to describe and elucidate social phenomena in all their facets, for as a filmmaker she does not feel she is qualified to point out solutions. Rather, she feels that her role is to be the chronicler of her time, for she describes life situations that could have existed as she portrays them. In the process, social relevance and references to reality are not only important criteria that determine the topics she chooses, but also constitute her guideline for treating a topic and for translating it into artistic terms as a whole.

As she writes her scripts and makes preparations for a film, she attaches importance to thorough research of the social background, drawing on the experience of persons with first-hand knowledge and experts. The results of these investigations enter into the films via documentary material, dialogues, behaviors of film characters, the exact representation of the locale, and occasionally through the reconstruction of historical events, thus giving her work an unambiguous social and political chronological specificity. For the same purpose, she uses documentary films such as Alain Resnais's documentation about National Socialist concentration camps *Nuit et Brouillard* (*Night and Fog*) in *Die bleierne Zeit* (*Marianne and Juliane*) and a film about the dying of the forests in *Paura e amore* (*Love and Fear*), archive photos from old newsreels (of the trenches in World War I and the 1918 November Revolt in *Rosa Luxemburg*), excerpts from TV newscasts and reports (about the Vietnam War in *Die bleierne Zeit* (*Marianne and Juliane*); the 1961 building of the Berlin Wall, the 1968 invasion of Prague, organisations who helped people escape from East Germany, and the demonstrations on the 20th anniversary of the Berlin Wall in *Das Versprechen* (*The Promise*), dubbed sections of commentaries by politicians (*Il lungo silenzio / The Long Silence*, *Das Versprechen / The Promise*), fictional TV interviews about the deployment of nuclear weapons in the Federal Republic of Germany in *Heller Wahn* (*Sheer Madness*) and about racism in *L'Africaine* (*The African Woman*), or radio broadcasts about the capacity of rats to survive a nuclear war in *Schwestern* (*Sisters*) and the Italian bribery affair in the early '90s in *Il lungo silenzio* (*The Long Silence*). Even her so-called »private« films, in which not political events, but private experiences set the action going, contain a large number of references to contemporary issues.

Yet even if the idea for a film is based on real, publicly known occurrences, the facts merely constitute the historical background for what chiefly interests Margarethe von Trotta: the con-

22. For the film *Das Versprechen* (*The Promise*) Margarethe von Trotta reconstructed the opening of the Berlin Wall.

crete effects of political events on the life and personality of the individual. In her opinion these are just as political as large-scale politics, and thus she agrees with the credo coined by Italian feminists in the early '70s, »Privato è politico« (»The personal is political«). Behind this view is the realization that the separation of the private and the political is a typically male perspective, while women, who were banished from the public sphere for thousands of years, perceive the world as a constant interchange between the society and the individual, between the public and the private sphere. It is this world view that Margarethe von Trotta incorporates in her films.

When choosing a film subject, to be sure, she normally starts out from a complex of social problems, yet she always seeks the subjective truth behind the public news item, the personal story behind the scenes. The predominant theme that keeps recurring in her work is the investigation of the scope of an individual's development, and of that individual's attempts to cross the boundaries imposed by personality structure and by social circumstances. Here she focuses on persons who suffer the process of history. Social reality, for her, is reality as the individual experiences and uses it. Behind it is the central question: What constitutes a person's existence, and what significance do social conditions and historical processes have for that person? – Margarethe von Trotta realizes that even when our entire lives are overshadowed by major political events, as she shows in *Die bleierne Zeit* (*Marianne and Juliane*) and *Das Versprechen* (*The Promise*), all of us continue to strive to achieve our idea of happiness, for each individual does not perceive history as a historian, but, in most cases, sees it as it is filtered by the mass media or by seemingly disconnected personal experiences. Historical events are reflected in everyday life, they determine our living conditions, demarcate the boundaries within which a personality develops, and shape our ideas, feelings, and actions.

The position Margarethe von Trotta takes in her films is in keeping with women's experience of life, for from time immemorial women's traditional role in society has denied them the illusion that they are able to determine the course of their lives themselves, and has sharpened their awareness of the fact that the vast majority of human beings does not consist of movers and shakers, but of followers at best, while as a rule people are victims who are at the mercy of decisions made by others. More than men, women perceive the effects of political happenings on daily life, and for women surviving catastrophes means, first and foremost, to go on living, to cope with everyday life, and to make sure their own and their family's basic needs are met.

It is this female sphere of experience that Margarethe von Trotta represents in her films. Subjective experience determines the action: the actual drama takes place in camera – in the private sphere, the workaday world. She shows her protagonists on the job, preparing meals, eating at home or at a restaurant, watching TV, reading, in bed at night, shopping, driving or going by train, visiting friends and family, going for walks, or on vacation. However, conflict smolders behind the apparent normality. Social contradictions come to light in relationship with other people, in the confrontation between opposing attitudes toward life, and initially manifest themselves only subliminally, in barely noticeable daily irritations, hidden meanings in conversations, small gestures, moods, nuances in people's behavior, memories, fantasies and dreams that are all too often nightmares. The curve of tension follows the development of the private conflict that constitutes the center of the plot. Yet, again and again, the public sphere irrupts into the private existence, causing consternation, fear, catastrophes. Surveillance and persecution by the police, the destruction of the environment, the standardization of living creatures by genetic engineering, racial or sex discrimination, the arrests of friends and relatives, political assassination or war disturb the characters' inner equilibrium. The media assume the role of the messenger who brings news of a death, and destroy the painstakingly maintained semblance of normality: In *Die bleierne Zeit* (*Marianne and Juliane*) Juliane, vacationing in Sicily, hears of her sister's death through a TV newscast. In the same way, the prosecuting attorney's wife in *Il lungo silenzio* (*The Long Silence*) finds out that her husband has been murdered. The loss of a close friend or relative derails the lives of characters, forces them to make decisions, and makes a conflict come to a head as no other event could, until the tension that has been bottled up for a long time is finally discharged. The eruption takes the form of aggression against one's own person or against others, and reaches its most violent form in the private confrontation with the sister (*Schwestern / Sisters*, *Die bleierne Zeit / Marianne and Juliane*, *Paura e amore / Love and Fear*), the partner (*Rosa Luxemburg*, *L' Africaine / The African Woman*, *Das Versprechen / The Promise*, *Winterkind* / »Winter Child«), the husband of the woman friend (*Heller Wahn / Sheer Madness*), or the Stasi informer (*Das Versprechen / The Promise*). Thus individual social relationships mirror societal dependency relationships and constraints.

For Margarethe von Trotta individual destiny is part of a vast mosaic – contemporary history, composed of countless such fragments. This idea is the theme of *L'Africaine* (*The African Woman*), where the central locale consists of two apartments facing each other across a courtyard. The point here is to observe people from a distance and to reconstruct a more or less random segment of life. In the process reality and imagination merge into a story that contains a piece of social reality. The repeated look across the yard into the neighbor's windows leaves its stamp on the frames of this film, as the narrative point of view increasingly shifts to two old men who, from the detached position of observers, watch from the window of their apartment what is going on behind the other windows , make comments on what they see, and intervene when they consider it necessary. This way, it becomes clear that the story that is being told is one of many. Another scene in the same film underlines this view: From the roof of the editorial office building where he works, Victor, lost in thought, gazes across the roofs of Paris, and the camera follows his gaze. It pans across the long row of closed windows in the courtyards, suggesting that a story is concealed behind each of them. There are similar frames in *Die bleierne Zeit* (*Marianne and Juliane*) and in *Das Versprechen* (*The Promise*), where, through pan shots over the façades of windows, it is suggested that the happenings depicted in the film are about one case among many.

Because attention is directed to private life and day-to-day existence, the film characters are given traits that emphasize their ordinariness. The bank robber, the revolutionary, the militant prosecuting attorney do not want to be tragic heroes, but – like the bank clerk, the secretary, the scientist, the university instructor, the doctor, the housewife, or the journalist – are merely trying to realize their ideals, longings, and dreams, however different these may be. Like all other people, they, too, are faced with existential crises when they become aware of the limits of their potential for development. The ending is left open: the protagonists of Trotta's films gain a partial victory at best, or draw their personal conclusions from their experiences, conclusions that do not rule out hope for the future. This is what gives her characters a common human dimension that makes them representative, and allows members of the audience to recognize their own experiences. In this way Margarethe von Trotta prevents the audience from experiencing cinema as a flight from reality and release of aggression. Instead, she confronts them with reality, causing consternation, but also frequently provoking resistance.

The objective dimension of the subjective point of view

At the beginning of each film there are persons whose special circumstances arouse the filmmaker's interest because they have an inherent potential for conflict. The story comes into being around these people as the auteur endows them with characteristics and distinctive features, as she imagines what their lives might be like, what problems, needs, and wishes they have, and how they relate to other people. At the same time, she is not interested in creating faithful portraits of these persons. Rather, she mixes the characteristics and experiences of a number of persons with her own experiences and enriches them with her imagination in order to show her protagonists in the complex context of their professional life, family, friends, and public and private activities. Only the figure of Rosa Luxemburg is an exception: Here, it was Margarethe von Trotta's purpose to represent the richness of this personality in a portrait. As she does this, living spaces and a web of relationships develop, providing the basic pattern for the story.

Particularly in the films she made during the '70s and '80s, she uses a large number of subsidiary aspects, »piling up as many of the motifs of life as possible around a particular theme«,[2] as Wolfram Schütte remarked, in order to illustrate the multilayered nature and complexity of existence. For Margarethe von Trotta, a character's early history and inner world help constitute this complexity, and she includes these in the form of flashbacks, dream sequences, and visions. She does not avoid inconsistencies and contradictions, but emphasizes them, for she wants to show people with all their good qualities and weaknesses, to understand them, and to make their attitude clear. At the same time, she approaches her film characters with fundamental sympathy. It is true there are negative figures in her films, yet no villains, but also none of those exemplary heroes and heroines who overcome all obstacles à la Hollywood in order to help good to emerge victorious. She neither glosses over human inadequacies, nor does she minimize social obstacles.

An important aspect in creating characters is the authenticity of their experiences. Margarethe von Trotta's film characters are always found rather than invented figures. If the subject of the film is based on contemporary political issues, the director, during the making of the film, works as much as possible with people who have first-hand knowledge of the subject, and includes their experiences and emotions in the film. Thus, in *Das zweite Erwachen der Christa Klages* (*The Second Awakening of Christa Klages*), she used the experiences of Munich nursery-school teacher Margot Szenki, who was a personal acquaintance – in several of her films, Szenki, as a script girl, had been part of the team. She wrote the script for *Die bleierne Zeit* (*Marianne and Juliane*) in collaboration with Christiane Ensslin, whose sister Gudrun, together with other prisoners, died at the high-security prison of Stuttgart-Stammheim in fall 1977. While making *Il lungo silenzio* (*The Long Silence*), the film director drew on the experiences of judges, attorneys, and bodyguards, and above all of family members of victims of the Mafia whom she had contacted. The script of *Das Versprechen* (*The Promise*) is based on countless true occurrences about which Margarethe von Trotta and her co-author, Peter Schneider, learned in conversations with people in both East and West Germany, while the film *Dunkle Tage* (»Dark Days«), which deals with the problem of alcoholism, is based, among other things, on reports by former alcoholics, their family members, and therapists. And even when she creates fictional characters, she uses the behavioral patterns and characteristics of living models: Thus the character Anna in *Schwestern* (*Sisters*) is modelled on a woman friend who committed suicide. Ruth in *Heller Wahn* (*Sheer Madness*) has some of the traits of a female acquaintance whose brother killed himself, and for the figure of Ana in *L'Africaine* (*The African Woman*) she drew on the behavioral patterns of a woman friend who died of cancer.

In this creative process she uses much of the material after careful consideration, combining it in such a way that the audience can recognize connections and understand hidden motives. Other material is adopted simply because it is a given. Often, in interviews, she has been asked about the meaning of certain elements of the plot, and her answer has usually been that she didn't think about it, but borrowed the behavior patterns of real people. Intuition plays a far more important role in this than intellect. The film director rejects everything constructed or intentional as superficial, artificial, and inauthentic. First and foremost, the artistic design of a film is determined by whether Margarethe von Trotta feels a frame, a scene, a character, and the action as a whole hangs together. Like Ingmar Bergman, who once said, »I am a radar unit that registers events and objects and that gives back mirror images of events and objects, mixed with memories, dreams, and ideas. A longing and a striving for form«,[3] she sees herself as a medium that absorbs what is going on around her with open pores, filters it in her subconscious as it were, and transforms it in the film into images, language, and movement. Facts, personal experiences, stories she has heard, many seemingly random and often contradictory impressions mix and fuse with images stored in her subconscious and take on artistic form. Once in a while long-forgotten events reappear as ideas for making a film. Thus Ruth's idiosyncratic habit in *Heller Wahn* (*Sheer Madness*) of making black and white copies of colored pictures goes back to an experience Margarethe von Trotta had in the early 1960s in Paris. Since she was studying art history at the time, she regularly went to the Louvre and often saw an old lady there who copied the works of art in black and white. Not until some time after she had incorporated the motif in the film did she recall where she had had the experience. This is also true of her fascination with the question of sisters. In her films there is a number of similarities with the life of her actual sister, of whose existence she only learned by accident after her mother's death – a circumstance the filmmaker herself attributes to unconscious memories from early childhood.

Thus, in keeping with the perception of the film director as an »auteur«, she claims the right to a completely personal standpoint of her own in order to show her way of seeing reality. As for many women filmmakers who were associated with the women's movement of the '70s, the creative process, for Margarethe Trotta, is always also a way of processing personal experiences, a search for her own identity, a conscious act of dealing with and overcoming problems. One important function of her films is that they are a way of exploring her own self and of sharing information about herself by bringing up problems that are weighing on her mind. The questions and doubts after a friend's suicide, a critical look at problems with personal relationships, the fear that she is incurably ill, her grief after her mother's death, tied to feelings of guilt for leaving her mother alone when she was dying, but also her uneasiness regarding genetic engineering, her fear of dying of atomic radiation after the power plant accident in Chernobyl, or her disappointment about the futility of her generation's attempt to bring about political change – these are only a few of the thematic aspects of her films that can be linked to her biography.

On the other hand, the subjective point of view always has an objective dimension for her as well, for like all other people she sees herself as someone who is socially conditioned, whose perception is founded on a social reality that has concrete existence, that she shares with others, and that is therefore representative. In other words, she adopts one of the great discoveries of the 1970s women's movement as her own: that many other women share your seemingly very personal feelings and your discontent with your own life situation. Emotions, secret desires, memories, and fantasies are thus the key to your own identity and must be taken just as seriously as the external circumstances of your life. Because she trusts her own sensitivity and consciously allows emotion-based decisions to be made as the film takes shape, a great many unconscious elements – ambiguities and contradictions – flow into her films. Thus a second subliminal level of meaning comes into being. What it says was perhaps not meant that way at all, but nevertheless it communicates a multilayered picture of society, of vital consciousness, of the historical moment, and especially of the development of the generation of women to which Margarethe von Trotta belongs.

Films for the cinema

Das zweite Erwachen der Christa Klages (*The Second Awakening of Christa Klages*)

The first film Margarethe von Trotta directed herself reflects the high spirits of the women's movement in the '70s. This film, which she was later to describe as naïve, already introduces a central subject of her work: the exploration of women's living conditions caught between social conventions and constraints on the one hand – in this case, a bourgeois marriage and traditional ideas about childrearing – and striving for self-realization and emancipation on the other. The film met with the general approval of the public and critics alike. It won the Filmband in Silber (»Filmstrip in Silver«) award of the German Filmpreis (»Federal German Film Prize«) for the production, and the Filmband in Gold for Tina Engel's portrayal of the title character.

The focus of the film is the story of Christa Klages, who, together with two friends, Wolfgang and Werner, robs a bank in order to save the child-care center she and a group of women have built up. During her subsequent flight, her path crosses that of two other women: her former schoolmate Ingrid, whose absentee husband is an army officer, and who lives in a new housing development, and Lena, the conservative and overly correct bank clerk whom Christa took hostage during the robbery. As they learn from each other, this encounter causes all three of them to change their outlook on life.

Christa represents the type of woman produced by the women's movement of the '70s. She has broken out of an unsatisfactory marriage to create a new way of life together with other

23. Margarethe von Trotta with cameraman Franz Rath during the shooting of *Das zweite Erwachen der Christa Klages* (*The Second Awakening of Christa Klages*).

women. She and her five-year-old daughter live in a women's communal household, and Christa works as a preschool teacher in the day-care center the women run jointly. Her attitude toward social institutions like marriage, state, and church is critical. She deliberately disregards conventional feminine patterns of behavior. When the day-care center is in danger of being closed because the women can no longer scrape together the rent, Christa, without further ado, decides to rob a bank. By doing so she intends to defend her hard-won way of life, yet during her subsequent flight she realizes that her action has had the exact opposite result. Gradually she loses all she has. Wolfgang is arrested by the police soon after the robbery. Since she and Werner are subsequently connected with the bank robbery and are sought by the police, she can no longer return to her women friends and her daughter. So as not to be recognized, she is forced to dye her hair and to change the way she dresses; as a result, even her external appearance becomes more and more unfamiliar to her. Moreover, she is unable to use the stolen money for the intended purpose. Wolfgang's friend Hans, a small-town clergyman at whose house she and Werner first take refuge in order to persuade him to give the money to the day-care center as a supposed donation from his church, refuses to support them. Her former schoolmate Ingrid, at whose house the two then hide out, does agree, after initially dragging her feet, to pass the money on to Christa's friends, but the friends do not want to accept it. Soon after this, she loses Werner as well. He is shot by a policeman when he draws attention to himself by a stroke of bad luck, and Christa has to continue her flight by herself. With the help of Hans and Ingrid, she leaves Germany to find a home in one of the agricultural communes in Portugal founded after the Carnation Revolution. There, though she is living in a community again, she continues to be a stranger, an outsider, particularly because she doesn't know the language. When Ingrid visits her, the peasants are upset by the friendship between the two women, and they have to return to Germany. As a last act of self-surrender, Christa leaves behind the money. In Munich, she rents an empty apartment and lapses into bouts of depression that almost drive her to suicide. At the last minute, she comes to realize that she must face reality, and she goes back to her daughter at the commune. Soon thereafter, she is recognized and put under arrest. But when she is confronted with Lena, Lena surprisingly declares that Christa cannot possibly have been the bank robber. Now Christa finally realizes that the only chance for women to oppose the restrictions they are subjected to in a male-dominated society is in solidarity and in acting together, and that for this they need to be stubborn and patient, for, to quote Hans, »... utopias, too, run according to schedule.«

The film takes a clear position on Christa's situation: Social problems cannot be solved by violent means. However, her motive is not without moral justification. She acts out of a need to help, while the motives of the other side can be reduced to pure greed. This is clearly illustrated by the fact that the day-care center is evicted to make room for a sex club, or that the bank's branch manager profits from the bank robbery by using it for an insurance fraud. This is why Christa gains the sympathy of the other women, and becomes a positive leader for them. When Ingrid meets Christa again, she recognizes the loneliness of her own existence, which is totally subordinated to the needs of her husband. She becomes aware once more of her own desires and expectations from life. This is reinforced by a budding affection for Werner. Now at last she finds the courage to question her marriage, to overcome her fear of material insecurity, and to act independently. Finally she separates from her husband and moves into Christa's commune. Lena's interest in Christa is aroused by the fact that Christa does not fit her idea of a bank robber at all, and she begins to examine Christa's motives. She feels responsible, as she says, for whether Christa is punished or not depends on her. That is why she begins to make inquiries on her own, and while doing so encounters different lifestyles that women have: the communal household in which Christa once lived, her daughter's child-care center, the small-town life of Christa's mother, who lives alone, Ingrid's stunted existence in her suburban apartment. At the same time, she discovers the attitudes of the other side: the reaction of the landlord when the child-care center is evicted, of the bank manager, of the police. Her final decision therefore has to do not only with Christa, but with her own life as well.

While it is true that the main conflict that sustains the action and moves it forward is Christa's wish to preserve her hard-won way of life, which is why she runs foul of the law, the real subject of the film is women's learning process. Starting with the question to what extent it is possible to change women's circumstances under existing social conditions a number of different women's lifestyles are examined. In this examination, an important role is played by the critical investigation of the relationship between women and men. Conventional marriage, where the wife submits to her husband's wishes and is at his disposal whenever he needs her, while in return

24. Hans (Peter Schneider) confronts Christa (Tina Engel) and Werner (Marius Müller-Westernhagen).
25. Christa and Ingrid (Sylvia Reize) in Portugal.

she receives a questionable material security, is unmasked as a dependent relationship, arising, on the part of the woman, from her fear of taking her life into her own hands. A relatively free relationship, like that between Christa and Werner, fails because of lack of commitment, especially because it, too, is burdened with an unequal balance of give and take, and there are outbursts of petty jealousy and possessiveness. In positive contrast to this, there is the budding relationship between Ingrid and Werner, for his spontaneity and the fact that he is able to show his feelings contrast pleasantly with the machismo and the emotional coldness of her husband and arouse maternal feelings in her. Since, on the other hand, she has a weaker and more emotional personality than Christa, Werner begins to develop a sense of responsibility toward her. There are indications that the mutual respect that exists between Christa and Hans is a potential basis for a satisfactory couple relationship: they share moral values and ideals, are committed to serving other people, and both have the same cultural interests. Moreover, this relationship is strengthened by the fact that he supports her independent way of life on principle. This is the film's contribution to the discussion within the women's movement at the time about whether an equal and satisfactory relationship with men was possible. The possibility of such a relationship was not dismissed as unattainable, and similarly the film leaves open the prospect of a closer relationship between Christa and Hans.

Schwestern oder Die Balance des Glücks (*Sisters or The Balance of Happiness*)

While Margarethe von Trotta still presents relationships between women as totally positive in *Das zweite Erwachen der Christa Klages* (*The Second Awakening of Christa Klages*), this attitude changes in her second film *Schwestern* (*Sisters*), which she made in 1979. The notes in her journal about the genesis of the script reflect a swing in public opinion that took place in the Federal Republic of Germany at the end of the '70s and found expression in the film. The basic idea was still along the same lines as that set forth in *Das zweite Erwachen der Christa Klages* (*The Second Awakening of Christa Klages*). Starting out from the premise that women like Christa Klages, who together with other women have been able to create relative freedom for themselves, were a privileged minority, while the average woman's life is hardly affected by feminist ideas of self-realization outside traditional lifestyles such as marriage and the nuclear family, Margarethe von Trotta wanted to develop further the figure of the bank clerk Lena, in order to clarify the situation, growth opportunities, and longings of working women. Here she took up the feminists' struggle protesting job discrimination against women: women's generally poorer training and a lack of opportunities for promotion condemned them to monotonous scut work, a situation that helped reinforce conventional lifestyles, for a majority of women regarded marriage as a welcome chance to break out of an unsatisfactory professional life. The idea was to show this in the film, using the very different outlook on life of two women: a shorthand typist in an open-plan office and an executive secretary. While the former simply wants to use marriage to go from absolute dependency to a relative dependency, the other finds fulfillment in her profession. Thus marriage plays a different role in her life, since she does not need it to supply her needs and to provide an escape. The basic idea here is that equal opportunities for women not only promise a chance for self-realization through one's work but also offer a way to eliminate dependent relationships within marriage.

After a closer look at the subject, however, Margarethe von Trotta realized that the issue appeared to be far more involved, since, first of all, dependent relationships have not only a financial, but an emotional basis as well, and, secondly, the pressures of a competitive society deny a large majority of people personal growth through their profession. This was why, in the course of working on *Schwestern* (*Sisters*), the critical analysis of social behavioral roles and of pressures existing in this competitive society became more and more important. Margarethe von Trotta thus fell in with an emerging tendency of the New Left toward the end of the '70s: faced with the failure of the lofty ambitions of the movement of '68 and the gradual retraction of the little it had achieved, the New Left became more and more embroiled in defensive actions.

The movement of retreat went hand in hand with a general mood of crisis in the Federal Republic. Growing unemployment caused by downsizing, a falling standard of living, fear of the future, increased job pressures, growing awareness of the dangers of nuclear energy programs and of the destruction of the environment in the name of economic growth, and especially the so-called »German Autumn« of 1977 and the expansion of the »security state« that went with it paralyzed the Left and caused a change in orientation that took the form of general criticism of the growth ideology, protests against an achievement-oriented society, and a struggle for more »quality of life«.

Based on this development, a second aspect came to the fore as Margarethe von Trotta worked on the script for *Schwestern* (*Sisters*): the concept of alienated work, an idea to which the student movement of the '60s had already attached special importance, and which the so-called alternative movement during the late '70s made into the central tenet of their criticism of bourgeois-capitalist competitive society. But while for the movement of '68 alienation was only one reason for justifying the need for a fundamental social change, the alternative movement believed that the contradiction between the competitive principle and the pleasure principle was more important. The members of the alternative movement declared that the way to effect social change was to reject the competitive principle and to withdraw en masse from the power structure of the economy and of science. The result was that thousands of so-called alternative projects were created, all espousing what they regarded as dropping out of the competitive society. Along with this went a general depoliticization. Most of the large and small political groups into which the movement of '68 had split showed signs of disbanding. Where there had been critical examination of social constraints and concerted efforts to break these down, there was now a search on the part of individuals for ways of attaining a maximum of self-realization.

The women's movement, too, was not spared this development. At the end of the '70s an idea gained in influence that equated the achievement-oriented society with patriarchy and declared that competition was the masculine principle. Thus the women's movement legitimized the refusal to live up to societal expectations, and reinforced a tendency among women to withdraw into niche occupations, a tendency that soon manifested itself in a huge number of women's projects. The first signs of dissent among factions with different political agendas – lesbians and straight women, politically motivated and apolitical women – had already been present earlier; now, dissent deepened, causing increasing separatism, concentration on whatever partial goals happened to prevail at the time, and the fostering of a women's culture. New, basically conservative trends appeared – sentimental enthusiasm for nature, distrust of technology, antimodernism – the beginnings of a »new feminine mystique« and a »new motherliness.« While early consciousness-raising groups still claimed they were there to create a collective consciousness with a view to engaging in joint actions, later the view that feminine identity should no longer be defined socially but psychologically began to gain ascendancy. As a result individual women felt called upon to examine and change their own behavioral role, and the movement's unified political plan of action that had been manifested in previous nationwide campaigns and other initiatives was lost. Like women, men also began to call into question the role assigned to them, and encounter groups of all kinds were suddenly all the rage.

Schwestern (*Sisters*) is a reflection of this period. The central focus of the film is the contradiction between an achievement-oriented society defined by men and women's attempts at self-realization, while the question of a new feminine identity is specifically raised.

The film is set in a white-collar milieu during the '70s. As in *Das zweite Erwachen der Christa Klages* (*The Second Awakening of Christa Klages*), Margarethe von Trotta again examines the lives of three very different women. In the center is the relationship between the two sisters Maria and Anna. Maria, the older of the two, is a competent, ambitious, and successful executive secretary. Although she would have loved to go to the university herself, she stepped down in order to enable her sister to study. Ever since, she has been projecting her own wishes on her sister. Supporting Anna's career has become Maria's most important goal in life, and she expects the latter to live up to her expectations. Anna is a dreamer, emotional, needy, and unable to stand on her own two feet. Since childhood, she has been leaning on her big sister, and she is dependent on her both emotionally and financially. She studies biology more to fulfill Maria's expectations than by her own inclination, but in return she demands Maria's absolute devotion. Both force each other to assume a role that prevents the full development of her personality. Although they are aware of how restricting this situation is, they do everything to maintain the roles they have been assigned: Maria criticizes her sister for being dependent and for not wanting to face life's demands, but stifles Anna's every attempt to develop initiative and to take on responsibility. Anna for her part is overwhelmed by Maria's expectations and finds them intolerable, but clings to her and resists anything that threatens to take her sister's devotion away from her. The equilibrium of this relationship becomes shaky with Anna's approaching graduation. Anna begins to question the meaning of her studies and realizes that the career her sister imagines for her can only be attained at the price of giving up her individuality. When she expresses the wish to break off her studies, Maria exerts even more pressure on her. Anna's panic attacks and depressions intensify

26. Moment of harmony between Maria (Jutta Lampe) and Anna (Gudrun Gabriel).
27. Miriam (Jessica Früh) tells Robert (Konstantin Wecker) about her dream of being a famous singer.
28. Maria and her mother (Agnes Fink) after the two sisters' quarrel.
29. Miriam after her quarrel with Maria.

and change to overt resistance when she finds out that Maria has a relationship with Maurice, the son of her employer. She feels betrayed by Maria and commits suicide. Self-destruction, for her, is both an act of liberation and revenge against her sister. By killing herself she takes control of her sister's life and throws it off balance by pursuing Maria into her very dreams and temporarily preventing her from functioning normally in her professional life. In her despair, Maria takes refuge with Fritz, a childhood friend, who lives with his sister in a village by the North Sea. Fritz, a dreamer and, like Anna, afraid of people, spends most of his time writing books about his dreams in almost obsessive self-preoccupation. He tries to explain Anna's motives to Maria, but Maria does not want to accept them, for if she did, her entire world view would be jeopardized.

While in this state of mind, she finds Miriam, a younger colleague she has befriended who works in the open-plan office. Miriam is a happy-go-lucky person. Naïve and cheerful, she always tries to make the best of things. Office work bores her, and she dreams of marrying a rich man or becoming a famous singer to escape the treadmill of everyday life. She admires Maria, and is grateful to her for taking her out of the typing pool and making her her assistant. It is therefore a spontaneous act of friendship for her to hasten to Maria's side in order to comfort her when she hears about Anna's suicide. She discovers Maria, usually so self-assured and controlled, weak and desperate, and is glad to offer her her devotion and sympathy. It then occurs to Maria to compensate for Anna's loss and restore balance to her life by making it possible for Miriam to have a professional career. She offers to pay for Miriam's training at a language school and finally talks her into moving in with her. Miriam is happy to do so, for it means she doesn't have to return to the open-plan office. As they start living together, Maria tries to push Miriam into the same kind of dependent relationship as the one she had with Anna. But from the start Miriam shows signs of resistance: When she moves in with Maria, she paints the apartment according to her own ideas. Instead of learning vocabulary and cramming for the exam as Maria expects her to do, she would rather listen to music or go out dancing at night. Thus Maria fails to recreate the old configuration of roles, and she is increasingly less able to understand Miriam's joie de vivre and longings, while Miriam becomes more and more aware of the pressure of Maria's expectations and rebels against them. In this she is supported by her relationship with Robert, who has given up a secure existence as a bookkeeper to become a singer. Since it is not possible for Miriam to talk to Maria about Anna, she becomes curious, and begins making enquiries about Anna's death. She talks to Maria's mother, and finds Anna's diary. Reading it, Miriam realizes that Maria is trying to push her into Anna's role so as to be able to repress the guilt she feels at her sister's death, and to continue playing her accustomed role. On the day when Miriam successfully passes her exam at the language school and when Maria informs her she has already found her a position as a secretary, she rebels. There is a crisis: Maria reproaches her how much she has done for her, whereupon Miriam retorts that Maria is trying to drive her to suicide just as she did Anna. The result is that they break up for good, and Miriam moves out. This experience finally forces Maria to question her assessment of herself and to take a closer look at Anna's expectations from life. She learns that she must try to merge both world views if she wants to restore balance to her life.

The two sisters Maria and Anna represent two opposing attitudes: While Maria's sense of who she is comes from her professional position and her work, and she has internalized the competitive principle, Anna recoils from the demands of a career because she believes a career would mean giving up her individuality. The film makes it clear that either attitude is an expression of a warped personality. Maria represses her emotional and imaginative side in order to do justice to her professional role, while Anna is introverted and unable to cope with life. Miriam represents a third, much healthier point of view. Unlike Maria, she feels the professional world is constricting and work is something she is forced to do, but unlike Anna she directs her longing for a happier life outward. Even if her dreams are hardly realistic, they help her to keep alive her optimism and joie de vivre, while Anna's dream of life destroys her life, as she writes in her diary. Hope exists in Maria's realization: The balance of happiness lies in merging Maria's competence and will to succeed, Miriam's joie de vivre and vitality, and Anna's dream world. The question whether such a utopia is possible is left open, but at least the utopia indicates a direction.

Schwestern (*Sisters*) thus comments on the various positions that developed in the women's movement in the latter half of the '70s. Focusing on relationships between women allows the filmmaker to show dependent relationships and mechanisms of oppression that exist in the same way between women and men. Without another, new, feminine identity – this might be the message of the film – such behavioral rituals will keep recurring over the centuries according to the same old patterns. But what should this new identity be like? The film gives no definitive answer. One thing is certain: It must not be limited to those characteristics that are traditionally seen as feminine – emotionality, sensitivity, impulsiveness, helplessness, and a resulting inability to assert oneself in male-dominated society. As a result, women's continuing personal growth cannot be nurtured by opting out and by withdrawing into a female ghetto. On the other hand, the film clearly shows that it is not enough to demand equal professional opportunities for women, for this causes women to submit to the pressures of a masculine achievement-oriented society and to suppress part of their personality. In *Schwestern* (*Sisters*) Margarethe von Trotta rejects the new feminine mystique, the tendencies to opt out, and the idealization of relationships between women. The same goes for career women who believe women can attain self-realization if they are offered equal opportunities in the working world.

Die bleierne Zeit (*Marianne and Juliane*)

Margarethe von Trotta's third film was made in 1981. It examines the consequences of the so-called »German Autumn« of 1977, when a series of violent incidents aggravated the political climate in the Federal Republic of Germany and got the political left in trouble: the kidnapping and murder of Schleyer, the then president of the employers' association, the hijacking of the Lufthansa plane »Landshut« by a successor organization of the RAF to Mogadishu, where a commando unit of the German police freed the hostages, and finally the death of the RAF leaders in the high-security prison of Stuttgart-Stammheim. Margarethe von Trotta got the idea for the film when, during the funeral of Gudrun Ensslin, she met the latter's sister Christiane and persuaded her to work on a script with her based on Christiane's experiences. Thus the story is based on actual occurrences, which, however, are told from a subjective point of view, so that political events move into the background. The portrayal of what happens lays no claim to authenticity. Rather, it includes a large number of aspects, resulting in an extremely complex and multilayered statement.

Central to the action is the relationship between the two sisters Juliane and Marianne. After the two are both gripped by the excitement of the student movement of the '60s, each goes her separate way to translate her ideas into action. While Juliane gets involved in the women's movement and works as an editor with a feminist magazine, Marianne leaves her husband and child in order to change society by force. The film investigates how her action affects the lives of people who are close to her. Primarily, it is Juliane who is touched by her sister's decision: Ever since

30. Reunion at the museum: Marianne (Barbara Sukowa) and Juliane (Jutta Lampe).
31. Juliane, Wolfgang (Rüdiger Vogeler) and the parents (Doris Schade, Franz Rudnick) beside Marianne's coffin.
32. Juliane takes Marianne's son Jan (Patrick Estrada-Pax) home to live with her.
33. Marianne in the prison's visitors' room.

their childhood her ties to her sister have been very close. But there are also Marianne's ex-husband Werner, her son Jan, her parents, and finally Wolfgang, Juliane's partner. Although Juliane has dissociated herself from Marianne's actions, she learns that the sister's actions keep touching her life again and again. As long as Marianne is wanted by the police, Juliane, too, is subject to police harassment. When the sister arranges sporadic meetings, Juliane has to endure her hostile remarks. Marianne's ex-husband Werner commits suicide because he feels incapable of taking care of his son on his own, and leaves responsibility for the boy to Juliane. Since Juliane has made a deliberate decision not to have children, she finds a home for him with foster parents, and has to put up with Marianne and Wolfgang's accusations. Finally Marianne is arrested, and Juliane begins visiting her regularly. Gradually the relationship with her sister changes her life. It is true that the political differences between the two remain insurmountable, yet they become increasingly less and less important in view of Juliane's indignation about the degrading and inhospitable conditions under which Marianne is imprisoned. She also begins to show understanding for her sister, recalling their shared personal history: childhood and adolescence in the »leaden« '50s, Juliane's own rebellion against her parents and school, their horror when they learned of the mass murder in the Nazi concentration camps, their indignation at the way members of the older generation repressed their guilt, and finally the movement for change in the '60s when, as a result of the new state-authorized mass murder in the Vietnam War, young people gave vent to their anger, and this in turn led them to question existing circumstances and to confront their parents' generation with the guilt of the past. The sister's concerns occupy more and more space in Juliane's life and increasingly damage her relationship with Wolfgang, and her own work. When Marianne is found hanged in her cell, Juliane begins to identify with her sister completely. She questions the official version, according to which Marianne supposedly committed suicide, and is obsessed by the idea that she must uncover the truth about her sister's death. Her investigations into Marianne's death become her main purpose in life, and the relationship with Wolfgang breaks down in the face of this. She actually does find grounds for thinking that her suspicion is correct, but when she turns to the press with the evidence, she discovers that there is no more interest in the case. Finally she realizes that it is up to her to preserve for the future the memory of the true circumstances of Marianne's life and death. She decides to bring home Marianne's son – who has recently been the victim of an arson attack – to live with her, and to pass his mother's story on to him.

Margarethe von Trotta takes an unambiguous stand against violence as a way of changing society, yet she also tries to discover the motives and reasons for choosing that path. She finds these in the fact that the past was repressed by the older generation, finally causing the younger people to rebel. By portraying the despotic use of power by the state and, what is more, by showing the images of the victims and establishing a connection between the crematoria of the concentration camps, the napalm victims of the Vietnam War, the disfigured face of the dead Marianne in her coffin, and that of little Jan, scarred by fire, she makes it clear that this rebellion was justified and continues to be so. She also asks herself why two people with the same personal history follow such different paths, as Marianne and Juliane did. The explanation, she suggests, is that the sisters have very different personalities. It is easy to understand that Marianne, who as a child and an adolescent was always the more submissive and well-adjusted of the two, but also emotional and idealistic, resorts to the other extreme when she experiences injustice and inhumanity, while Juliane, who rebelled early in life, expresses her protest more prudently and moderately. Marianne fails because the path she follows comes more out of her own impatience than out of a clear political agenda. But Juliane's step-by-step work toward social change is also to no avail. In her horror at her sister's death she gives up her political work in the women's movement to devote herself exclusively to investigating the circumstances of the death. Beyond that, her experiences of the daily abuse of power, the repressive violence of the authorities, but above all the dead of Stammheim, in the circumstances of whose death the public lost interest only a short time later, all go to show that the new direction taken by the movement of '68 led nowhere. The conclusion drawn in the film is that as long as events like these can take place and be forgotten immediately afterwards, and questions as to who is to blame are repressed, nothing has changed in Germany.

Thus, the film is primarily an appeal against forgetting the past, something that Margarethe von Trotta regards as the cause of the immutability of German conduct, for only by remembering repressed guilt is it possible to process the past and to effect true change. The film makes a contribution to the struggle against forgetting. This struggle is portrayed in more than one respect: the film shows how the movement of '68 brought to light the National Socialist past and, on behalf of the generation of the fathers, began to reappraise it. There were great hopes that this would prove to be a new beginning, hopes that proved to be futile when the Stammheim events took place, if not sooner: for now the younger generation, too, practiced forgetting by once more sweeping the conflicts under the rug. It is Wolfgang, a sixty-eighter like Marianne and Juliane, who says, »I can't deal with it any more. This robbing of corpses.« And this refers to his own past political commitment as well, for Wolfgang's horizons, in the meantime, have shrunk, and encompass only his work as an architect and his life with Juliane in a nuclear family. Thus he represents an attitude that was widespread in the early '80s among members of his generation, whose »movement for social change ... fizzled out at some point«[4], as Margarethe von Trotta said in reference to the film. Here, the film also documents the relapse into a »leaden era«, when only a few scattered individuals like Juliane still ask questions. What is disturbing are Juliane's moments of isolation as she investigates her sister's death. These are mitigated only by the support of her friend Sabine, who, however, helps her because she is her friend and not because she shares her political motivation.

An inventory of the political situation in the Federal Republic after Stammheim has pessimistic results, and thus mirrors the paralysis of the Left. Any hope of change must be directed toward the future, and in the film this function is served by Marianne's son. Related to this is Juliane's learning process, as she initially tries to deny responsibility for the boy by giving him to foster parents. The reasons she rejects the role of a mother are explained in a subplot, as the film takes up various aspects of the debate about motherhood that was going on at the time: women's struggle against Paragraph 218 and for the right to choose; the double burden of children and work, which Sabine knowingly takes upon herself; the lack of responsibility and inadequacy of fathers, as illustrated by the case of Werner; Marianne's opinion that in view of the plight of children in the third world her own child has lower priority; Wolfgang's wish for children, as a result of which Juliane feels pressured and forced into a role she rejects; the reactionary glorification of motherhood in the Third Reich, which Juliane researches for an article. What makes her decide to change her original attitude and to look after Jan is the realization that by shunting the child off to a foster family she has deprived him not only of his mother, his family, and his personal history, but also of his identity. The film illustrates this by pointing out that Jan has no memory of his mother or his aunt, and has been given a different name. Juliane gives him back all these things by taking him home to live with her and telling him the story of his mother. In this way she makes him the keeper of the remembrance of what really happened, and the bearer of hope for the future: since he is aware of his history, he will be able to protect the future against the mistakes of the past. The conclusion of the film should not be misunderstood: Margarethe von Trotta is not trying to assign Juliane to the traditional role of women, and neither does she present the case of a mythologically veiled »new motherliness«, as critics would have it[5], but she sees motherhood as an intentional act of taking responsibility for the future.

34. Margarethe von Trotta with Barbara Sukowa, Jutta Lampe and producer Eberhard Junkersdorf after receiving the Golden Phoenix for *Die bleierne Zeit* (*Marianne and Juliane*) at the 1981 Venice Film Festival. (Photo: Graziano Arici.)
35. Awarding of the Golden Lion (1981) by Liv Ullmann and Carlo Lizzani (at that time director of the Venice Film Festival).
36. Margarethe von Trotta with Angela Winkler, Hanna Schygulla and cameraman Michael Ballhaus during the filming of *Heller Wahn* (*Sheer Madness*).

Heller Wahn (*Sheer Madness*)

The film *Die bleierne Zeit* (*Marianne and Juliane*) was, for the most part, received enthusiastically by critics, and was given awards in Germany and abroad, including the Golden Lion of the 1981 International Film Festival of Venice. However, it was sharply attacked by feminist film critics. The reactions came from the radical wing, which accused Margarethe von Trotta of betraying the Left and the cause of women, since, according to the critics, she had reproduced clichés current among the establishment.[6] She was also reproached for not dissociating herself sufficiently from male-dominated society and not searching for a fundamentally new aesthetic. In the early '80s, the filmmaker for her part increasingly developed discrepancies with one part of the movement, since she disliked trends that equated emancipation with reproducing male behavior. It was the discussions in the political women's groups that particularly went against her grain, for the arguments presented there sounded as though women had to constantly prove to themselves that they had severed all ties to the traditional role of women and to their personal history. Margarethe von Trotta, on the other hand, observed that while it was true that under the influence of feminist ideas women had created stronger bonds among themselves, frequently new dependent relationships could be recognized behind these bonds. This issue is central to her fourth film *Heller Wahn* (*Sheer Madness*), made in 1982. Here she portrays the lifestyle and the state of political awareness in FRG left-wing liberal circles in the '80s. The people who are the center of the action belong to the generation of '68, which is around forty by this time and has come to terms with existing circumstances. Their political stance has become a part of their self-image, but over time it has turned into a posture, for these people prove incapable of putting it into practice in their daily lives. The film demonstrates how, subconsciously and often with the best of intentions, traditional behavior patterns are repeated in interpersonal relationships, even though their form has changed.

Again the action revolves around the relationship between two very different women: Olga, a self-assured, independent, and successful university lecturer in feminist literary studies, and Ruth, who is tormented by depression, fears, and fantasies of suicide, and is neurotically dependent on her husband. The two women meet when Olga and her ex-husband Dieter, after spending a vacation together, visit their friends Bruno and Erika in the couple's country house in Provence and meet Bruno's family, including his brother Franz and the brother's wife Ruth. Ruth, usually unsociable, feels drawn to Olga from the start. Olga's interest in her is aroused when she notices that Ruth is painting black and white copies of pictures in color. She finds Ruth's sadness and helplessness moving. They begin to come closer to each other when Ruth runs off after an argument with Franz and hides in the cellars where Olga finds her. Back in Germany, the two meet again by chance, and Ruth tells Olga she and Franz have separated, which turns out to be a lie, for when Olga visits her, she finds Ruth in perfect harmony with her husband. She is even more disconcerted when Franz asks her to befriend his wife. After this, Olga hardly feels inclined to continue the acquaintance. However, Ruth brings about a seemingly accidental meeting – in reality, she has been following Olga for some time without Olga's knowledge – and a friendship that continues to deepen develops between the two. Olga tries to strengthen Ruth's self-confidence by motivating her to paint her own pictures. She even succeeds in getting a gallery-owner friend of hers to organize a show of Ruth's paintings. When Franz hears of the plan, he opposes it, because Ruth's brother, a painter, killed himself after his first success. He fears that Ruth might react the same way, and prevents the exhibition. Ruth's newly awakened feeling of self-worth is shattered once more. Through her friendship with Olga, however, she not only overcomes her disappointment, but also becomes more and more sure of herself. Franz, who feels abandoned and excluded as a result, tells Ruth in his jealousy of Olga that Olga befriended her only because he asked her to do so. Ruth makes a suicide attempt. She is saved, and Olga succeeds in convincing her that she could never be forced into friendship by anyone. After his wife leaves the hospital, as a sign of his remorse, Franz allows her to accompany Olga on a lecture tour of Egypt. There, Ruth succeeds in completely overcoming her depression and shyness. On the trip back, the two decide to stop and visit Erika and Bruno in Provence, where Franz awaits them. Franz is not very pleased at the change in Ruth, for he feels she has broken away from her dependence on him and no longer needs him. There is a violent argument between him and Olga, during which Erika takes her side, while Bruno supports Franz. Panic-stricken, Ruth runs away. The next day, Olga, depressed, returns to Germany alone. There, to make matters worse, she discovers that her lover Alexej has left her. She enters a state of crisis, and has to face the fact that her son is the only person who supports her at this moment. Ruth returns together with Franz, but refuses to speak to him. Franz regrets his actions, asks Olga to forgive him and begs her to speak to Ruth. But Olga refuses to interfere, for she has realized that the two must clear up their relationship on their own. The film ends with Ruth's vision: When Franz comes home with an armful of flowers to effect a reconciliation with her, she shoots him and is brought to trial. In her final words to the judge she thanks Olga for helping her to kill her husband.

On the surface, the film seems to be a self-portrayal of the women's movement at the time. It addresses topics that were then the subject of public debate, such as the rediscovery of 19th century women's literature, psychic disfigurement or even mental illness in women whose individuality was suppressed, and tendencies toward esotericism and a new introspection in the women's movement. But above all, at first glance, it seems to reproduce one of the stereotyped ideas of certain subgroups in the women's movement: the wholesale glorification of relationships between women and the one-sided demonization of men's behavior, a reason many, predominantly male, critics used as a pretext for disapproving of the film. But Margarethe von Trotta was not prepared to accept this view, which was then very widespread in the women's movement, without questioning it. In *Heller Wahn* (*Sheer Madness*), as in *Schwestern* (*Sisters*), it is her opinion that there needs to be a new feminine identity if relationships between women are to improve. She clearly shows that while the friendship between Olga and Ruth apparently has a positive effect on Ruth's development, in the final analysis the relationship on which it is based is as dependent as Ruth's marriage to Franz. Olga needs Ruth because it gives her satisfaction to be there for others. Olga has always gathered people around her who lean on her – for instance, her husband, who has developed into a successful stage director with her help, and takes it for granted that she is at his disposal at all times with her advice even though they have separated. There is also her lover Alexej, an unemployed musician, for whom she provides financial and emotional support. She encourages Ruth to break away from Franz and to become less of an introvert, for she understands that Franz stunts Ruth's independent development because he is afraid of losing her. Yet she steers Ruth in a direction that corresponds to her own ideas of self-realization and overlooks the fact that no one can vicariously emancipate another, but that her friend must learn to make her way on her own. Ruth seeks Olga's friendship because she needs someone to give her support so that she can free herself from her husband's excessive solicitude and from his patronizing treatment of her. She replaces Franz with Olga, and thus goes from one dependent relationship into another to avoid having to assert herself.

When the crisis finally comes, this unhealthy equilibrium turns out to be unstable. Ruth falls back into old behavior patterns, with one difference: her destructive instinct is no longer directed against herself but against Franz. Olga recognizes her mistake when she realizes her own weakness, but the ending is left open. The true summing-up of the story is provided by an Adorno quotation with which Margarethe von Trotta prefaces the script: »Der nur liebt dich, bei dem du schwach dich zeigen darfst.« (»How do you know someone loves you? Only if you are free to show your weakness in that person's presence.«) The claim to another's genuine love and affection can be redeemed only by absolute renunciation of power over the other person, and this holds true for both men and women.

Even more than *Die bleierne Zeit* (*Marianne and Juliane*), *Heller Wahn* (*Sheer Madness*) conveys disappointment about the futility of the '68 generation's movement for change: That generation falls back into behavior patterns everyone thought had long been overcome. We are shown different facets of one left-wing development, facets that were already a secondary theme in *Die bleierne Zeit* (*Marianne and Juliane*): how the left wing adjusted to existing circumstances and secretly adopted conventional ideas about life. Political work is carried out inside institutions and has turned into a career: Franz works in an institute for peace studies and gives lectures about the need for peaceful communication among nations, Olga is involved in the women's movement and combines this with an instructorship at the university. For years, everyone has belonged to a cultural and intellectual elite whose standard of living is far above the average. Olga, a single parent, is able to afford a large apartment with stucco ceiling ornaments in an old building, and is able to support her friend financially, Ruth and Franz have a fine house in the suburbs, while Erika and Bruno own a country house in Provence, where they indulge in thoughts about living close to nature and the pastoral idyl of the extended family. And if Olga's husband lives in a furnished room, it is only because he wants to. Apart from that, the call for liberalization has long since given way to economic necessity, as in the case of the gallery owner, who, in contrast to the old days, now makes business interests her priority. People have made themselves comfortable in their little niches, and are now successful. Rebellion is something that takes place in the

37. New Year's Eve party: Olga (Hanna Schygulla) and Ruth (Angela Winkler) at Ruth and Franz's New Year's Eve party.
38. Franz (Peter Striebeck) and Ruth meet again in Provence.
39. Ruth's vision of suicide: A despairing Franz clings to her dead body.

private sphere at best, whenever stress and discomfort become unbearable, as in Erika's case when, following the argument between Franz and Olga, she screams her frustration at her monotonous existence as a housewife and mother into her husband's face, or in the case of Ruth, who rebels against her husband's patronizing behavior by running away and suicide attempts. These violent eruptions momentarily shatter the characters' conception of themselves, but after a short phase of remorse they go back to making the same mistakes.

The microcosm created in *Heller Wahn* (*Sheer Madness*) shows phenomena that are typical for the period when the film was made. In the early '80s, the élan of the great collective movements that emerged from the movement of '68 fizzled out, and the emotionalism associated with working for social change had become hackneyed. The alternative utopias proposed by the women's movement, the ecology movement, or the alternative scene disintegrated to the extent that the issues which even in the late '70s and early '80s had led to mass protests were now taken up by establishment organizations and parties and incorporated into official policies. Conflicts were defused by admissions on the part of the state, and the confrontation between the »system« and the movements became less well-defined. A pragmatic attitude now gained acceptance, and people began concentrating on things that were immediately practically feasible and that could be pushed through on a political level. As a result the spectrum of activities fanned out more and more, the unified program and the sense of having a clearly defined political opponent were lost, and increasing professionalization and institutionalization of political activities superseded the grass-roots organizations. The peace movement, which had attracted huge numbers in the early '80s, could provide no new impetus for social development because of its very nature. It was true that there were many links with the other social movements, but their cohesion was founded on a basic area of consensus, the struggle against the stationing of nuclear weapons in Central Europe. This is how it became possible to unite a broad political spectrum ranging from individual representatives of the conservative parties, to churches and labor unions, parts of the Social Democrat party and the Greens, and finally Marxist factions, yet there was no alternative project for social change.

As far as its goals were concerned, the peace movement was a survival movement, building on a multitude of fears to create political commitment, fears directly addressed in the film: fear of a third world war, fear that the environment would be destroyed, fear of technology and its uncontrollable consequences, fear of the unpredictability of politicians, bureaucrats, and scientists. Its organizational structure was determined by established organizations, prominent unifying figures, and full-time peace researchers, as well as by a large number of grass-roots initiatives that were only loosely connected with each other. As a result people no longer felt there was an »us«, and the depoliticization of everyday life increased.

At the same time the basis for a left-wing counterculture disintegrated, for cultural expectations were increasingly focused on repressing reality. This is why the New German Cinema movement also showed signs of decay. The starting point of this decay is often equated with the death of Faßbinder in 1982, although this surely did not cause it, for Schlöndorff, Wenders, and Herzog had already left Germany by that time. The group of Munich filmmakers began to break up. The fact that the filmmakers wandered off to other countries is symptomatic of the crisis of the New German Cinema, a sign that times had changed. There was no longer any demand for a critical analysis of reality, for a »cinema of experience«, as Thomas Elsaesser characterizes the movement in his extensive study.[7] The New German Cinema was gradually losing its public. This meant that not only the filmmakers' political conception of themselves, but also their artistic concept began to waver. A final blow was the filmmakers' discomfort at concealed criticism by public sponsors of the cinema who, after the CDU/CSU (Christian Democratic Union/Christian Social Union) coalition came to power in 1982, changed their guidelines, so that films that were critical of society were denied access to public funding. Artistically and thematically ambitious films continued to be made, but these were largely the work of a relatively small number of established directors who could rely on their reputation and financial reserves, and who had access to international co-productions. The many filmmakers who could not achieve large-scale success were forced to drop out. At the same time younger directors who produced apolitical films whose goal was pure entertainment were promoted. These tendencies, which were to increase in the years that followed, were already in evidence at the time *Heller Wahn* (*Sheer Madness*) was made – for example, when promised funding for Herbert Achternbusch's film *Das Gespenst* (»The Ghost«) was denied, supposedly because the film attacked religious values. In her film, Margarethe von Trotta makes the contradiction between high artistic standards and financial necessities her secondary aspect, emphasizing her point of view by having the stage director Dieter say, »Bei unseren Kulturärschen hat doch jeder seine Chance ...« Whereupon Olga answers, »wenn er sie bedient.« (»Everybody's got a chance with our cultural assholes ...« – »Yes, if you brown-nose them.«)

No other film by Margarethe von Trotta has been attacked as *Heller Wahn* (*Sheer Madness*) was. German reviewers in particular reproached the filmmaker for reproducing the women's movement's clichés, and claimed that she advocated banishing men from women's lives. Many women, on the other hand, recognized their own experiences in the film and defended it vehemently. For instance, one group of women entered the offices of the editors of the Berlin city magazine *Tip* after it had published a completely irrelevant, scathing review, and covered the walls with protest slogans. Since *Heller Wahn* (*Sheer Madness*), if not before, many German film critics have stubbornly insisted on regarding Margarethe von Trotta as a manhater. Hardly any of them, however, took the trouble to analyze the film in detail. If they had, they would have learned, no doubt, what reviewers abroad had recognized perfectly clearly: namely, that the director here draws a keenly observant and clearly differentiated portrait of German society in the early '80s that does not exclude relationships between women from its critique.

40. Rosa Luxemburg (Barbara Sukowa) and Leo Jogiches (Daniel Olbrychski) at work together. (Photo: Margarethe von Trotta and Christiane Ensslin, *Rosa Luxemburg. Das Buch zum Film*, Nördlingen 1986.)
41. Warsaw prison, 1905: Rosa Luxemburg (Barbara Sukowa) on her way to an interrogation.

Rosa Luxemburg

The idea for the film *Rosa Luxemburg* is based on a posthumous project by Faßbinder. When it was offered to Margarethe von Trotta, she saw it as a challenge, but felt that Faßbinder's plan did not do justice to Rosa Luxemburg's personality as a whole, for he had intended to make her love relationship with Leo Jogiches central to the action. After careful research, she decided to base the project on Rosa Luxemburg's prison letters, which had just been published at the time. She wanted to draw a portrait that would take into account both the private and the public Rosa Luxemburg. Her starting point was a problem that concerns her in all her films: What is the interaction between the private and the public, and what conflicts arise from it? In the specific case of Rosa Luxemburg she discovered a contradiction between the longing for harmony, beauty, peace, and private happiness, the bouts of dejection and private loneliness, but also the serene patience and joie de vivre expressed in the letters, and the image of the militant, uncompromising, and radical communist – the version that has gone down in the annals of history. In her film, Margarethe von Trotta wanted to examine this apparent contrast by confronting Rosa Luxemburg's political work and her private life.

In a complicated narrative structure consisting of flashbacks and leaps in time that extend from childhood memories until 1916, she develops the conflicts that shape Rosa Luxemburg's

life: collision with the power of the state, chiefly as it relates to her protest against World War I; her conflict between her longing for private happiness and the necessities of her political work, illustrated by her relationship to Leo Jogiches and Kostja Zetkin; and her conflict with the Social Democrats, alluded to in her relationship with Bernstein, but primarily shown in her increasing differences of opinion with Kautsky. The pivotal points of the story of Rosa Luxemburg are the times she spent in prison, with which the film begins and to which it keeps coming back.

Imprisonment, isolation, separation from family, comrades, friends – especially her women friends – and loneliness are thus shown as continuous components of her life, a situation that eventually comes to an end in the events that immediately precede her death, and in her assassination. In a first, introductory part, the film represents the conflicts that dominate her life: imprisonment in Warsaw in 1906, the interrogation, and a feigned execution, all of which she faces with the determination to die for her principles; her relationship to Leo Jogiches, in which he gives top priority to their political work, while she hopes for middle-class family life and children, and finally, on the occasion of the New Year's Eve celebration in 1899, her relationship to the German Social Democrats, whose future development is already indicated in her differences of opinion with Bernstein. Central to the second part is the inner contradiction in Rosa Luxemburg's personality – her longing for personal happiness on the one hand, and her political commitment on the other. We see happy moments with her friend Luise Kautsky, her work for the *Neue Zeit* (»New Era«) together with Karl Kautsky, her inflammatory speeches at workers' meetings on the occasion of the1905 Russian Revolution, and her first disagreements because of the fatalistic attitude toward the war among factions of the Social Democrats; the high point of this part of the story is Leo's return to Berlin in 1907 and the breaking-up of their relationship. A third part describes how the conflicts come to a head: there is her struggle against war in particular, conducted on two fronts – agitation against the state's warmongering, and against the executive committee of the Social Democrats, especially against the position of Kautsky, who is increasingly willing to sacrifice the Second International for the national interests of the German bourgeoisie. In her private life Rosa learns to come to terms with the fact that her private longings and the demands of her political work are incompatible. At first she still savors brief moments of happiness in a romantic relationship with Kostja Zetkin, but after the break-up with Kautsky, in 1910, her life becomes more and more lonely. Then come the events of 1914/15: the disintegration of the Second International, the outbreak of war and Kostja Zetkin's conscription, Rosa's arrest and the founding of the Spartacus league together with Karl Liebknecht, and thus the formal break with the SPD (German Social Democratic Party), all of which turn into a great political and personal defeat for Rosa. From this point on, the action follows the chronological course of events: her imprisonment until the end of the war in 1918, Rosa's release in November, her illegal work together with Karl Liebknecht as leaders of the Spartacus league and editors-in-chief of the

Rote Fahne (»Red Flag«), the November Revolution, and finally Rosa's assassination. In portraying her time in prison, the emphasis is on Rosa's loneliness and her grief for the victims of the war, alleviated only by the visits of her friends Luise Kautsky and Sonja Liebknecht and her friendship with the young prison guard Elisabeth. She looks for consolation in her books and in nature by cultivating a little garden in the Wronke prison yard, or by observing the tomtits outside her cell window. Although prison clearly weakens her physically and emotionally, she keeps encouraging herself and others and pointing to a better future. When she is released, she is ill, a shadow of her former self. And yet she immediately plunges into political work and takes on responsibility for the *Rote Fahne*. There are incipient open conflicts with Karl Liebknecht, for whom the November uprising signals the moment of revolution, while Rosa believes that the situation is not yet ripe and tries to avoid unnecessary bloodshed. In the last months of her life, Leo Jogiches and Mathilde Jacob become her most important political and personal mainstays. They are concerned for her safety, worry about her health, and make sure she eats and sleeps enough. The film ends with Karl Liebknecht's and Rosa Luxemburg's arrest and assassination by units of the Reichswehr.

The action first focuses on Rosa Luxemburg's inner conflict, caused by the incompatibility of her political conviction with her wish for middle-class happiness – a home, husband, and children. This is clearly shown in the relationship with Leo Jogiches. After the dissolution of her relationship with Leo, her struggle against warmongering and particularly against the stance of the Socialist leadership becomes the focal point. In its last third, the film then becomes a plea against war: Rosa's humanity and her appeal against violence are contrasted with the effects of destruction. Rosa suffers one defeat after another. At first she has to accept the fact that the personal wishes she has regarding Leo are incompatible with her political conviction, not only because Leo is opposed to them, but because, unlike the people who head the Social Democratic Party, both she and Leo always come into conflict with the government on account of their political single-mindedness and their uncompromising attitude. Rosa is still filled with unfulfilled yearning whenever she sees her brother's family life in Warsaw or that of Kautsky in Berlin. Her second, far greater defeat comes when she must accept that she has lost the fight against the war, for she does not succeed in enforcing her position within the Social Democratic Party and in organizing effective resistance – in her opinion, a general strike. This defeat is personal as well as political, for she not only loses her political home, but is also aware of her increasing personal isolation, beginning with a lonely Christmas in 1914, up to her prison term, shown in the film. And finally there is her last and greatest defeat, her assassination. However, what has failed is not only Rosa Luxemburg the person, but the utopia she represents in the film: a fulfilled life as a woman in which personal happiness and political commitment can be fused; a more just society, combining democracy and socialism; a more humane world without violence or wars. Margarethe von Trotta once mentioned that the film had unwittingly turned into a requiem for Rosa

Luxemburg, a fact she did not realize until after the film was completed. But more than that it is a swan song for a utopia that is identical with the vision of the future held by the movement of the '68ers and the women's movement. In its passionate plea against the war it supports the goals of the peace movement and raises the problem of nonviolent resistance, once a contentious issue for pacifists. In addition, the film also reflects the driving force of this movement: fear of the horrors of war, especially the terrible thought that humanity could be annihilated in a nuclear war, and despair because the politicians refuse to listen, alluded to in the film when it gives prominence to Rosa Luxemburg's speech about 40 years of peace after the war of 1870/71 in which Germany was involved. When people became aware of the dangers of the arms race – an important factor that contributed to the founding of the peace movement and promoted the movement – they also became hopeless, for the movement was based on an essentially pessimistic attitude, since, unlike *Rosa Luxemburg*, they lacked a positive utopia. This explains the pessimism about history that underlies the film and that says so much more about the Federal Republic in the '80s than about Rosa Luxemburg's own time. However, the film is a call to follow Rosa Luxemburg's example – a woman who in spite of all setbacks and defeats kept fighting to the end, »in spite of everything«, as she writes in her letters – and here is one of its hopeful elements. Another is friendship between women, Rosa's relationship to Luise Kautsky, Clara Zetkin, Sonja Liebknecht, and Mathilde Jacob, to whom the film devotes considerable space. These friendships are based more on trust and affection than on political agreement, and from them Rosa Luxemburg draws the joy, consolation, and energy she needs to survive and to continue her struggle. In this film, however, there are also the beginnings of a new, more mature relationship between men and women – that between Rosa and Leo in the later years, which, like her friendships with women, is free of expectations on either side, and is founded on equal give and take.

As with hardly any other film directed by Margarethe von Trotta, the reviewers of *Rosa Luxemburg* became deeply engrossed in an idle debate about whether the plot of the film corresponded with historical reality. Among other things, reviewers criticized the fact that important events in the protagonist's life had been left out – the founding of the KPD (German Communist Party)[8] and Rosa Luxemburg's differences of opinion with Lenin[9], and that her political importance had been reduced by concentrating on her private life.[10] The latter statement can be proved to be untrue, even if one sets aside Margarethe von Trotta's view that political circumstances are reflected in private existence. A further argument used by critics was that the filmmaker had moved Rosa Luxemburg close to the ecology and the peace movement, which was seen by some as glorification,[11] while others saw it as disparagement.[12] An added objection – interestingly, by male reviewers – was that she had neglected to criticize Rosa's views on women's issues.[13] In response to this debate, it must be mentioned that Margarethe von Trotta intended to make a film that touched on the political problems of the 1980s. Accordingly, certain points were emphasized, a practice granted to artists when they deal with historical materials.

42. Rosa Luxemburg (Barbara Sukowa) and Clara Zetkin (Doris Schade) at a workers' rally.
43. Rosa Luxemburg and Karl Liebknecht (Otto Sander) in 1919 after being arrested by the German army (Reichswehr).

Felix

In 1986, in Germany, Margarethe von Trotta together with Helma Sanders-Brahms, Helke Sander, and Christel Buschmann made the episodic film *Felix*. The idea originated that same year at the Munich Film Festival: The producer Theo Hinz thought it would be interesting to have these four directors, who had specialized in women's topics, make something about a man for a change. If, as was conjectured in the press, it was his ulterior motive to capitalize on the success of Dorris Dörrie's *Männer* (»Men«) made the same year, the four filmmakers certainly had no such intention. They saw the project more as an exercise about a theme none of them had worked on until then.

It was Christel Buschmann who had the idea of using a central figure throughout – a young man whose wife has walked out on him – and to show in four episodes how he reacts to this. The first part, directed by Helma Sanders-Brahms, introduces *Felix* in a monologue in the course of which he ranges from wounded vanity to self-pity, obstinacy, pretended indifference, and feeling down in the dumps, while during his attempt to remove traces of his ex from the apartment everything literally breaks apart. At the end he decides to take a trip, whereupon in the next episode, contributed by Helke Sander, we see him on the beach in Sylt. Here he talks two girls into having sex, but they refuse to use contraceptives, and his plan falls through. In Margarethe von Trotta's episode Felix bumps into a crying woman on the street. The woman spatters him with ice-cream and finally reveals that she has been deserted. Sympathetic and understanding, he gives her advice without admitting that he is in the same boat. Then it becomes apparent that she is crying for a woman, with whom she makes it up again shortly thereafter. The humor is in the dialogues, and is created by the misunderstanding and the different reactions the two have to a similar experience. In the last episode Christel Buschmann sends *Felix* on a crawl through the bars and pubs of the Reeperbahn in Hamburg, where he meets all sorts of remarkable and bizarre figures and finally, soliloquizing about the meaning of life and love, lands in a hotel room with a girl.

In the last scene of the film, the beginning episode is taken up once more. Felix returns from the trip, goes into raptures telling a woman friend on the phone how well he is doing, and suddenly his wife stands in the doorway. In spite of the way the episodes are bracketed, and the attempts to create transitions between them, the individual segments are so different that the story is not unified or connected, as was originally intended. In other words, Felix is interesting mainly as a cinematographic experiment, for the film impressively illustrates the individual style of each of the four filmmakers and gives the audience an idea of the diversity of so-called »women's cinema«.

Paura e amore (*Love and Fear*)

Margarethe von Trotta's next film, *Paura e amore* (*Love and Fear*), was made in Italy in the latter part of 1987. At this point she was still officially living in Munich – she did not give up her apartment until after her divorce from Volker Schlöndorff in 1991. However, in 1988, after she received another offer from an Italian producer, she decided to take up permanent residence in Rome. In part, there were personal reasons for this decision, but no doubt increasingly more unfavorable conditions for auteur cinema in Germany were a contributing cause. The New German Cinema movement had finally disintegrated, and feminist cinema, too, was in retreat. Also, the change in the political climate was responsible for an increased trend toward light entertainment. It was harder for a politically motivated cinema to find an audience now, especially since after World War II, in contrast to other European countries, no audience had developed for art films. Besides, state funding for highbrow films was lower, while at the same time production costs were rising. The filmmakers who had emerged from the New German Cinema thereupon took two main directions: Either they gradually moved closer to the mainstream, and finally merged with it, or they made films within the relatively limited framework of the subculture. This situation was one reason that Margarethe von Trotta seized the opportunity when she was given the chance to work in Italy.

Paura e amore (*Love and Fear*) is based on a concrete offer by Italian producer Angelo Rizzoli to make a film version of Chekhov's *Three Sisters*. This meant that, in contrast to her preceding films, Margarethe von Trotta would be bound to a thematic original, which, to be sure, fit in with her own interests. The central themes of Chekhov's play, the question as to the meaning of life,

44. Eva (Eva Mattes) and Felix (Ulrich Tukur) run into each other on the street. (Photo: Filmverlag der Autoren.)
45. Maria (Greta Scacchi), Sandra (Valeria Golino) and Velia (Fanny Ardant) greeting Massimo (Peter Simonischek) at Sandra's birthday party. (Photo: Bioskop Film.)

the longing for happiness, disillusionment, resignation, and loneliness were problems that were also on Margarethe von Trotta's mind.

In her adaptation, on which she collaborated with the Italian writer Dacia Maraini, she keeps the problems and basic constellation of the play, but moves the action to the academic milieu of the North Italian university town of Padua in the 1980s. Central to the action is the story of three sisters and a brother, Velia, Maria, Sandra, and Roberto, who are trying to come to grips with their life within the boundaries set by bourgeois conventions, and to realize the happiness they long for. The reasons for their failure are their own inability to change, the egotism of other people, or the fact that social constraints are insurmountable. The same conclusion is drawn in the film as in Chekhov's play: Happiness does not exist, only the longing for it.

However, while in Chekhov the sisters' ideas of happiness focus on breaking out of the constricting and monotonous small-town milieu and a return to bygone, happier times in Moscow, each of the three sisters in *Paura e amore* (*Love and Fear*) represents a certain type of woman in the 1980s, and each strives for happiness in her own way. The ideas of Velia, the oldest, have been shaped by the reform mood of the '60s and '70s, the women's movement, and the hopes these raised. She is an instructor of women's literature, and finds her satisfaction in her work. While she takes critical note of the fact that there is discrimination against her as a woman in an academic career, and realizes that the university has become depoliticized, she has actually come to terms with this. Her political commitment continues – she supported the Red Guards and is active in the ecological movement – but she has long since given up the hope that her work might have any social effects. In the meantime her life revolves chiefly around her family and her profession. When Massimo, an astrophysicist and student of her late father, returns to Padua, and a love relationship is in the offing between them, she draws new hope for her happiness through love for a man. On the other hand she feels her relationship with Massimo is a betrayal of Erika, his wife, and her own behavior, which runs counter to her ideas of female solidarity, troubles her. Some time later Massimo discovers he is interested in Maria, the middle sister, and begins an affair with her behind Velia's back. Without suspecting Velia's relationship with Massimo, Maria tells her sisters that she has fallen in love with Massimo, whereupon a violent argument erupts between the two older sisters in the course of which Velia accuses Maria of acting selfishly in regard to Erika. She thus expresses her own pangs of conscience, mingled with her disappointment at Massimo's betrayal and her destroyed hopes. This experience brings Velia to the realization that it is senseless to wait for a happier relationship with a man.

For Maria, the middle sister, happiness is associated with the dream of a great, romantic love. She longs for a man with whom she can share her thoughts and feelings. She's never wanted anything but marriage, but her marriage to TV comic Federico, a somewhat naïve, unattractive man, turns out to be a disappointment. It's true that he is gentle and faithful; he adores her, and also he offers her a life of comfort. She, however, finds the monotonous, unfulfilled existence of

a housewife unbearable, and becomes increasingly apathetic, melancholy, and depressed. In Massimo she believes she has found the man of her dreams, but basically she is only projecting her wishful thinking on him, while he feels that in her need for absolute intimacy she expects too much of him, and shrinks back. Still, he lets Maria go on believing that he is going to leave his wife and live with her. But when she starts taking concrete steps in that direction, he balks at the decision. Instead, his interest in Erika is rekindled. Finally he leaves Maria and destroys her dream of the love of her life.

Sandra belongs to a younger generation of women than her sisters. The film begins with a celebration of her 18th birthday. She has just graduated from secondary school, is full of enthusiasm, energy, and joie de vivre, and has firm ideas about life: Her future plans include not only a fulfilling professional life but also marriage and a family. Wishing to do something meaningful with her life and to help other people, she has decided to study medicine. But she feels that her life dream is endangered by science's unquestioning belief in progress and misanthropic thoughtlessness, which she has encountered among researchers and students at the university – an attitude she also senses and criticizes in Massimo. She feels fear and dejection at the sight of environmental destruction and war, which she translates into anger and political involvement in the ecological movement. She also chafes at the discrimination she is exposed to as a woman, and the competitive atmosphere at the university, and she keeps falling prey to self-doubt. Velia, who has been her confidante ever since their mother's early death, comforts and consoles her. It is mainly with her and later with Nicola, a young instructor she has met at the university, that she shares her fear of the future and her despair, but also her ideals and her moments of joy and happiness. As Sandra's final examination approaches, she and Nicola decide to marry after her graduation. But her dream of happiness is also shattered when Nicola is killed in an auto accident.

Like the three sisters, their brother Roberto, too, has to bury his dream of the future. Of course, in contrast to his sisters, he does not see his life's fulfillment in love, but in his profession. He is a talented violinist, and aspires to a career as a musician when he falls in love with Sabrina. She is the feminine counterpart of Massimo: Egotistical, she thinks only of herself, disregards the needs and feelings of others, is vain and ambitious. Her goal in life is a husband, children, a social position, and a secure existence. After her marriage to Roberto she pushes him into a career as a bank official, manipulates him into turning away from music, and alienates him from his sisters while at the same time she is cheating on him with his boss. It does not take Roberto long to regret his marriage and to rebel; but he is too weak to assert himself against his wife, and finally bows to his fate.

Thus the siblings are disappointed by life, each in a different way. They have to come to terms with the facts of life and try to make the best of things. Velia learns to accept her loneliness and to be content with whatever good moments life has to offer: pleasure at getting professional recognition and at her promotion to the rank of a professor, her affectionate relationship with her sisters, and friendship with other women, including Erika, to whom she has drawn closer. It is this attitude that finally also allows her to forgive Massimo and to remain on friendly terms with him. Maria buries her dream of the great love and stays with her husband, knowing full well that life with him condemns her to boredom and monotony. Her dark predictions for the future are mitigated only by the fact that her sisters have decided to go to live with her. Sandra's consolation is that she is still young and has her whole life before her. She will concentrate on her profession and get over the loss of Nicola. And Roberto learns to howl with the pack by extorting a promotion from his boss because Sabrina is carrying the latter's child. It is Velia who has the last word when she says, in a tone of calm resignation: »Nothing has changed, everything still revolves around money and success just as it did in the '50s, and if you've got that it helps you to forget.« This insight is underlined by the final scene, which establishes a parallel between the present and the past: Everyone has gathered for an evening of music during a family celebration. Roberto plays the violin, and Maria accompanies him on the piano. Slowly the color fades, the camera finally stops on Maria's face. A similar image appears in an eight-millimeter film that Velia and Cecchini, an old family friend, watch in an earlier scene. It shows the mother, played by the same actress who also plays Maria, listening to music with Roberto, still a child at the time.

These scenes emphasize Chekhov's message that happiness only exists as a pipe-dream. As always, however, the filmmaker touches on a number of aspects that provide complex insight into the period. The play is used as a framework for examining the issues that are close to her own heart: women's existence in the so-called postfeminist period, their relationships with other women and men, their state of mind, their hopes and dreams. And she asks herself: What is left

46. The three sisters visiting the convent. (Photo: Bioskop Film.)
47. Sabrina (Agnès Sorel) and Roberto (Sergio Castellitto).
48. Concluding scene: musicale at the family gathering. (Photo: Concorde-Film.)
49. Margarethe von Trotta and her partner at the time, Felice Laudadio, Rimini 1986.

of the struggles, expectations, and hopes? In order to answer this question, she introduces a number of plot elements that do not exist in the play. The most important concerns the character of Massimo, which in the play is drawn far more positively than in the film: In the film, both through his work as a scientist and through his personal conduct, he becomes the embodiment of the masculine principle of thoughtless destruction, as Sandra puts it. His affair with Velia – something that was added in the film – refers to this, as does the fact that he leaves Maria to devote himself to his wife again. In Chekhov, on the other hand, the cause for the separation is his transfer. Another additional element characterizing masculine behavior is the way Roberto adjusts to prevailing corruption. He is capable of profiting by his wife's infidelity, and now that he has proved he is able to assert himself, he gains the respect of his boss and even of his wife. On the other hand, the female characters are given more importance. The sisters have a more positive outlook on life, and they are also more active. Besides, there is an added character, Massimo's wife Erika, who is only mentioned in Chekhov. While in the play she is characterized as someone who is emotionally disturbed, who makes her husband's life hell, the film shows her as an insecure, dependent woman who, however, thanks to her friendship with Velia and other women, succeeds in gradually freeing herself from the dependency on Massimo.

In an interview, Margarethe von Trotta described the film as »an overall balance of emancipation.« The balance is predominantly negative. While it is now a matter of course for younger women like Sandra to aspire to a career as well as a family, women are still professionally discriminated against, and even younger men like Nicola try to restrict them to the role of a mother. At least women have made some gains, like Velia's instructorship, which allows her to explore the history of women and provides recognition for her. As in the case of Maria and Erika, marriage is still a more or less luxurious prison in which women become emotionally and intellectually stunted. But the filmmaker asks another question as well: Is living alone a desirable alternative? Satisfactory relationships with men seem impossible as long as the men are thoughtless and egotistical, as long as they are concerned only with their convenience and their career, and prove to be incapable of expressing their feelings. On the other hand the film also suggests that masculine behavior is the product of expectations placed in men. Thus disappointment and fear of emotions appear behind Massimo's cynicism – »fear of life«, as he says. A positive element portrayed in the film, as in *Rosa Luxemburg*, is a new type of female friendship, free of the pressure of expectations and competition, founded on tolerance and mutual understanding. However, these rarely transcend the personal level and are predominantly apolitical, for politically there is resignation and stagnation everywhere. The Red Guards are as good as crushed. The environmental and peace movements now engage only in defensive actions, which spring from the rage of despair. That is the situation with which women are confronted in *Paura e amore* (*Love and Fear*) and which they must learn to accept.

This last statement is emphasized by the old family friend, Doctor Cecchini, whose role throughout is to comment on the action, just as it is in the Chekhov play. However, while in Chekhov he appears as a drinker who, though wise, is disappointed by life, in the film he turns out to be the only positive masculine figure. As the siblings' intimate friend and adviser, he shares his wisdom with them, encourages them, and helps them to deal with their disappointments. His attitude is without illusions, but in a positive sense, for he has no more lofty expectations. The fact that his hopes were disappointed has taught him to be content with little. All his life he was in love with the siblings' mother, but could only admire her from afar. In his old age he lives on his remembrance of her, and he has learned that true love is completely selfless and is based on an unlimited willingness to give. Since he makes no claims of ownership regarding women, he does not feel his interests are threatened by the emancipation of women, and can state with honest conviction: »The women's revolution is the greatest event since the French Revolution.« Margarethe von Trotta has this character embody the positive utopia for a new type of interpersonal relationships, free of dependencies and claims to power.

L'Africaine (*The African Woman*)

Margarethe von Trotta's next film is based on a screenplay that had been in her drawer for a long time, but whose production she had had to put off because of *Rosa Luxemburg* and *Paura e amore* (*Love and Fear*). Here she again treats a very personal, private subject: a reflection on the betrayal of love and friendship in a story about the eternal triangle. Like *Paura e amore* (*Love and Fear*), *L' Africaine* (*The African Woman*) was also made as a German-Italian-French co-produc-

tion. This meant that, as in her previous film, the film director had to work with actors from three different countries. That circumstance had caused difficulties during the making of *Paura e amore* (*Love and Fear*), since the story took place in Italy, while not all the actors spoke Italian, so that they had trouble with the original text and their parts had to be dubbed. That is why there is no original version, but several dubbed versions in different languages. Because of this, Margarethe von Trotta moved the scene of *L'Africaine* (*The African Woman*) to Paris, where people of many different nationalities live together, and made the original version in French.

The film takes up the central theme of earlier Trotta movies and develops it further. It focuses on the friendship between two women who are each other's antithesis: the German physician Martha, a strong, unsentimental, intellectual person, uncompromising toward herself and others, and the feminine, emotional, impulsive, and dependent Italian Ana. In flashbacks we discover how their friendship is shattered when, after a failed love relationship, Ana takes refuge with Martha and begins an affair with Martha's partner Victor behind her back. One evening Martha discovers the two without their noticing. Her pride wounded, disappointed about the double betrayal, she doesn't waste any words, but leaves France to work as a physician in Mali.

The story begins when, years later, Ana is in the hospital after an operation, afraid that she is terminally ill. In the meantime she has married Victor, and has guilt feelings toward Martha, expressed in a recurrent nightmare: It is night, she runs down a hospital corridor into her room and finds Martha in her bed. Ana drags Martha out of the bed, there is a bitter struggle that Ana wins, but when she lies down in bed in Martha's place, she feels the imprint of Martha's body like pinpricks. Ana, who tends to believe in miracles and esoterica, is firmly convinced that she must die if she does not succeed in bringing about a reconciliation. Encouraged by Jan and Andrej, two fatherly friends from the neighborhood, she feels her illness is the result of disharmony in her life caused by her betrayal of Martha, and believes she can regain her health only if she restores the harmony again and lives at one with herself and nature. The illness becomes a metaphor for the lack of inner balance, the »balance of happiness«, as Margarethe von Trotta called it in her film *Schwestern* (*Sisters*). The solution she indicated in that film was to fuse emotion and intellect, vitality and yearning for death. In *L'Africaine* (*The African Woman*) she equates healing with becoming reconciled oneself and with the world. As a result, reconciliation with Martha is a matter of life and death for Ana, and that is why, after years of silence, she takes the first step. She sends for Martha. Martha returns, and now finally the repressed conflicts erupt. Ana begs Martha to forgive her, and makes it clear how much her forgiveness means to her. This is how she succeeds in making a crack in Martha's protective shield of rejection and coldness. Behind it, Martha's bitterness becomes apparent, but also her longing to be healed, for, as Martha realizes herself, she, too, is sick. Her suffering comes from repressing her feelings, which is how she turns her pain against herself. Although she initially rejects Ana, she secretly uncovers facts about her life. She discovers the strange marionettes Ana has been making, her books about

50. Ana's nightmare: She discovers Martha (Barbara Sukowa) in her bed.
51. Ana (Stefania Sandrelli) informs Victor (Sami Frey) of her travel plans.
52. Martha and Victor on the morning after their reconciliation.

esoterica, her contemplation of death; she remembers their friendship and the events that led to the breakup, and gradually gives up her hostile attitude. The fact that they are coming closer to each other becomes apparent in looks, in small gestures, in the worry on Martha's face, in the peaceful way they sit next to each other smoking a cigarette, or when Martha covers up for Ana because the doctor does not want Ana to smoke. Finally Ana is on the road to recovery. She is released from the hospital and would like to include Victor in the reconciliation in order to restore the harmony they once had, but the conflict is not over yet. It is true that Martha has overcome her resentment against Ana and Victor, but she hates to see them together and feels excluded. Ana is convinced that she can definitely be healed if Victor and Martha are reconciled as well, and vows to bring them together again if she regains her health. For her the only thing that counts is her will to live. Now that she is free of all other expectations, healing becomes a process of purification for her, a search for new harmony within her. She hopes for ultimate healing from an old Celtic holy well in Brittany, to which she travels with Jan and Andrej's help. When she returns she is forced to acknowledge that in the meantime Victor and Martha have rediscovered their love for each other. Suddenly it is she who sees herself as the one who was betrayed, as Martha did before her, and she reacts the same way: She is deeply hurt by the breach of trust, retires to Andrej's apartment, and refuses to speak to Victor. Martha on her part feels shame and remorse for having done to her friend what she most hates herself – betraying their friendship – and she wants to return to Africa. Victor convinces her to remain for Ana's sake. He has realized that the two need each other, and accepts a job abroad so as not to stand between them any longer. The two old men interfere once more and arrange a meeting between the two women friends during which Martha begs Ana to forgive her. Only by switching roles like this do the two women gain deeper insight into each other's feelings, so that the conflict between them can be resolved. At the end there is complete reconciliation, a new element for Trotta's films.

Another new element is the fact that the man is included to a greater extent in the women's relationship, that his motivation is scrutinized, and that there is understanding for his point of view. The reconciliation between Victor and Martha is here the prerequisite for that of the two women. It takes place as they clarify their positions, first cautiously feeling their way, then reproaching each other violently, and finally rediscovering what they have in common. When Martha arrives, she reacts coldly when Victor tries to convince her, for Ana's sake, to take a conciliatory stance. In order not to have to be alone with him, she finally leaves the apartment to take a solitary walk through the dark streets, which becomes a habit of hers from this time on. During her walk she discovers an African café, where she makes friends with a group of men from Mali. The café becomes a home away from home for her, a retreat. But to the degree that her inner hardening dissolves as she comes closer to Ana,disappointment about Victor's infidelity also erupts from Martha. In the bitter argument that follows it turns out that the conflict between Victor and Martha did not begin when Victor started an affair with Ana. That becomes clear when the two of them reproach each other for provoking this affair because they were looking for a pretext for separating without having to admit to themselves that they had become estranged years ago. Martha accuses Victor that he never loved her, while he retorts that she believed she was the only one capable of really loving someone. He says she always acted as if she were unassailable and morally superior, something that causes admiration, but not love. We begin to understand what attracts Victor to Ana – the characteristics Martha does not possess: gentleness, helplessness, the need to lean on someone, admiration. On the other hand, in Martha's presence, he notices how much he has missed her uncompromising ways and her consistency, the discussions with her and her criticism. Both of them rediscover their shared political interests. Martha finds the video recording of a TV interview in which Victor violently objects to racism, and is impressed by his attitude. Their bonds become stronger when he accidentally discovers her in her African café, and she introduces him to her friends. But for a complete reconciliation, the conflict needs to erupt in all its violence, revealing Victor's dilemma, for he loves both women and would not like to hurt either of them. Not until Martha sees that the situation is as painful for him as for her does she throw off her armor and admit to herself her pain at the way he betrayed her. This helps her to overcome it and to forgive Victor. Later she realizes that her behavior is not in accordance with her ideas of friendship and absolute fidelity, and that she has to give up her uncompromising attitude and look for a different way. Thus reconciliation with Ana becomes possible, but also the prospect of a different kind of relationship with Victor. It is left open what such a relationship might look like. One thing is certain: The two women give priority to their friendship and decide to go to Africa together, but they leave an invitation for Victor to join them there, in other words, they do not exclude him.

With Victor, Margarethe von Trotta develops a positive male image only tentatively present in her other films. Like Trotta's earlier male characters, he, too, derives his self-esteem primarily from his work as a journalist, but he is willing to cut back on his professional life in favor of his personal life. He tries to respond to the needs of the women and to understand them, respects their friendship, and is even capable of placing it above his own interests by withdrawing in order to make a reconciliation between Ana and Martha possible. But above all he is allowed to show his weakness and vulnerability, and that is the decisive factor in the reconciliation between him and the two women.

The film outlines a positive vision of a more satisfactory way for people to live together. A constant thematic element is the search for harmony as a symbol for life, while discord means death: Ana tries to establish harmony between herself and nature to escape death; Martha returns from Africa because her anger against Victor and Ana has become an unbearable burden for her that prevents her from living. Victor looks for a harmonious relationship with both women, and again and again the healing force of music is conjured up as a symbol of beauty and of psychic equilibrium. Harmony has both an inner and an external dimension. For the individual it means living in agreement with oneself, accepting one's own identity with all its inadequacies, while in one's attitude toward others it means respecting their otherness. This is Margarethe von Trotta's provisional answer to the question that constantly recurs in her films: What is a fully developed feminine personality? But it is also her attempt at offering a solution to the question: What is a harmonious relationship between people, one including both men and women? Her answers are also politically relevant to the contemporary problem of xenophobia, a problem that is raised in the film. Victor's plea against racism, in which he draws a parallel between present-day phenomena and the German Nazi past, is underpinned by Martha's experiences in Africa and with her African friends in Paris. The friendliness, helpfulness, and respect with which the Africans treat Victor and Martha is contrasted with the conditions under which African emigrants live in Paris, and make it clear why Martha feels at home in Mali, while she has the sense of being a stranger in France. Home is here defined by the quality of interpersonal relationships.

In contrast to earlier Trotta films, the social background in *L'Africaine* (*The African Woman*) is examined relatively little, and the film's political dimension predominantly consists of a plea for more respect and more tolerance toward others. As for the rest, the story concentrates on the emotions and insights of the three protagonists. A special role is played by the two old gentlemen from the neighborhood, who, like the chorus in Greek tragedy, comment on the action and occasionally intervene in it as well. From a dramatic standpoint, they provide a distancing element that enables the filmmaker to contrast the close-range perspective of the camera reading emotions on the faces of the characters, and the observant perspective of the voyeur. As regards content, the old men are associated with Ana, whose interest in esoterica and the supernatural they share. With their crystal ball and other hocus-pocus they pass on home truths – frequently accompanied by a dash of kindly irony – that spring from the serenity of old age, and they let their listeners know in no uncertain terms that as they grow more aware of mortality, relationship problems will come to seem more and more trivial. In all this, there is clearly also a sly comment on a phenomenon that was very widespread in the early '80s: the endless, and usually fruitless, discussions about relationships.

Il lungo silenzio (*The Long Silence*)

Margarethe von Trotta's next film is an exclusively Italian production and deals with contemporary political events: the 1992 murder of the investigating magistrates Giovanni Falcone and Paolo Borsellino, which triggered rage and indignation in Italy. Both judges were in charge of inquiries against the Mafia during the course of which a network of criminal relationships among the Mafia, politicians, and the economy came to light. The public was worried by a series of revelations about the corruption of the political elite that shook their trust in the Italian government. The film here is a means of reacting directly to a concrete political situation. The screenplay was written by the Italian journalist and film critic Felice Laudadio, Margarethe von Trotta's partner at the time. It was completed only a few months after the two magistrates' deaths, in May and June 1992. Shooting began as early as September of that same year, and the premiere took place in Palermo, in April 1993, in the presence of many widows of Mafia victims.

Margarethe von Trotta's interest in the Mafia issue was focused on the perspective of victims who were innocent bystanders: the wives, children, and mothers of the murdered men. The pro-

53. Walk on the beach: Carla (Carla Gravina) and Marco (Jacques Perrin) surrounded by bodyguards.

tagonist in *Il lungo silenzio* (*The Long Silence*) is the gynecologist Carla Aldrovandi, wife of the prosecuting attorney Marco Canova who, together with his colleague Francesco, is investigating a case against the Mafia. Surrounded by security precautions, the couple has been vacationing at the seaside in Ostia when Marco is called back because the suspect Fantoni has decided to testify, a significant breakthrough in the investigations. There are indications of large-scale illegal arms deals, in which important personalities seem to be involved. At the same time the magistrates receive murder threats, and security precautions are stepped up. Marco and Fantoni travel to Zurich to take a look at the suspects' bank accounts. During the return flight the plane is blown up, and all the passengers are killed. Marco's colleague Francesco continues the investigations, but he and his superior Tommasco are subjected to increasing political pressure. Soon thereafter Francesco, too, is murdered, and Tommasco submits his resignation because he is facing the overwhelming power of patronage, nepotism, and corruption that make a continuation of the investigation seem hopeless. Carla decides to do something. She turns to the press in order to vent her indignation about the behavior of the authorities. With the help of a journalist friend, she arranges TV interviews with the wives of Mafia victims who support her campaign. Meanwhile she continues the investigations on her own, using the personal notes left behind by her husband. After initially refusing to help, Fantoni's wife agrees to let Carla have her husband's papers. Together the two women succeed in reconstructing important connections in the case. One day Carla's mother finds a candle of the type used on graves in front of her apartment door – the Mafia death threat that also announced Marco's murder. When Carla hurries to her office that night in order to take the documents to a safe place, she discovers that they are gone. Instead she finds another murder threat, and the telephone line has been cut. As she tries to call for help from a phone booth, she is shot. Maria, Francesco's daughter, has until then refused to support the campaign by family members of Mafia victims. Carla's death causes her to bring before the public a cassette on which Carla left her important information.

As Margarethe von Trotta tells this story, her main emphasis is on the personal drama. In the first part of the film she studies the effects of the Mafia's threats on the couple's feelings and daily life. With oppressive images she describes how the security precautions condemn Carla and Marco to living like prisoners. They are forced to take their vacation in the off-season when aside from them nobody is at the resort. Moments of intimacy become impossible because they are constantly surrounded by bodyguards. A walk along the deserted beach is a security risk, and after dark they can no longer leave the house. When they return to Rome, they are accompanied by a police escort with flashing lights and wailing sirens, are led into the house like prisoners and are allowed to enter their apartment only after a policeman has searched the rooms. Their windows are shuttered even during the day, they are not allowed to go to the cinema or theater because the risk is too great. When they eat at a restaurant, the other guests leave in a hurry as soon as they recognize the magistrate. Danger, invisible and diffuse, seems to be lurking everywhere. A man in front of the house, a phone ringing, or the creaking of a door in their apartment cause them to panic.

Added to this there is continuous fear and worry about the other partner. It casts its shadow over the couple's relationship. When Carla looks out the window in the morning, watching the convoy of vehicles that takes her husband to the law court, or sits alone in the apartment and nervously waits for his return, she is filled with worry. Yet while they are together, she avoids showing her feelings in order not to burden him even more. When the pressure is too much to bear, she seeks refuge with her friend Rosa or goes to the woods to shout out her despair. Marco for his part tries to downplay the danger and acts optimistic, although he is only too aware of the meaning of the anonymous threats on the phone, which do not stop even after they change the unlisted number, and especially of the grave candle that Carla finds outside the front door shortly before his death. Yet all their attempts to give their life a semblance of normality fail. The TV interview of a politician, a radio newscast, or a newspaper item are enough to remind them of the threat, and every conversation with friends or with Carla's mother sooner or later revolves around the danger Marco is in and the fear it triggers.

One of the observations the film makes is that the greatest burden, the one that is hardest to bear, is fear for the person one loves, worry about one's partner, family, or friends. Thus Marco realizes that he can be attacked through his love for Carla, and tries to convince her to move to her mother's until the case is closed. But she refuses to leave him, for the love, the moral principles, and the loyalty that unite her and her husband carry more weight than her fear for herself. It is the bond between them that gives her strength to endure the confinement and the terror. After her husband's death the fear leaves her, for she has nothing left to lose. Rage and despair are the reason she does not shake hands with certain people at the funeral, thus revealing that she knows who is behind her husband's murder, and they are also the reason she continues her husband's struggle in spite of all warnings by friends and in spite of the anonymous threats she has received. What motivates Carla to act is not just political conviction, but also her love for Marco and her fear that his death and Francesco's might have been in vain. On the other hand she does not see death as something alarming, because for her it represents a way of being reunited with her husband, and this is the basis for her strength, which becomes a shining example for other women. Her actions set off a chain reaction, and this is precisely why her dying is not meaningless. It contains a message that is expressed in the final sentence of the film: »True happiness can be built only on the foundations of despair.« This realization is radically different from the pessimistic view Margarethe von Trotta held a few years earlier in *Rosa Luxemburg*, where she equates death with final defeat. Here, however, it is death that shakes people up as only such a profound experience can, and causes them to start fighting back. The final scene underlines the exemplary effect of Carla's actions: It shows a wall with rows of screens on which women can be seen speaking out.

The central conflict whose different aspects the film explores is the problem of fear, which only too often leads to silence in the face of threats, harm, and injustice. *IL lungo silenzio* (*The Long Silence*) is here shown both in its private and its political dimension. Silence in many different forms dictates the behavior of the victims: Carla and Marco keep silent about many things in order to protect each other. Carla tries to silence her mother when the latter speaks of her fear for Marco. Later, when her own life is threatened, she keeps the danger a secret from her mother. Francesco's wife falls silent out of concern for her family. The widows of the Mafia victims report that after their husbands were killed they were incapable of sharing their grief and pain with others. Maria refuses to speak publicly about her father's death in order to be able to forget the sorrow she associates with it. Fantoni's wife at first does not want to tell Carla what she knows because she fears for her children. After Marco's death Carla, too, at first lapses into silence and retreats into herself: Wordlessly, she lets the expressions of sympathy wash over her at the funeral. Mute, she stands next to Marco's coffin. When the testament is read, she receives her husband's last message without comment; only the tears that run down her cheeks show her pain. She does not say a word about her grief and hides away in her dark bedroom to cry. For all these reactions, the film shows deep understanding, for they are human.

But *Il lungo silenzio* (*The Long Silence*) also clearly shows that in the long run it is »omertà«, the wall of silence, that actually makes possible the criminal machinations of the Mafia, for – and this is the realization whose significance goes far beyond the subject matter of this film – only a silent majority creates the conditions for social injustice. It is not her knowledge of the background of the crimes that condemns Carla to death. She does not become a threat to the Mafia until the moment she breaks through the wall of silence that has protected the machinations of

54. Carla escapes the claustrophobic atmosphere in the vacation home. (Photo: Bioskop-Film.)
55. Carla and Marco discuss their anxiety about each other.
56. Escape through the sewer.

this secret society for centuries. In her action there is an appeal to resist not only the Mafia, but a state that is rotten to the core and whose top representatives are the first to trample on the moral and political principles they claim to protect. When Carla is offered the chance to run for parliamentary representative, she declines as follows: »I believe in democracy, but not this democracy.« As in the '60s, only the extraparliamentary way seems to offer a possibility of social change, yet in contrast to that period people have lost faith in the effectiveness of demonstrations and meetings.The strategy of fighting back that the film offers consists of an appeal to break the silence and to make the protest public, for only the fate of the individual can still rouse people to action. Thus the film particularly addresses women, for, more than men, they are reluctant to raise their voices against social injustice, because as long as patriarchal society has been in existence they have been barred from the public sphere. On the other hand, »after a certain point, women simply have more courage«[14], as Margarethe von Trotta noted in a conversation about the film, even if this courage – as in this case – springs from despair. That is why speaking out, in *Il lungo silenzio* (*The Long Silence*), represents far more than a means of political resistance. The end of silence means an act of emancipation for women through the conquest of public space.

Das Versprechen (*The Promise*)

The idea of making a film about the division of Germany was proposed by Italian producers. After the fall of the Berlin Wall in November 1989, they believed that this unique political phenomenon would provide a good subject for a film. In 1989, at a chance meeting between Margarethe von Trotta and the writer Peter Schneider in Rome, the producers convinced the two to write a screenplay. The first version was ready in 1990, but the Italian production company got into financial difficulties, and the making of the film had to be postponed until new funding could be found. The film was finally made in 1993 as a German-French-Swiss co-production. After a pre-release screening in Leipzig, in September 1994, it premiered as the opening film of the 1995 International Film Festival in Berlin. Limited by its subject matter, the story is interwoven with its political background as in no other Trotta film to date, and keeps returning to it. By means of the love story between Sophie and Konrad, adolescents separated in 1961 shortly after the construction of the Wall, the film shows the effects of separation on people in East and West Germany. It describes how over a period of 28 years the relationship of the two toward each other changes, a change that is applicable to all Germans in East and West. Politics at large determine the couple's fate, and they are at the mercy of political developments without a real possibility to make their own decisions about the continuation of their relationship. Between 1961 and the fall of the Wall in November 1989 they meet only twice: in 1968, when during the Prague Spring

there is a relative opening-up of the Eastern Bloc, and after the basic treaty, in 1980, between the governments of the FRG and the GDR as a result of which regulations controlling travel into and out of the GDR were relaxed. The film picks up on the couple's meetings in order to represent the different realities and attitudes in East and West.

The story begins in 1961 a short time after the completion of the Wall. Sophie and Konrad, who have just graduated from secondary school, decide, together with a few friends, to escape to the West through the sewer system. Konrad stumbles over his shoelace just before he reaches the manhole, an army truck approaches, and he is forced to remain behind. From this point on the lives of the couple develop in different directions. Sophie and her friends at first live with Sophie's aunt, who has a fashion salon in the center of West Berlin. The glittering world of the years of the West German economic miracle are in sharp contrast to the gray monotony in the East. While Sophie works first as a dresser and then as a model in her aunt's salon, Konrad is interrogated by the Stasi after his father reports the escape to the police in order to »set things right« again. Soon after this he is drafted and posted to guard the Wall. The two miss each other and suffer from the separation, but any contact between them is ruled out. Sophie's letters are intercepted. Her mother, who works as a schoolteacher in East Berlin, is pressured to break off contact with her daughter after Sophie's stepfather, who is loyal to the East German state, comes to the West and tries in vain to talk her into returning voluntarily to the East. Sophie finally contacts an escape organization that will help Konrad flee to the West. The organization is busted shortly before Konrad reaches the agreed-upon meeting place. Yet another attempt to escape while on guard duty by the Wall is thwarted by a fellow soldier, but has no serious consequences for Konrad, who is able to talk his way out of his predicament. Sophie, who knows nothing of these events, begins to doubt Konrad's love for her.

The couple's next meeting does not take place until 1968 when Konrad, by now a successful young astrophysicist, is allowed to travel to Prague to give a lecture at an international conference. With the help of his sister Barbara, a Protestant pastor, and his brother-in-law Harald, who as a dissident has contacts in the West, he smuggles out a letter to Sophie asking her to meet him there. In view of new possibilities opened up by the Prague Spring, Sophie and Konrad make plans to live together in Prague. Sophie, who has never quite felt at home in the West, sees the promise of life in a better social system in the combination of democracy and socialism propagated by the Czech government. Moreover, Konrad has hopes of getting a position at an institute in Prague. Their plans are shattered by the Soviet invasion of Czechoslovakia in August 1968. Sophie returns to West Berlin, while Konrad is at the mercy of Stasi investigations in East Berlin. He has aroused suspicion not only because of his meeting with Sophie, but also because he refused to sign a declaration in support of the invasion. Also, his sister and brother-in-law have been arrested and sent to prison because of an action protesting against events in Czechoslovakia. In the meantime Sophie has discovered that she is pregnant after her reunion with Konrad in Prague. She keeps trying to get a visitor's visa for East Berlin. Finally she is allowed to cross the border, but only because the Stasi wants to investigate her relationship with Konrad. In the interim she has decided to return to the GDR so as to be able to live with Konrad. He, on the other hand, is so disillusioned by the regime that he offers to defect to the West during an already authorized trip to Stockholm. But this plan fails, for Konrad's travel permit is rescinded. After Sophie vainly tries countless times to visit Konrad again, she gives up her dream of a life together with him and decides to raise her child on her own.

They do not manage to see each other again until 1981, when Konrad, who has in the meantime become the director of the Astrophysical Institute and has married a colleague, travels to a conference in West Berlin. Sophie is now working as an interpreter and living with Gerard, a French journalist. Konrad finally meets his son Alexander, who is already 12 years old by now. Alexander welcomes him with childlike nonchalance and curiosity, while the relationship with Sophie is burdened by her lost hopes and her suspicion that years ago he gave her up for his career. The two discover that in spite of their doubts and disappointments their love for each other is still alive, but they have resigned themselves to their separation and have settled into their respective lives.

After his return, Konrad is taken to task by the institute's cadre leader because of his meeting with his son. The cadre leader offers Konrad regular opportunities to see Alexander in East Berlin if in return Konrad toes the line politically. Konrad agrees, and his son receives a visitor's permit. However, the first visit is problematic for Konrad's wife Elisabeth, since Alexander tells his half-sister Lena about a life that, as a result of the political situation, she is not familiar with, and Elisabeth is afraid of embarrassing questions. She asks Konrad to meet his son alone in future.

57. Sophie (Meret Becker) and Konrad (Anian Zollner) with Konrad's department head Lorenz (Otto Sander) in Prague, 1968. (Photo: Concorde-Film.)
58. Reunion in Berlin, 1981: Konrad (August Zirner) with Sophie (Corinna Harfouch) and her partner Gerard (Jean-Yves Gautier).
59. Konrad and Sophie saying goodbye to each other, 1981.
60. Opening of the Berlin Wall in 1989.

Shortly thereafter Harald undertakes a spectacular protest action on the anniversary of the building of the Wall. He is arrested and pressured to emigrate to the West together with Barbara, who plays an important role in the GDR peace movement. Barbara refuses, for she is confident that Harald will be released because of public pressure. Konrad, too, when asked by his cadre leader to talk to her, is unable to convince her. Harald is deported against his will and shot as he tries to reenter the GDR one night by going over the Wall. All these events graphically demonstrate to Konrad the repressive character of the GDR regime once more. His critical stance changes, among other things, when he visits the peace group led by his sister. This causes a fight with Elisabeth, who reproaches him for endangering her and Lena without including them in his decisions, because all his thoughts revolve around Sophie and his son. When soon thereafter Alexander's visitor's permit is revoked, Konrad vents his rage against cadre leader Müller and knocks him down. This incident results in his social demotion: He loses his position, and from then on works as a caretaker at an indoor swimming pool. His marriage falls apart, and he lives alone in a shabby rented room. Sophie and Konrad do not meet again until the day the Wall is opened, in November 1989. As they stand facing each other on the Bornholmer Brücke amidst a jubilant crowd, they vacillate between joy, sadness, and hope. Only their son Alexander, now a young man twenty years old, is able to look into the future with optimism.

As the story unfolds, the film increasingly concentrates on Konrad's conflict between rebellion against the state and adaptation to the conditions. As the conflict grows we are shown to what mechanisms of oppression people in the GDR were exposed, and how different were the attitudes provoked by oppression. By nature, Konrad tends not to be interested in politics; he is a hesitant dreamer who adapts, though reluctantly. But as the pressure on him grows and his conflict with the regime is exacerbated, his resistance increases until at last he rebels openly. At first his opposition has predominantly personal reasons. The driving force for fleeing to the West is Sophie, who does not want to let herself be »walled in«, while Konrad actually wants to flee only because of his love for her. He has far closer ties to his family, and the political convictions of his father, a communist of the old guard, also influence him to some extent; that becomes apparent when he later tells his son, »Remaining here was a gamble, an adventure. We wanted to build something totally new here.« Therefore it is relatively easy for him to adapt for the sake of his professional interests after all attempts to reach the West fail. Initially the Prague Spring only has personal meaning for him, for it gives him hope that he and Sophie can live together. When his hope is shattered by the Soviet Union's military intervention and, at the mercy of increasing political pressure, he is also spied upon and subjected to restrictions, he openly opposes the GDR regime for the first time. Now he wants to defect to the West not only because of Sophie, but because he is repelled by the methods of those in power. But his escape plans are foiled and Konrad becomes resigned. He tries to make the best of his situation both on a personal and on a professional level, he marries and has a family, concentrates on his career, and enjoys a number of privileges. The conflict does not break out again until he sees Sophie and gets to know his son, whom the Stasi uses as a way of exerting political pressure on him. »A signature for a son«, is the offer cadre leader Müller makes him. His contact with the GDR peace movement through his sister, the Stasi's blackmail attempts, and Harald's deportation and death increase his inner revolt against the state, and this turns into open opposition when his son is no longer allowed to visit him. The price he pays is political ostracism, which condemns him to an isolated, marginalized existence.

Konrad's attitude is representative of that of the great majority of East Germans, and it explains why the East German state could remain in existence as long as it did, but also why it finally came to an end under pressure from a fast-growing opposition movement. The film examines the reasons for, and consequences of, conformity and revolt in their various manifestations, and tries to explain them. On the one hand there are those who are convinced that the GDR system is superior – party secretaries, Stasi collaborators, or members of the Volksarmee (»the GDR People's Army«) and judiciary, but also representatives of the common people. Their views have been shaped by the experiences of the Nazi period and the wish to create a new and better state in which the crimes of the National Socialists cannot be repeated. When the Warsaw Pact countries march into Czechoslovakia, if not sooner, this hope turns out to be illusory. It turns into disillusionment, uneasiness, and inner opposition, as was the case with Konrad's father. But the most important mainstay of the state is the silent majority of those who »keep still and sign on the dotted line«, as it says in the film. There are many motives for their conformist behavior: They do not resist because they have become resigned, or see no alternative, or because of personal advantages, for fear of the consequences of revolt, because they make their

professional interests a priority, or else, like Konrad's superior Lorenz, they feel the German Democratic Republic is the lesser of two evils. For those who resist risk being discriminated against socially, being persecuted, spied upon, arrested, forcibly deported, or killed, as Barbara and Harald, the escape helpers and the victims by the Wall, and finally Konrad himself are forced to discover. If people still keep on rebelling, it is because in certain situations the pressure increases and indignation gets the better of them, say, after the Wall was built, or after the invasion of Czechoslovakia, or when personal needs are used to blackmail someone, as in Konrad's case.

The film compares Konrad's experiences and the development of Sophie. The latter is sketched only in general outlines, mainly to emphasize the contrast between East and West. Sophie's lifestyle has been shaped by the Western consumer society and the liberal social ideology that evolved in the '70s and '80s. If, after her flight in 1961, she reacts with something like amazement to the status symbols of those years, she takes them all for granted twenty years later. When Konrad visits her in 1981, she is living in a studio furnished with designer furniture, while Konrad's apartment is barely different from his parents' home in the '60s, furnished in typically petit-bourgeois taste. Sophie is living with a man to whom she is not married, while Konrad *is* married. At Sophie's house, the cooking is done by her partner Gerard, while at Konrad's house it is his wife who cooks. In the West, there is boeuf à la bourguignonne, in the East they eat beef rolls. Even the language has gone off in two different directions: In the East, pizza is called *krusta*, and hamburgers are called *grilletta*, as Alexander reports with amazement after his first visit there. Sophie is a self-confident independent woman who knows what she wants, while Konrad takes things as they are and does not react until he can no longer stand the pressure. The way the two of them act expresses a character difference which the film attributes to their different family and social backgrounds. Sophie's father was opposed to the regime and was driven to suicide in prison. This experience is expressed in her rebellion against her stepfather, who becomes, for her, the embodiment of the hated regime, particularly because she suspects that he had a hand in her father's death. It is experiences like these that have molded her into a strong, rebellious person. Moreover, she has internalized the attitude of protest characteristic of the young generation in the West. Her views on the Prague Spring show the influence of the social reform movement of the '60s, for unlike Konrad she welcomes it not only as a chance to achieve personal happiness, but as a way to create a better society by political means. When the Soviet tanks pull up in front of her hotel, she fights her way through to the protesting crowd on the street, while Konrad watches from the hotel lobby, helpless and indecisive, for he is used to ducking and conforming, a habit that imperceptibly becomes a character trait for, as we hear toward the end of the film: »When the cage is opened thirty years later, the bird can no longer fly.«

Sophie's perspective on her relationship with Konrad reflects the general attitude of Westerners toward German partition. At first it makes her unhappy, and like many others she hopes that the Wall will be of short duration. But then she reconciles herself to the separation and buries her dream of a life together. And finally both sides get accustomed to the abnormal situation and learn to live with it. At the same time Sophie has less and less understanding for the situation of people in the GDR, although she still has a feeling of connection and longs for a future together. The film leaves open what such a future might look like. It does make it clear that there was more separating the Germans than the Wall, and that there is new potential for conflict in the reunification of Germany.

Margarethe von Trotta and Peter Schneider saw *Das Versprechen* (*The Promise*) as their personal contribution toward the critical appraisal of the partition of Germany as a phenomenon of contemporary history. They thought that after the fall of the Berlin Wall there would be many other films dealing with this topic. However, they underestimated the public tendency to suppress all memory of historical events. The film turned out to be the only attempt to take a serious look at the recent German past, and thus was assigned an importance it had not sought. It became the »Wall film« par excellence and provoked a heated debate among film reviewers on whether life in the GDR had really been the way it was portrayed in *Das Versprechen* (*The Promise*). The film had been planned as an ordinary personal story, portraying a segment of reality in the form of a few individual lives; critics demanded from it the total social truth of an era – the kind of achievement that can at best be accomplished by a great historical epic. But *Das Versprechen* (*The Promise*), like all of Trotta's films, places primary emphasis on exploring the inner conflicts and reactions of people whose lives are derailed by historical events, and in this way tries to shed light on the interplay of the personal and the political.

Films for television

Personally and professionally, *Das Versprechen* (*The Promise*) marks a turning point in Margarethe von Trotta's life. The subject unavoidably brought her back to Germany, which has again been the focus of her work ever since. This circumstance coincided with a personal decision to leave Italy, which had been the idea of her partner Felice Laudadio. Like many left-wing intellectuals, he felt that the swing to the right of Italian society after Berlusconi's electoral victory was dangerous and intolerable. The couple decided to move to Paris, where Margarethe von Trotta has an apartment she received when she and Volker Schlöndorff divided their joint property in their divorce. The move from Rome to Paris took place at the end of 1994. But while Margarethe von Trotta settled down quickly, feeling that she finally had a home again, the new surroundings were hard on her partner. Several projects he had hoped to work on fell through; there were also language difficulties, and since, moreover, the political situation in Italy changed when Berlusconi was removed from office, he decided to return to Rome, which resulted in the couple's separation. Thus Margarethe von Trotta is now living alone for the first time in many years, which she considers a challenge. Since then she has been more active than ever before.

Already during the production of *Das Versprechen* (*The Promise*), she began preparations for a new film: the story of the women from Rosenstraße in Berlin, who, in the 1930s, fought successfully against the deportation of their Jewish husbands to a Nazi concentration camp. This project was suggested by Volker Schlöndorff, who felt the topic was ideal material for her. He thought the story could be made into a lavish film on the financial scale of *Das Versprechen* (*The Promise*), and he promised to obtain the necessary funding through the Babelsberg Film Studios, which he headed at the time. Thereupon WDR (Westdeutscher Rundfunk / »West German Radio and Television«) offered to participate in the project and made available funds for a co-production. Margarethe von Trotta was fascinated by the subject, especially since it brought her a step closer to her dream of creating a kind of cinematic chronicle of the twentieth century. She began her research. The determining factor in her decision to make the film were meetings with the documentarist Daniela Schmidt, who had studied the events of that period in detail and had, among other things, made a TV documentary about them, and conversations with survivors who had been personally involved and who were deeply moved by the idea that a film would again focus public awareness on their experiences. With this in mind, she wrote the screenplay, but after completing it she was told by Volker Schlöndorff that the money for the planned »big« movie was not available and that she should downsize the project to fit a lower budget. She then changed her concept of the story and wrote a new screenplay. Finally the project fell through completely because it turned out that the Babelsberg studios had no funding available at all at the time, and that WDR could not hold back the authorized funds any longer. Instead, WDR asked Margarethe von Trotta to direct the TV film *Winterkind* (»Winter Child«), based on a book by Nicole Houwer. Although the offer came at very short notice – WDR made the proposal in October 1996, and shooting began the following January – she agreed. Thus, for the first time, she directed a film without having been involved in writing the screenplay. Since that time, she has made two more TV films in quick succession: the comedy *Mit fünfzig küssen Männer anders* (»At Fifty Men Kiss Differently«) and the drama *Dunkle Tage* (»Dark Days«), which were both produced in 1997. Immediately after this she began preparations for a four-part TV adaptation of Uwe Johnson's *Jahrestage* (*Anniversaries*).

In many ways, working for television means an adjustment for the filmmaker. For one thing, there is her conceptional approach. Since the beginning she has always seen her films as a contribution to the analysis of social problems and a way to facilitate collective experience. This approach can be translated into television terms only to a very limited degree. It is true that television makes it possible to reach a larger audience right away. But unlike the cinema, a television film carries less weight, and its effect soon fizzles out. Viewers choose a TV film less deliberately, often more by chance; even if a film manages to shake up the audience, something else will be on TV the next day, and impressions are forgotten quickly. On the other hand, the reason people go to the cinema is that a film interests them. When the movie is over, they talk about what they've seen and think about it critically. With television, there is none of the direct exchange of opinion with the audience and other filmmakers that Margarethe von Trotta always looks for at public screenings of her films and discussions at festivals and other events because it helps her to develop artistically and personally.

Also, TV producers have different expectations. Their most important criterion for a film is that it should work and lure viewers to the screen: The reason is immaterial. The artistic standard of the film may be less important. Moreover, there are formal restrictions and financial limits. Budgets are lower and the time spent shooting is quite a bit shorter than with films made for the cinema. This creates pressure, and there is even more stress when, as in the case of *Winterkind* (»Winter Child«) and *Dunkle Tage* (»Dark Days«), the cast includes children, who are allowed to work only three hours per day. Thus the need for artistic perfection is often less important than the demand that the schedule be met. What is more, there are time limitations, for if the film is to be shown during the peak period of the evening schedule, its length needs to fit pre-existing blocks of time. For this reason Margarethe von Trotta was forced to cut *Dunkle Tage* (»Dark Days«) to 88 1/2 minutes, although she felt that the 15 minutes longer original version was ideal. Also, TV films are usually specific offers to produce already existing screenplays, or screenplays about circumscribed subjects which leave only little room for the kind of subjective statement that is possible in an auteur film.

All these factors imply a different approach. There is typically less personal involvement, and artistic sights are lowered. On the other hand, a director like Margarethe von Trotta needs to think of her reputation as an artist. She has vast professional expertise, and she has developed her own style, which shows in the standard of her television films as well. Thus, for instance, the program advisory council of WDR described *Winterkind* (»Winter Child«) as »one of the television high points of 1997«, and said that watching it »almost made up for the burdensome task of monitoring programs.«[15]

Winterkind (»Winter Child«)

When WDR asked Margarethe von Trotta to produce *Winterkind* (»Winter Child«), they were aware that the screenplay had its weaknesses, and their offer included the stipulation that she would rework it. However, although she made innumerable changes and kept hardly a single dialogue, she still felt she was tied to the original basic pattern, and thus the story is by far less realistic, and the problems less complex than in Trotta's other films. The plot is based on a coincidence of dramatic events that feel artificially constructed and resemble the clichés of a soap opera. The film portrays an unusual case, allowing the viewer to generalize its central problems only to a limited extent, and thus barely contributing to the critical analysis of a specific social situation. Unlike in other Trotta films, the conflict situation does not come from the contradiction between social and personal limitations, and the ideas and desires of the protagonists, but from the confrontation of good and evil. Events are triggered by the egotism, unscrupulousness, and weakness of two men who destroy the lives of two women, a child, and an old man. Only because of the magnanimity and understanding of the woman who has lost the most is it finally possible to keep even more mischief from being done.

Even the events that precede the story – gradually brought to light in the course of the action – show a clear separation into victims and perpetrators: The young Russian woman Jelena loves the German engineer Michael, who is working on a bridge-building project in Sverdlovsk. Jelena gets involved in the criminal machinations of his superior Georg Berger, and as a result is condemned to several years in a labor camp because of a breach of money exchange regulations. Her lover deserts her and their son Boris, and marries Elke Berger, his boss's daughter. When it turns out that his wife is unable to have children, he brings the baby to Germany in order to adopt it. He tells Elke that the child was placed with them by an agency.

The film begins when Jelena arrives in Germany after her release from the camp in order to look for her son, who is now ten years old. Although she has very little information, she finds out the truth, falls in love with Michael again, and has hopes of getting back not only her son, but his father as well. She fails with Michael, for while he feels attracted to her again, he has no intention of breaking off with Elke. However, their son, now called Daniel, finally decides to leave the parents he has had up to this point and to go to Russia with Jelena. His wish is motivated by his difficult relationship with Elke's father, whose malice causes the death of Daniel's best friend Jonathan, an eccentric old man who lives in a trailer on the adjoining property and is Daniel's favorite playmate. Jonathan has an ongoing feud with Georg Berger, and accuses him of having robbed him by trickery of the land on which Elke and Michael run their nursery. During one of their regular clashes, in the middle of winter, Georg Berger destroys the electric heater in Jonathan's trailer home, whereupon Jonathan contracts pneumonia and finally dies. Daniel blames not only Georg Berger for the old man's death, but Elke as well, since she always disapproved of his friendship with Jonathan and tried to undermine it. She also refused to let the old man spend the night in

61. Elke (Lena Stolze) and Michael working in the nursery. (Photo: Westdeutscher Rundfunk.)

the greenhouse as her son asked her to do. This incident shakes his trust in his adoptive mother and benefits Jelena. However, during the first night Daniel spends with Jelena before they plan to leave for Russia, she realizes that he will suffer if he leaves the family he has had so far. She decides to give him back to Elke and Michael.

Aside from the one-dimensional and stereotyped conception of the characters, the story suffers from the fact that it raises a number of serious conflicts, but they are not analyzed in depth or developed. Jelena's and Elke's struggle for Michael and Daniel, Daniel's conflict with his grandfather, which he transfers to Elke, the problems between Elke and her father, and between her father and Michael are merely touched on and remain static for the most part, because the course of events is determined not by the development of inner conflicts, but by unexpected turns and coincidences. For instance, as Jelena searches for her son, all kinds of obstacles are first placed in her path. These go against the laws of logic and only create artificial confusion. For example, one cannot help wondering why she never connects the only piece of information she has on her son's whereabouts – the fact that he was adopted by a family called Berger from Cologne – with Michael's father-in-law and former boss, whom she knows from Russia. And – wouldn't you know it! – when Michael got married he took his wife's last name, or else Jelena would have realized at once who is behind her son's disappearance. If Michael did this to make it harder for Jelena to find her son, as she suspects, it was a very clumsy maneuver no matter how you look at it. He obviously didn't bother to hide his new last name when he adopted Daniel, for Jelena heard it in the Russian children's home. If the plot were not full of such dodges, the search would have been simpler, and it would not have been necessary to fall back on a lucky coincidence to keep the plot moving. In the end, Jelena only finds the Bergers because during a visit at the youth welfare department she manages to catch a glimpse of their name and address on the social worker's computer screen, and again she is lucky it's such a small town, where there are few families with this name. Also, her visit at the nursery would probably have been unsuccessful if she hadn't accidentally caught sight of Michael in the yard as she left the place. Another thing that makes no sense is why she doesn't immediately see the connections, but allows Michael to put her off. After all, at this point she already knows that the Bergers have a ten-year-old son. It is yet another »act of providence« that the quarrel between old Jonathan and Georg Berger comes to a head at the very moment when Jelena appears to assert her rights to her child, for initially the two conflict situations are not connected in any way. In contrast to this, it is almost plausible that Jelena is on the spot right when Daniel, who has run away from his grandfather's house, returns home alone and discovers Jonathan seriously ill in his trailer, thus giving her the opportunity to help the boy in this difficult time and to win his sympathy.

In her adaptation of the screenplay Margarethe von Trotta strives to offset the weaknesses of the plot and to get rid of a few of the biggest inconsistencies. Since it was decided that Jelena would not have a Russian accent because supposedly the audience would not like it, Margarethe von Trotta made her an interpreter, and engaged Susanna Simon for the part – an actress who has a Russian mother and speaks both Russian and German without an accent. Also she tried to give Jelena's behavior a realistic background, and to take away some of her character's naivety by juxtaposing her with the figure of the Italian Ana, temperamental, eccentric, but extremely practical when it comes to emotional matters. Ana has had an affair with a former fellow prisoner of Jelena's, Sergio; while Sergio has left Ana to go to Italy, he keeps enlisting her for his work with Amnesty International. After arriving in Germany Jelena turns to Ana for help because Sergio gave her Ana's address. Ana puts Jelena up at her place and becomes her support and her confidante. In terms of the drama Ana has a similar function as the two old men in *L'Africaine* (*The African Woman*). She is the one to whom Jelena tells the story of her time in the camp, her life in Russia, the search for her child, and her dream of new happiness with her son and Michael, details that explain the motives for her actions. Ana also creates a distance to Jelena's behavior, for she forces Jelena to face facts whenever Jelena begins to dream of an illusionary happiness with Michael and their son: for instance, she reminds her that Michael abandoned her and deceived her, or challenges her by asking if it is really the best thing for Daniel to tear him from his familiar surroundings. Apart from this, at the end, Ana offers her hope for a new life by suggesting that they can go to Italy together. In this way Jelena's inner conflict and her decision to give up her son become easier to understand.

In characterizing the other figures, the director also makes every effort to explain the behavior and psychological processes of the protagonists, and to show their inner development. She succeeds in clarifying the motivation for their actions and in breaking through the oversimplifying constellation of good and evil. She takes away the one-dimensionality of the two villains, Michael and Georg Berger, by showing that both become guilty because they cannot overcome the limitations of their personality. The reason for Michael's conduct is his weakness. Because he is weak he takes the line of least resistance and gives in to outward pressure, whether it comes from the two women or from his father-in-law. His tendency is to avoid problems whenever possible. At the same time, he has some very positive traits. He is a good father, a loving husband and a decent person who realizes he has done wrong and tries to make up for it. Georg Berger is portrayed as a strongman who forges ahead without thinking, used to getting his way without scruples and, if need be, by force. But he is also very fond of his daughter and he has his sentimental moments – for instance, while celebrating Christmas with Michael and Jelena as he remembers the old days in Russia and the three begin to sing a soulful Russian song – another element Margarethe von Trotta added to the plot. At this gathering, for Daniel's sake, a reconciliation of sorts takes place among all the characters, a stalemate situation in which the final decision is left up to the boy. Yet another change made by the filmmaker is that the figure of Jonathan, originally stereotyped as an eccentric, somewhat childish old man, is given an added dimension of wisdom but also of melancholy, as she shows him deeply engrossed conducting a classical aria against a background of old family photographs.

The most important change undertaken by Margarethe von Trotta was that she accentuated the problem of adoption and analyzed it from different perspectives in order to give the story greater social relevance. In the process she focused the action on the conflict between Elke and Jelena and brought out the tragic nature of their situation by showing that these are two women who fight for the fulfillment of their dream of an intact family and are both forced to acknowledge that this is possible only at the expense of the other woman.

It is true that initially the main conflict seems to lie in the struggle of the two women around Michael. For instance, Elke has no idea that Daniel is Jelena's son, and she is merely jealous. But this aspect retreats into the background when Jelena provokes open confrontation between them by suddenly holding a photograph of her, Michael, and their newborn son in front of the other's face. In this crucial scene, which Margarethe von Trotta added to the screenplay, Elke realizes, from one moment to the next, that her whole life is built on lies. From this point on the struggle for the child becomes the focus. The culmination comes as the two women literally tug Daniel back and forth between them when Jelena tries to get in the ambulance with him as Jonathan is being taken to the hospital, while Elke wants to prevent the boy from going.

In the course of the story it becomes clear that both are morally entitled to the child. Not only is Jelena the boy's biological mother, but she is also convinced that in spite of their long separation there is a »sacred bond« between her and her son. Actual facts at first seem to confirm that this is so. She succeeds in appealing to the boy's imagination and in imbuing him with a fascination for Russia which will later become one of the motives for his wish to go there with her. However, the determining reason for his decision is that, unlike Elke, Jelena understands how much

62. Daniel (Benjamin Kaatz) pushes away Elke and drives to the hospital with Jelena (Susanna Simon). (Photo: Westdeutscher Rundfunk.)

his friendship for Jonathan means to him, and is at his side when the old man dies, while Elke lets him down at this crucial time. Still, Jelena, too, is making a mistake. When Daniel voluntarily comes back to her as she had wished, she is forced to realize that she overestimated the bond between them. Just in time, she sees that she will be as guilty as Michael if she deprives Daniel of his family.

Elke's relationship with Daniel has solidified in the long years they have lived together, and has stood the test of time. It is based on familiarity, the little habits and rituals between a mother and child emphasized by the film, and therein lies its strength. Still, daily life does not consist of happy moments alone, but also problems that might lead to inappropriate behavior. The story illustrates how an adoptive mother who looks at her failure immediately doubts whether she is fit to be a mother and has the right to raise another woman's child. In this particular case, there are also guilt feelings, for because of her desperate wish for a child, another woman's son was taken from his mother without her consent. These circumstances help us to understand why Elke and Michael are prepared to yield to Daniel's wish to go and live with Jelena, and even plan to help them financially.

Between the two women there is the child, whom the conflicts of the adults plunge into a chaos of emotion in which he is in danger of losing his way. Margarethe von Trotta gives depth to this course of events by associating the image of a labyrinth with Daniel. This image becomes a leitmotif for the entire film. Its symbolic content is revealed when Elke asks Daniel about the meaning of the drawings in his school notebook, and the boy answers that this is the labyrinth of the Minotaur and asks her to stretch a golden thread for him like Ariadne so that he won't get lost. The image also refers to the child's imaginary world, which he shares with his friend Jonathan. For in contrast with the original book, where the friendship between the boy and the old man implausibly began with the gift of a video game, in Margarethe von Trotta's adaptation the special relationship between the two is founded on the fascination Daniel feels when he hears Jonathan tell the story of Theseus and Ariadne and other myths from antiquity. When Daniel sees how, after Jonathan's death, Elke's father has the old man's belongings moved out of the trailer, it therefore makes sense that he expresses his pain at his friend's death and his rage at his grandfather by falling back upon the ritual of a game he used to play with his old friend: Wearing a steer mask, he goes for Georg Berger with a dagger, feeling like Theseus attacking the Minotaur – an action by which, in the final analysis, he is also defending the fantasy world of his childhood, which he feels is being broken up along with Jonathan's trailer home. After this experience, he demands to go with Jelena to Russia, the land of wolves and endless frozen rivers which to him seems a promise of new adventures.

By her complex portrayal of characters, the psychological exploration of their behavior, and the symbolic deepening of events Margarethe von Trotta gives the story a tragic dimension like that of classical Greek tragedy, and the issue of guilt is pushed into the background. All the characters act correctly, from their perspective, and want only the best, creating a conflict from which all of them are in danger of emerging as losers. A halfway happy solution is possible only through sacrifice, and at the end all those involved are willing to choose this way out.

Mit fünfzig küssen Männer anders (»At Fifty Men Kiss Differently«)

The film *Mit fünfzig küssen Männer anders* (»At Fifty Men Kiss Differently«) is in every respect an exception in Margarethe von Trotta's work. Firstly, she did it purely on commission, and made practically no changes in the screenplay – written by Alistair Beaton and Martin Hennig, based on Dorit Zinn's novel of the same title. Secondly, except for the episode she did in the joint production *Felix*, this was the first time she had directed a comedy. Margarethe von Trotta accepted the offer to produce this film mainly because of her friendship with Senta Berger, whom she had known since their collaboration in *Der plötzliche Reichtum der armen Leute von Kombach* (*The Sudden Wealth of the Poor People of Kombach*) in 1970. But she was also interested in proving to herself that she could handle comedy material.

Mit fünfzig küssen Männer anders (»At Fifty Men Kiss Differently«) is a summer film, as the director said. In unusually luminous, colorful scenes, it describes how a fiftysomething married woman sets about giving her life new content and because of this clashes with her husband's resistance and indifference, which leads to a marital crisis and the couple's separation. Not until then do both of them realize what they have in each other, and their love manages to overcome their differences.

63. Gerd (Konstantin Wecker) talking with Marie (Senta Berger) about the flaws of her paintings. (Photo: Ziegler Filmproduktion.)

The protagonist, Marie Mechlenburg, studied art in her youth, but gave up her studies when she married, and has been a housewife ever since. Now that the children have left home, she begins to paint again and tries to become established as an artist. Now she discovers that her husband Dietrich, a management consultant who is absorbed in his work, is not only completely uninterested in her wishes and needs, but also constantly stands in her way. When she has an important meeting with the owner of a gallery, he insists that he needs the car, and later accuses her of being a spendthrift because she took a taxi. Besides, he claims that she spends too much time on her hobby and that she neglects her housewifely duties. Also he disapproves of her friendship with the sculptor Gerd, a »boozing would-be artist«, according to him. She feels ignored and neglected, and begins to call her marriage into question.

After Marie is devastatingly rebuffed by the gallery owner Dorit Mertens – »Art is not for bored housewives« –, she meets Dr. Eugen Hülsenberg, an ear, nose, and throat specialist and art collector. She is very receptive to his obvious interest in her as an artist and a woman. Encouraged by her friend Ada, the wife of Dietrich's former university classmate Udo Kötter, she therefore accepts Eugen's invitation to spend a weekend in the mountains, where Eugen will introduce her to an influential art historian. Marie has high hopes not only of an important contact for her career as a painter, but also of a romantic adventure. But Eugen proves to be an even bigger pedant and egotist than her husband, and so she leaves earlier than planned.

Shortly thereafter she rents an old loft where she wants to set up a studio so as to be able to paint undisturbed. On the day of the move she falls apart and burns her paintings after Gerd tells her they are not good enough for a show, since they lack a style of their own, passion, and excitement. That same night she responds to the advances of Kevin, an art critic and amateur saxophone player who is temporarily living at Gerd's house because he is having problems with his girlfriend. Marie sleeps with him. Dietrich, who notices she is becoming estranged from him, waits at home for her meanwhile, and discovers a video from Eugen in which Eugen invited her to their weekend together. When Marie comes home, Dietrich reprimands her and asks her to leave. She moves into her studio, continues her affair with Kevin and begins moving in different circles. Suddenly she has other images in her head, and her style of painting changes. Kevin again brings her into contact with Ms. Mertens, and talks the gallery owner into organizing an exhibition of Marie's paintings. At a garden party at Ada and Udo's house, Marie meets Dietrich again. He tries to get closer to her. She does not respond, but instead accuses him because he is to blame for Udo losing his job. The two do not bury the hatchet until he appears at her art exhibition, which is an overwhelming success, and congratulates her.

This conflict, which in itself is serious, is embedded in a series of events where the humor of the dialogues, the comicality of the situations, interspersed gags, but particularly the caricature of the protagonists' behavior, peculiarities, and weaknesses overlay any hint of tragedy with pointed witticisms. All sorts of innovative staging and structural details underline the absurdity of what is happening. The couple's squabbles, Marie and Ada's scuttlebutt about their marriages, the little secrets and escapades of the women, and the ironic juxtaposition of male and female behavior, which reaches its peak at a barbecue on Ada's birthday, all go to show that men are like grown-up kids, who are, of course, full of their own importance, and show off in front of each other to prove they are somebody, but whom you shouldn't take too seriously. The description of Dietrich's professional activities in great detail provides an opportunity for poking fun at masculine competitiveness and pushiness. With Udo's help Dietrich is hired to give his expert opinion on the effectiveness of the company in which his friend is the head of the data processing department. Like his friend Bernhard, Udo hopes that he will be given a positive evaluation that will get him a promotion, and the two keep trying to influence Dietrich to speak in their favor. At a strategy course for managers organized by Dietrich, grown men lapse into the behavior of little boys while Dietrich stands there watching with an air of importance taking notes. Underscored by martial drums, the men line up in single file in front of the trainer, a short, skinny squirt in battle dress at least 10 to 15 years their junior, and, for the sake of their career, allow him to bawl them out and to order them about. The men build huts, go on the night watch, and play other boy scout games, at which they cut ridiculous figures. Udo turns out to be an eager beaver who almost masochistically always exceeds his quota, while Bernhard gets bonus points because he is the only one who won't stand any nonsense and always looks for the easiest way out (»War is change that is accelerated by technical means. And the technical means I need right now is a beer«). At the end, the conclusion Dietrich reaches in his expert opinion is that his friend Udo's lack of effectiveness is his company's main trouble. Although his boss, Dr. Heinrich, advises him to focus his report on raising the sales volume – which means he need not identify the problem too accurately so that he will be given follow-up jobs, Dietrich sticks to this opinion and refuses to change it. Now the career carousel begins to turn: Udo loses his job, but is hired by Dietrich's company, which in turn fires Dietrich, while Bernhard is promoted and now wants to hire Dietrich as a consultant.

In addition, the film's humor is based mainly on the contrast between various types of persons with distinctive, somewhat crazy characteristics. First, there are Marie and Dietrich: He is a know-it-all careerist, full of himself, egotistical, pompous, and obsessed with separating the garbage for recycling, someone who scolds his wife because he found a yoghurt container in the wrong recycling bin, and who flinches even as his boss informs him he is fired because the man throws a beer bottle in with the regular garbage; a type who cuts the hair in his nostrils while his wife is standing next to him, and can't stop himself from emphasizing as he hands Marie a bouquet that it came from the most expensive florist's in town. She, on the other hand, is spontaneous, impulsive, and unconventional, an »anarchist artist«, as she calls herself; she gets up-set about his quirks, but also smiles at his faults, knows how to manipulate him and, behind his back, does what she feels is right. The contrast between the two of them constantly creates amusing incidents and battles of words: She secretly smokes in the bathroom and then hectically sprays room deodorant when he knocks because she is wanted on the phone. He indignantly asks whether she has been smoking, and she, outraged, denies it. Later he finds a cigarette stub in the garden, brings it to her gingerly and says, »Look what I found.« Laconically, she answers, »Hunted for.« While his boss is at their house, she comes home tipsy in the middle of the afternoon, and when her husband asks where she has been, replies giggling, »With my lover.«

Ada and Udo complement Marie and Dietrich. They are extremes as regards both their outward appearance and their character. He is short, bald, hyperactive with a hint of neuroticism, and sometimes behaves distinctly childishly, for instance, when, criticized by his friends for the way he prepares the barbecue, he answers defiantly, »It's my garden party, you know.« She, half a head taller, blond, attractive, self-confident, tends to take life as a game, and treats him like a big baby. Although she has come to terms with her situation and admits that she is actually quite satisfied, she thinks nothing of plunging into a sexual adventure with a young Polish blue-collar worker, »bargain-priced Polish manpower«, hired by Udo to make a fishpond in the middle of Ada's flowerbeds, to fulfill an alleged dream of his youth, as she remarks sarcastically. Meanwhile Bernhard's wife Petra represents another type of woman: Exaggeratedly feminine, flirtatious, apparently madly in love with her Bernie, she seems even more obsessed than he that he should make a career for himself, which doesn't keep her from retiring into a corner on the sly with Kevin in the final scene, the party that celebrates the opening of Marie's exhibition. The differences between the three couples are satirized in the farewell scene at the train station when the men leave for their strategy course: Petra and Bernhard embrace each other amorously, one of her

hands clings to his neck while the other reaches up one leg of his shorts as she laments how much she is going to miss him, finally exclaiming encouragingly, »The important thing is for you to prove what you're worth.« Meanwhile Ada asks Udo anxiously if he packed warm socks and enough underwear, and cautions him to make sure he doesn't get an inflammation of the bladder, which visibly embarrasses him, while Dietrich and Ada stand watching the others as she eats an apple and he manages in the nick of time to keep her from throwing the core in the wrong garbage bin.

One variation of the behavior of these fiftysomething men, who constantly have to prove to themselves how youthful and dynamic they still are, is represented by Marie's temporary suitor Eugen, who plays the woman-chaser and weekend Casanova, but is constantly unmasked by the vagaries of real life as a show-off and narrow-minded philistine. At a romantic dinner by candlelight he fancies himself as another Humphrey Bogart. He lowers his voice to a seductive murmur that sounds rather out of place in view of the banality of the conversation and with the expression of a man of the world, cigarette stuck nonchalantly in the corner of his mouth, utters highfaluting commonplaces such as »Life is risk«, and the like. But romance vanishes as quickly as his posturing when it starts raining, and the two make a dash for the car. For the hike in the mountains, he appears in full hiking gear with knee breeches, traditional hat, first aid kit, rope, survival kit, flashlight, and binoculars. Only unfortunately none of this saves him from losing his way and finally wandering with Marie in the dark on stony mountain paths. And the night of love he had planned finally falls through because she refuses to shower first as his partner was in the habit of doing for seventeen years. He has already destroyed what is left of the romantic mood by lingering over his personal hygiene and, one foot on the night table, removes a hangnail before joining Marie, who has been waiting for some time in bed dressed in a seductive negligee.

Meanwhile representatives of the art scene like Gerd and Kevin appear as completely normal, sensible people contrary to generally accepted clichés. The important exception is the eccentric gallery owner Ms. Mertens, a »monster« according to Marie, stuck-up, arrogant, and conscious of her power, capable of cold-bloodedly telling somebody to get lost, a woman who surrounds herself with a harem of handsome young men whom she allows to pay homage to her while admitting of no doubt that she values her dog more than them, and who loves to make scintillating, razor-sharp statements about art that demonstrate her expertise. For even Marie finally realizes she is right in spite of her overbearing manner, and therefore again seeks her acquaintance. Since the exhibition of Marie's paintings is such a success, even the severe gallery owner develops some sympathetic traits. Come to think of it, Margarethe von Trotta manages never to make

64. Angela Rinser (Suzanne von Borsody) waiting for her daughter in front of the school. (Photo: Westdeutscher Rundfunk.)
65. Role reversal of the mother and daughter: Felicitas (Stefanie Stappenbeck) becomes her mother's protector. (Photo: Westdeutscher Rundfunk.)
66. Leaving the clinic: Felicitas and Angela with another patient (Wolfgang Packhäuser). (Photo: WDR.)

complete fools of her characters, for behind their weaknesses she always allows their humanity to show through. In her portrayal of Marie and Dietrich she is particularly successful in walking the thin line between the comic and the serious, which is why the action becomes plausible and realistic, and the movie never becomes boring. On the contrary, it is an entertaining study of society that conceals a number of profound truths.

Dunkle Tage (»Dark Days«)

Immediately after completing *Winterkind* (»Winter Child«), Margarethe von Trotta received another WDR offer to make a film, using her own script, about the problems of children of alcoholics. The result was *Dunkle Tage* (»Dark Days«), the harshest and most somber film she has made to date. While the story is fictional, it is founded on true events and realistic patterns of behavior, which it took her months to research. Although in this case she could not fall back upon her own experience, she began to identify with the topic more and more as her work progressed, so that the film turned out to be very personal.

The story centers around young Felicitas Rinser, who has to answer for her mother's death before the juvenile court. At the hearing she tells her story. Until she was twelve, she, her parents, and her brother Max were a happy family. Her mother, Angela Rinser, worked as an executive secretary and earned a good salary, while her father, an ornithologist, took care of the household and the children and was at work writing a book. However, when the father suddenly dies of a virus he brought back from Africa, Angela Rinser starts drowning her sorrows in alcohol. Her relationship to the children has always been rather distant, and now she makes their life a hell. At first she drinks on the sly, but soon her alcoholism can no longer be concealed. She loses her job because she becomes undependable and forgetful, and they begin to go downhill socially. The daughter carries the main burden. She takes care not only of the mother, but of her younger brother as well. She tries to keep her mother from drinking by hiding the bottles, throwing them away, or diluting their contents with water. At night she is often sent to the gas station to buy brandy, and she has to relay to their neighbor, a piano teacher, her mother's complaints about the playing of his students. Angela's drinking reaches its height when she ruins Max's birthday party because she is lying in bed drunk. At the party, in a fit of rage, she also scares away her last remaining friend Alexandra Schmanke, the wife of her former boss, who until then has still been looking after her and her family. Because of this incident, Max is beside himself with hatred and tries to put a hex on his mother with one of his father's African dolls. After this, for two years, she manages to pull herself together again. She gives up drinking and finds a new job. Five years later the situation is worse than ever. Max can no longer stand his mother's constant alcoholic excesses and the messy apartment, and moves into a commune. Felicitas, now seventeen, is left alone with Angela and takes care of her as though she were a child while trying to preserve an outward semblance of normalcy. When her mother is asked to come to school because Max pulled a knife during a fight and is in danger of being expelled from school, Felicitas rehearses the visit with her. But instead of keeping the appointment, Angela gets drunk and lands in detox. Felicitas threatens to leave if she does not go into treatment. Afraid that she will be abandoned, Angela agrees. While her mother is at the clinic, Felicitas runs into Fabian, a student of her former neighbor, who is now studying at a conservatory and earning his living playing the piano in a bar. The two fall in love, and he moves in with her. Her mother is not very pleased, but she has become accustomed to Felicitas making her own decisions, and furthermore is full of optimism that now that she is »dry« everything promises to go back to normal. Felicitas tries to keep Fabian from finding out that her mother is an alcoholic, and at first all goes well. But when Angela begs her former boss in vain for a job, she has a relapse, and Felicitas tells Fabian the truth. For her sake, Fabian tries to put up with the situation a while longer, but then he moves out. After an ugly scene with Angela's mother and one of her drinking buddies he is able to persuade Felicitas to come with him. At this point, Angela Rinser begins to hound her daughter to try and get her to return. But Felicitas remains adamant even though her mother threatens to kill herself. Finally Angela actually does make a suicide attempt, and Felicitas feels compelled to give in if she doesn't want to become partly responsible for her death. Fabian leaves her because he doesn't want to watch her destroying herself. Felicitas no longer has the strength to fight her mother's drinking, and now begins to drink herself in order to be able to tolerate the situation. During one of their drinking sprees Fabian happens to see the two on a park bench, and urges Max to get Felicitas away from her mother. Max is reluctant at first, but then he goes to the apartment and finds his mother and sister drunk in the corner of the living room looking at old photographs. When he tries to convince Felicitas to come with him, she resists. He tries to drag her from the apartment by force, her mother clings to her, whereupon he hits her on the head with an empty bottle, and she dies. Felicitas tells him to run away and takes the blame for her brother's action. When the judge is about to announce the verdict, Max jumps up and shouts that he was the one that killed his mother. At that moment, to his astonishment, he hears that his sister has been acquitted.

Margarethe von Trotta here focuses on problems that have been foremost in her mind in most of her films: the conflict between self-destruction and affirmation of life. The film shows very vividly how a successful, self-confident, and good-looking woman is suddenly thrown off the track and becomes a wreck both physically and mentally. In spite of transitory periods of recovery, which are largely omitted in the portrayal because of the way the story is told, she is beyond saving. She is inevitably doomed, and is in danger of dragging her children down with her. Her situation is hopeless and shocking, but the real, terrible tragedy is the conflict of the children who see themselves torn between their love for their mother and their sense of duty on the one hand, and hatred toward the mother, who is destroying their childhood and youth with her alcoholic excesses, on the other hand. They have the choice of abandoning their mother to her fate and becoming guilty, or being destroyed themselves – a problem that in the long run becomes a question of life and death.

Max, of whom it is said that he used to be especially close to his mother when he was younger, becomes emotionally detached from her even as a child and directs his aggression outward, for he understands that either he must destroy her or she will destroy him. He continues to believe this. On the day he moves out, he screams at Felicitas furiously, »Why don't you let her starve!«, when he sees she is trying to pour some soup down their mother's throat. Later he carries out his death threat by actually killing her. Meanwhile Felicitas has seen herself as her mother's and brother's protector since she was a child, and in this role she is self-sacrificing to the point of self-destruction. Only her relationship with Fabian temporarily gives her the courage to get away from her mother, and she adopts her brother's attitude. When her mother says, while drunk, that she could jump out the window, she retorts, »Go ahead.« And when her mother threatens to commit suicide if Felicitas does not come back, she screams, »Why didn't you do it long ago?« However, confronted with the choice between her mother and Fabian, she capitulates. Her love for her mother triumphs, and she develops a perverse kind of bond with her on the way down into the abyss which she experiences almost as a relief, as she admits herself. It turns out that her struggle against her mother's addiction is identical with the struggle against her own tendency toward self-destruction, to which she at last succumbs.

But it must also be said that Felicitas's behavior expresses far more complex factors than mere feminine masochism. For one, she has guilt feelings in connection with her father's death. On the day he dies, her mother reproaches her for not informing her and also not calling an ambulance when his fever rose. If her father's death triggered her mother's alcoholism, Felicitas must inevitably feel she is partially responsible for it. In addition, she is childishly jealous of her mother for disturbing her close relationship with her father – for instance, when Felicitas goes to him because she cannot sleep and he rocks her like a baby until her mother comes and sends her back to bed. Afterward, through a crack in the door, she watches her parents embrace. After the father's death, when the mother tries to get closer to the children and to share the imaginary world that united them with their father, they are cold toward her, and she blames them, as she later tells them under the influence of alcohol, »I drink because you treat me so badly.« Later, with Fabian, the feeling of jealousy is again visible through Felicitas's fear that she will lose him because of the mother's alcoholism. Felicitas sits as if paralyzed on a wall and watches her mother nestling against him and leading him away from her around the corner, dancing on unsteady legs. In the next scene Fabian carries the mother into the bedroom and lays her on the bed while Felicitas watches from the doorway and then closes the door from the outside, just as she did in her childhood. On the day she moves out, the mother, tipsy from wine and carried away by her feelings, tries to paw Fabian, and Felicitas screams at her, »Don't you touch Fabian!« These scenes express rivalry: the daughter feels ousted by her mother, and must oust and destroy her if she is to maintain her position – something that is made easier by alcoholism. But since this is a forbidden wish, she compensates for it by solicitude and affection, though in the final analysis these conceal guilt feelings. Thus, at the end, she shoulders the blame not only to protect her brother, but also because she herself wished her mother would die, and could have killed her just as easily.

Guilt finally overwhelms Max as well, though initially it seems he can free himself from the catastrophe that love for his mother implies: for he must face up to the realization that he let down not only his mother, but his sister as well. After assuring Felicitas one moment that he would do anything for her, he refuses to support her yet again when, in her despair, she begs him to look after their mother instead of her so that she can stay with Fabian. He does not act until he realizes that Felicitas is at stake, and he is able to save her, but at the same time takes on an even greater, double guilt: He becomes his mother's murderer, and once more leaves the burden of responsibility to Felicitas. The horror at his action is condensed in the scene after the mother's death, in which he races wildly through the streets and is pursued by a group of little boys who finally pounce on him – a motif taken from the story of Orestes, who is pursued by the Erinnyes after he kills his mother. Just as Orestes is finally acquitted by the gods, Max, too, receives his acquittal once he is finally ready to admit his guilt publicly in the courtroom.

In addition, the film examines the reasons for the mother's alcoholism. Her drinking is triggered by the father's death, but what is the underlying cause? Is it the fact that her children rejected her, and panic fear of being alone? Is it guilt feelings because the very night her husband was feeling ill she accepted her boss's invitation and came home late, so that the ambulance did not arrive in time? Is the reason hidden in her nightmares and the visions of her dead husband that haunt her? Does her boss share the blame because after her husband's death he does not agree to her request to work part-time, makes a lot of demands on her, and after her treatment for alcoholism is not willing to give her another chance? Does the widespread consumption of alcohol in society seduce people to abuse it? Or is it a combination of all these factors? The question is not definitively resolved, and Angela Rinser herself does not know the answer when they ask her at the clinic to give the reason for her addiction. The motif to which the film keeps returning when the subject of alcohol addiction comes up is the curse that emanates from the African masks and dolls the father used to keep in a locked closet. As a child Felicitas firmly believes that they caused the father's death and also put a hex on the mother. She gets them out of the house in order to avert disaster. Yet demons and spirits in Margarethe von Trotta's work also always represent the unknown, something that cannot be understood rationally, that is menacing, the subliminal fears that cloud consciousness, throw people off balance and propel them into self-destruction. The opposite of these forces is the circle as a symbol of unity, of spiritual harmony, of perfection which appears in the final scene of the film when Fabian forms a circle with his thumbs and index fingers in order to capture Felicitas's face in it.

With *Dunkle Tage* (»Dark Days«), regardless of the limitations inherent in a TV production, Margarethe von Trotta succeeded in making a film which, because of its intensity and expressiveness, gets under your skin and leaves you shaken. Her extraordinary skill in directing her actors once more comes to fruition here and makes it possible for the cast to do their very best. It is also striking that the film contains a series of deliberate quotations from the director's earlier films. This is how she leaves her own mark on the film, something akin to a trademark, thus expressing an insight she was reluctant to admit to herself for years: namely, that her permanent stock of ideas and visual motifs, to which, often purely intuitively, she returns in all her work, is not a sign that she lacks imagination, but is an integral part of her own style, evolved over more than 25 years of artistic creation as a film director and author of screenplays.

3. Characteristic features of Margarethe von Trotta's artistic direction

The dialectics of contemporary events versus state of mind as a formal principle

There is no doubt that Margarethe von Trotta's films are subtly drawn pictures of society, and as such are products of their time. This is also true of her latest works for television in which there are no references, or only minor ones, to contemporary political issues. Therefore many elements of meaning can be properly interpreted only in a sociopolitical, cultural, and historical context. But there are also a number of thematic and structural constants that run like a red thread through her work, independent of the period. This repertory of means of expression characterizes her unique artistic style, her own film language, and gives her films the classic format on which her artistic reputation is based.

One such distinctive feature is the fusion of external events with the description of states of mind. The interrelation between individual and society, between inner and outer world, and the subjective standpoint and concentration on the personal that determine the narrative structure extend to the artistic form. The question »What's it like to live with somebody like Falcone?« that Margarethe von Trotta asked herself as she was making *Il lungo silenzio* (*The Long Silence*) is applicable, in modified form, to all her stories. She wants to know: How do people deal with the suicide of somebody they're close to, with the ostracism and unexplained death of a sister, with a lover's betrayal, with knowing that their personal desires are incompatible with their political goals, with losing their illusions of a better world, with being separated by force from their lover, their child, their parents, or with living with an alcoholic mother? This way of formulating questions places psychological processes and interpersonal dynamics in the center and relates them to external events. For Margarethe von Trotta many of the answers are found in the inner world of her protagonists, in their thoughts, feelings, and moods; she tries to make these visible by using all formal elements – starting with the choice of locale, decor, makeup and costumes, the work of the actors, the way scenes are resolved, the use of color and light, and including camera settings and movement, and editing – to represent the interaction of external events and her characters' states of mind. This is why the atmosphere in her films is extraordinarily compact. This compactness is communicated as psychological tension, and is an essential distinguishing feature of her style.

Striving for historical authenticity

A differentiated representation of her protagonists' social context is indispensable for the filmmaker, for this is a prerequisite for the realism and the social relevance of her message. Especially the space where her film characters live and their outward appearance are intended to establish their social milieu and the historical framework in which events take place as accurately as possible. Here we are struck by the painstaking attempt to make sure that external details are authentic and that what is typical can be recognized. Both aspects are present and in the foreground when the story takes place in the past, as in the case of *Rosa Luxemburg*, the first two sections of *Das Versprechen* (*The Promise*), or the flashbacks in *Die bleierne Zeit* (*Marianne and Juliane*). Thus, for *Rosa Luxemburg*, using photographs and descriptions in letters, Margarethe von Trotta had Rosa's Berlin apartment reconstructed in the studio to look like the original; this excellent work was done by her set designer Monika Hasse although she was fatally ill and died of cancer while shooting was still going on. Later the film director dedicated the film to her, and she still grieves the loss of an outstanding collaborator and friend. Costume design was also based on contemporary pictures, for example, the Japanese geisha costume that the film character Rosa wore on New Year's Eve 1899 was copied from a photograph of the real Rosa.

In *Das Versprechen* (*The Promise*), sets and costumes serve above all to emphasize the contrast between East and West. On the one hand all the fashions and status symbols that are typical of Western lifestyle during each particular period are displayed: The bulky TV cabinet with its little screen, the up-to-date elegance in Aunt Sophie's living room; the classic, modern designer furniture, French doors, and wide windows with a view of the Gedächtniskirche and the Kurfürstendamm in the showroom of the fashion salon; the fashion show in front of select women customers; suits in pastel colors or with huge checks; tight skirts; dresses with fitted waists, bows, and piping; short or three-quarter-length swinging jackets and coats; matching gloves and hats; pointy high-heeled shoes; drainpipe pants – the stretch pants that were very fashionable with teenagers at the time; frilled shirts, narrow ties, and conspicuously patterned jackets and overcoats; and Ford Taunus and VW Cabrio accurately represent the period of the German economic miracle. The close-fitting red patent leather coat, the miniskirts, colorful tights, short, tight blouses and shirts that Sophie wears in Prague in 1968 show the typical fashions of the late

67. Rosa Luxemburg at the 1899 New Year's Eve party in a geisha costume based on a historical model. (Photo: Ivan Minar.)
68. Fashion show in the sixties (*Das Versprechen / The Promise*). (Photo: Bioskop-Film.)
69. The bourgeois palazzo as a symbol for tradition: festive dinner in the house of the sisters' parents in *Paura e Amore* (*Love and Fear*).

’60s, while the bright and spacious factory floor where she lives with her son and her partner in the early 1980s with its stylish black-and-white furnishings attests to prosperity, and in its informality reflects the casual manners and the lifestyle that gained acceptance in the West after the revolt of 1968 and are similarly depicted in *Die bleierne Zeit* (*Marianne and Juliane*) and *Heller Wahn* (*Sheer Madness*). On the other side of the border, in the house of Konrad’s parents, we see the unimaginative, sober ambience of the first postwar decades as it is also shown in the flashbacks of *Die bleierne Zeit* (*Marianne and Juliane*): boring patterned wallpaper, net curtains with drapes over the windows, the big dining-room table complete with white tablecloth, stuffed chairs, the seven-armed chandelier with cone-shaped lampshades, the brown varnished living-room sideboard with rounded edges and glass doors in its central section – all fastidiously tidy, unadorned, in dreary shades of brown, beige, and white. The style of the East Berlin apartment where Konrad and his family live 20 years later is hardly different from that of his parents’ place and shows that Western fashion has to a large extent bypassed the citizens of the GDR.

In *Das zweite Erwachen der Christa Klages* (*The Second Awakening of Christa Klages*), furnishings and costumes are intentionally used to contrast the social milieus and lifestyles of women in the 1970s. Christa’s casual, unconventional clothes and the milieu of the communal household are in complete contrast with the impersonal, unimaginative modernity of Ingrid’s apartment, which could have been taken from a magazine on contemporary living. Her middle-class, formal clothing and her neatly pinned-back hair characterize her orderly, emotionless life, which is adjusted to the needs of her husband. A disconcerting note is introduced by the stuffed bats mounted in all the rooms – her husband’s hobby. In this case the apartment and the wife serve as status symbols. They demonstrate a certain level of social prosperity and material security, for »after all, Heinz has a permanent position«, as Ingrid says. She leads the kind of life Lena, the bank clerk, dreams of when she sits alone at night in her equally impersonal, but much more cramped, studio apartment, and hopes for a winning lottery ticket. The longing to escape the rut of her job is present in a single personal household article, a lamp on her night table, a kitschy replica of the Niagara Falls. America here represents the dream of breaking out of the workaday world, of freedom and happiness – something that members of the young generation of that period typically longed for. (Margarethe von Trotta again takes up this idea in *Schwestern* (*Sisters*) where Miriam has a pencil sharpener shaped like the Statue of Liberty.) Lena’s visit at Ingrid’s house is one of the reasons she begins to doubt her own ideas about life: She sits on the modern couch and scrutinizes the bats with surprise and is just as amazed and disturbed by what she finds in Christa’s mother’s apartment: the little rooms, the outmoded furniture, the potted plants on the windowsill, the orange and white wallpaper with its big overpowering patterns, and, to top it all, the mother in the ridiculous costume of a medieval chatelaine that she is trying on for a performance by her amateur theater group. The spaces where these women live help Lena to look at her own ideas about happiness, and cause her eventually to begin to question these ideas.

In the above cases the world of objects emphasizes the social and historical component, and is used mainly to place the film characters in a social context. This context is important in making plausible the characters' experiences, their state of consciousness, the way they deal with problems, and their patterns of behavior. Also, depending on the film's subject, the set and costumes to a greater or lesser degree have the function of underscoring the individual characteristics and state of mind of the characters. On closer inspection each detail turns out to be carefully thought through and chosen with regard to its wider significance. Colors, forms, lighting, presentation, the coordination of clothing, the placement of the furniture, objects of daily life, décor such as flowers, objets d'art, photographs, or knicknacks – often symbolically condensed – give added depth to the characterization of persons or life situations.

The bourgeois palazzo – the main locale of *Paura e amore* (*Love and Fear*) that Margarethe von Trotta had built in the studio – defines the social milieu of the story, the old-established bourgeoisie, anchored in conventions. At the same time the palazzo emphasizes the fact that the siblings are trapped by traditional structures. Although it is spacious, there is something oppressive and constricting about it. Dark and lusterless colors dominate the scene:Wood panelling, heavy, old furniture, a set of chairs covered with dark green velvet, leaded stained-glass windows, valuable old carpets, bookshelves, and a marble fireplace give the house an atmosphere of quality and distinction, refinement, and sense of tradition that overlays any personal note of its inhabitants. Only the piles of books in Velia's bedroom and the music stand in Roberto's Spartan room point to individual preferences. As he plays his violin there in one of the first scenes, an abstract painting hanging behind him shows a shape resembling a spiderweb; this symbolically alludes to his approaching misfortune – being captured in a woman's net. The style of the clothing is also conservative and discreet. Muted colors – black, white, and gray – are preponderant at Sandra's 18th birthday celebration in the initial scene, and appear again in the final scene. In particular the clothing of Velia, who always wears long, full skirts and high-necked blouses and dresses with a preference for brown, beige, and gray, has something nunlike about it that lends an almost religious character to her secluded life, her renunciation of worldly happiness, along with – one might say – self-imposed celibacy and an interest in the writings of medieval mystics. This analogy becomes especially pronounced when she sits alone in a café in one scene and is addressed by a nun whose dark gray habit with its contrasting white coif and veil parallels the clothing of Velia, who is wearing a jacket and scarf in the same colors. Because the nun, who has been following her lectures, invites her, Velia goes to the convent in a later scene to give a talk – a scene in which during a long shot across the hall she can hardly be distinguished from her listeners. Sabrina is out of place in this conventional milieu: the garish color of the light blue dress she wears during her initial visit breaks through the melancholy mood optically as well as in other respects. With her love of gaudy colors and her loud, vulgar behavior, she destroys the tradition-laden atmosphere that surrounds the lives of the brother and sisters, and takes possession of their home by introducing signs of modernity. After she moves in, a TV set suddenly appears in front of the beautiful old window in the living room; later the shouting of children replaces the former peace and quiet; under Sabrina's direction what was once the sisters' room has turned into a nursery with light blue walls and modern furniture. In the final scene modern paintings suddenly hang on the walls here and there, and a new white sofa appears in the living room. On the other hand Sabrina gradually adapts as far as her outfits are concerned. While in the beginning she mostly appears in baby-doll pink, fuchsia, or orange, she later comes to prefer white and black. In this way Sabrina, planned as a negative figure from the point of view of behavior, takes on a positive complexion, for she shatters the deathly silence that weighs heavily on the house and that belies the youthfulness of its inhabitants. A contrast to the parents' house is provided by Maria's apartment, as luxurious as theirs to be sure, but much brighter and friendlier. Here Velia and Sandra find shelter after Sabrina has driven them out of the house by her obnoxiousness, though this has its positive side as well: In the end they are liberated from the cage of conventions their parents' house represents.

Much more explicitly than here, where captivity is concealed behind the outward appearance of distinction and quality, the representation of the empty apartment to which Christa retreats (*Das zweite Erwachen der Christa Klages / The Second Awakening of Christa Klages*) conveys the idea of being shut in. This apartment is a bare, isolated, dark room, more prison than refuge. Juliane's place in *Die bleierne Zeit* (*Marianne and Juliane*) at the end of the film has similar characteristics: it is so gloomy and austere it resembles a prison cell and is markedly different from the bright, friendly, two-story penthouse apartment and the carefully assembled furnishings of the home she once shared with Wolfgang. The few items of furniture – a desk and a chair, a

Moments of light and darkness

70. Constitutional in the prison yard.
71. Vacation near Lake Garda (Photo: Margarethe von Trotta and Christiane Ensslin, *Rosa Luxemburg. Das Buch zum Film*, Nördlingen 1986.)
72. Joie de vivre: Colored lights above Miriam's bed (*Schwestern / Sisters*).

bookshelf full of files with dates on them, a pile of books on the floor, the walls bare except for a lot of pieces of note paper and a large photograph of Marianne – document the focal point of her life: her obsession with shedding light on her sister's death.

Marco and Carla's apartment in *Il lungo silenzio* (*The Long Silence*) feels just as dark and oppressive. They live there like prisoners. The closed shutters keep out daylight, so that the rooms are always plunged in semidarkness; this affects the mood in the apartment and constantly brings home to them the fact that they live like prisoners. The apartment contains a mixture of solid wooden furniture and modern pieces of an unconventional elegance befitting the social status of a senior official and a physician, yet the colors intensify the gloomy atmosphere: In addition to the white of the walls and the medium brown wood of the floors and doors, the colors of mourning – dark brown and black – predominate. The only spots of color in the apartment are two red easy chairs and two paintings. One painting is all in shades of blue, which have their analogy in Carla's favorite color of clothing, the other, its symbolic meaning far more unambiguous, shows a bright red spot on a white background, suggesting blood.

The symbolism of the world of objects – colors and shapes, worlds of light and shadow

The conscious use of colors and light to emphasize inner developments recurs in all of Trotta's films. Light and shadow characterize the contrast between joy and sadness, energy and exhaustion, vitality and discouragement, life and death. A salient example is *Dunkle Tage* (»Dark Days«), where the darkness of the frames deepens as the mother deteriorates physically and mentally. A similar process may be observed in *Rosa Luxemburg*. As Rosa's resignation and disillusionment and her physical and emotional exhaustion grow, and she approaches her end, the atmosphere of the film darkens. The costumes, too, express this. While in her youth she still wears mostly light colors, with occasional frills – for example, in the relaxed atmosphere vacationing at Lake Garda with Luise Kautsky – her dresses become plainer and darker as the years go on. The beginning sequence is significant: Accompanied by a tame, black raven, Rosa walks in the snowy prison courtyard dressed all in black. The color of mourning as well as the symbolic raven, considered to be an omen of bad luck in all cultures, and the long shot from above across the yard stressing her isolation and forlornness concentrate in a single frame the disaster that lies ahead of her. In the last scene of the film, when she is killed, she wears brown, once more a color of mourning that, even more than black, underscores how pale and exhausted she looks.

The counterpart to these mainly dark films is *Mit fünfzig küssen Männer anders* (»At Fifty Men Kiss Differently«), where, except for a brief dark moment, the atmosphere is characterized by serene brightness, color, and vast sunny expanses usually reserved for the depiction of Mediterranean countries in other Trotta films. In *Winterkind* (»Winter Child«) similarly vivid colors are employed in creating little Daniel's room and costumes, and – curiously – in Ana's apartment, where a wall painted orange juxtaposed with a dark blue coverlet creates a strong contrast of color that is heightened even more by a bunch of primrose-yellow balloons. In the living room, the orange of a sofa is intensified by bright blue cushions. These colors correspond to Ana's character – extroverted, full of joie de vivre – as does the big Father Christmas doll opposite the front door, the lifesize display figure in one corner, and the rhythmically blinking star in the window, which add original accents to the otherwise clear lines of the apartment's furniture. Elements like these also indicate that a person like Ana, whose character traits Margarethe von Trotta added to the screenplay, is something new in the director's repertoire. The only parallel in her work is Miriam in *Schwestern* (*Sisters*) who, to express her joie de vivre, paints the walls a luminous red when she moves into Maria's apartment and hangs a chain of lights over the bed. Ana, however, is no longer a young girl like Miriam, but a woman in her thirties with a great deal of life experience. Thus, Ana also has a serious, reflective side that finds expression in a large granite-colored painting covering one wall of her living room. The painting comes from her friend Sergio and conveys the mood in the camp where Jelena met him. The joylessness of the painting establishes a connection with Jelena's past and – like the dreariness of her beige and white knit dress, her shabby tweed coat, and the heavy brown boots she was wearing when she first arrived – is a reflection of her frame of mind. A black suit and a beige coat – items of clothing Ana gives her later – pick up the same colors again and, like the clothes she wore before, underline the character's seriousness and melancholy. Elke, too, at first dresses just as unobtrusively and inconspicuously, though in her long, full skirts, heavy sweaters, jackets, and the lace-up boots she

wears at work she tends to look girlish. However, after she discovers the truth about her son's origin, she sees herself in competition with Jelena and begins to make changes in her appearance. When she visits Jelena, she is suddenly wearing a stylish coat, and later, at the Christmas celebration, in her red dress, she is a brilliant focal point in an environment that is optically muted in tone. Her house, and especially the nursery with its glazed greenhouses, big cold frames, tall non-flowering plants, stacks of crates and big flowerpots, has something of a junglelike labyrinth about it. Models of bridges placed between the plants as decoration hint at Michael's actual profession, but also allude to Jelena, whom he met while building a bridge. This setting is the background for the eruption of conflict among the protagonists. It represents the dark, serious part of the film.

The symbolic content of contrasts between light and dark and of colors used in Margarethe von Trotta's earlier, so-called »private« films is even more clearly apparent. In *Schwestern* (*Sisters*) even the screenplay emphasizes individual characteristics and psychological processes when detailing the women's appearance and the physical space where they live. Pale, classic suits with simple lines, and hair severely pinned up characterize Maria, the rational career woman, while the place where she lives is decorated in shades of brown, the color of autumn and of the earth, but also, until the Middle Ages, of mourning. The more emotional Anna, on the other hand, wears flowing, loose-fitting dresses in dark colors, and her hair is worn loose; the predominant color of her workroom is green, the color of hope and renewal, but, like black, it is associated with yin, one of the fundamental cosmological principles in Chinese philosophy corresponding to the negative, feminine, dark side. Her room is full of houseplants that cast filigree shadows. In a terrarium, she keeps iguanas, whose ugliness is reminiscent of the terrifying pictures she pastes into her diary. Her mascot is a ceramic owl, a night bird that has been considered to be an omen of misfortune and death from antiquity until today and creates a link to the cries of the screech owl in the frightening fairy-tale forest she remembers from her childhood. The dark and eerie aspect of the place where she lives is underscored by an intimate twilight that sharply contrasts with the scene directly after her death when Maria and her mother clear out her room, which is now empty and plunged in harsh white light.

The juxtaposition of the worlds of light and shadow as an expression of different world views and characters is found in *Heller Wahn* (*Sheer Madness*) as well. The pair of opposites – the golden girl and the pitch-covered girl from »Mother Holle« – in the therapy scene of the beginning sequence refers to the external characteristics of the two women protagonists; it suggests the basic pattern of their personalities, repeated in their outfits and apartments. Ruth's color is black, the color of night, of negation, of the occult, and occasionally she wears red or orange-red. Only in two sequences is she dressed entirely in red: at the New Year's Eve party at her house, when, like Elke at the Christmas celebration in *Winterkind* (»Winter Child«), she outshines all the others – Olga wears a black pantsuit with a red rose in her lapel on this occasion – and during her visit in Egypt, when she temporarily overcomes her fears and fits of depression. Ruth's apartment, which she says was furnished by her husband's mother, feels like a tomb: Walls painted a brownish beige, decorated with Ruth's unusual black-and-white paintings, small windows, a winding staircase to the top floor, and dark, heavy furniture convey an atmosphere of gloom and closeness emphasized by muted lighting. The studio in the attic, however, the only space that belongs to her alone, is bright and spacious. Significantly that is where, together with Olga and the gallery owner, she celebrates the decision to organize an exhibition of her paintings. In another scene she is shown painting there in high spirits. But the studio is also the place where, in one of her visions, Franz finds her dead by hanging. A massive, black leather sofa opposite the front door plays a special role: this is where Franz lays her down when she comes home from the hospital after her suicide attempt. In her black dress, and surrounded by flowers that he has placed everywhere to welcome her home, she looks as though she were lying in state. This scene corresponds to one at the end of the film in Ruth's vision: Again dressed entirely in black, she is sitting on the same sofa holding a revolver as she waits for her husband. When he comes through the door with a bunch of flowers, she shoots, and he sinks to the floor amid the scattered flowers.

Olga, meanwhile, prefers light colors: white, natural, beige, and once even a strong yellow, the color of the sun and of light, the Chinese yang – the positive, masculine, active principle. Her apartment, with its high, wide windows that look out on a garden, feels spacious and bright, but above all, unlike the »house of the dead« inhabited by Ruth and Franz, it contains signs of life and of the activity of its inhabitants: The walls of the hallway and of Olga's study are covered with bookshelves right up to the ceiling, hinting at her work as a teacher of literature. In her son's

Rationality versus emotionality in *Schwestern / Sisters*

73. Maria's world is characterized by clear lines, firmly outlined forms, autumn colors, closeness to the earth.
74. Anna's space is characterized by broken lines, blurred and soaring forms, dark colors, twilight.

Contrast between figures of light and shadow

75. Olga and Ruth (*Heller Wahn / Sheer Madness*). (Photo: Filmverlag der Autoren.)
76. Ana and Martha (*L'Africaine / The African Woman*).
77. Franz places Ruth on the living room sofa after her return from the hospital (*Heller Wahn / Sheer Madness*).

room posters of James Dean, Jimi Hendrix, and Amnesty International testify to his interests; while the big black grand piano of her friend Alexej, which is in a room with a bay window, alludes to the fact that he is a musician. When he moves out, he takes it with him, literally leaving an empty space behind.

Similarly in *L'Africaine* (*The African Woman*) the rational Martha moves predominantly in an ambience characterized by light and brightness – the apartment that Victor shares with Ana. The style of the apartment is not different from the one he once shared with Martha, and is basically associated with her: Large rooms with high windows, parquet floors, white walls, glass doors between the individual rooms, a white marble fireplace with a mirror wall, modern, white upholstered furniture and glass tables create an ambience full of light and space that underscores Martha's personality. One reminder of her is a large abstract painting hung in an easily visible spot near the entrance. To her surprise, Victor has kept it although he never liked it. The painting states her colors – red, brown, beige to white – which are picked up again in a rust-brown sofa and a matching swivel chair, as well as on the walls of the African café where she takes refuge. And yet Ana is present here as well; for one thing, there is the room in which she makes her unusual marionettes and which really doesn't match the rest of the apartment. With the ghostlike puppets, the walls covered with scraps of paper, the big worktable full of paintpots and other tools of the trade, and the muted lighting, it feels like a cave and is part of the netherworld she enters with her belief in esotericism, magic, and supernatural powers. In the living room, there is yet another conspicuous abstract painting, in various shades of blue – colors that have their analogy in Ana's nightmare, which is shot with a blue filter; for blue, the color of the sky, of distance, of the divine, the irrational and the fantastical, goes with Ana, as does the blackness of night in which her memories and guilt feelings toward Martha break forth and in which she performs her spiritualistic rites. The realms with which she is associated in the film are the hospital, the holy well in Brittany, and later Jan's apartment, whose atmosphere resembles that of her workroom: Crammed with valuable old furniture – bookshelves, a flowered old-rose and beige chaise longue, chairs with carved backs, a piano – , books, his crystal ball, all sorts of magical stones, photographs, and memorabilia, plus the dark curtains, it conveys a cozy and intimate atmosphere that suits Ana's character far more than her own apartment, where she is shown in only two scenes, and gives the impression of being a guest. This is emphasized when Martha, looking for Jan, rings the neighbor's doorbell. The door is opened by children wearing masks, a reference to Ana's marionettes. The costumes in part take up the contrast between light and dark again, for instance, when Martha wears a yellow blouse at the party celebrating Ana's dis-

charge from the hospital, while Ana herself is dressed in black, or when the two walk in the Jardin du Luxembourg, one wearing a black coat, while the other wears a light-colored trench coat.

There is something special about Margarethe von Trotta's use of the color red, which appears rarely and always has a particular significance. She uses the color according to its traditional symbolic value both in a positive and negative sense: on the one hand as the color of life, of love, of warmth and passion, and on the other hand as a symbol for shedding blood, for fire and war, but also for the destructive power of emotions. In *Das Versprechen* (*The Promise*) red represents vitality and passion, and is Sophie's characteristic color. Starting with the ribbon which is torn off her dress during the escape through the sewers and which becomes the symbol of Konrad's longing, his »holy relic«, as his wife Elisabeth accuses him later, red is repeated in Sophie's clothing, though like her black and white woolen cap, which she wears in all three episodes, its function is also to make it easier to recognize the character, as the part is played by different actresses in the episodes from the '60s and from the '80s.

Red has a number of meanings in *Rosa Luxemburg*. On the one hand, the symbol assigned to the title character is a red rose, an allusion to her name, but also a symbol of love, and a reference to the nickname »red Rosa«, given to the revolutionary by the bourgeois press. Margarethe von Trotta provides additional associations for the rose by showing Rosa in a flashback as a little girl who refuses to go to bed because she wants to watch the opening of a rosebud. Her mother talks her into going to sleep, claiming that roses never open at night. The next morning, disappointed, she realizes she has missed the decisive moment. Later the rose motif is picked up again when, upon Rosa Luxemburg's arrival in Berlin after her release from prison in 1918, Mathilde Jacob hands her a red rose, which thus becomes a metaphor for patient waiting and unfulfilled longings (incidentally, the film's original title was *Die heitere Geduld der Rosa L.* (*The Serene Patience of Rosa L.*). The color red also serves to place Rosa Luxemburg's death in the context of militarism, fascist terrorism, and war, all of which have claimed millions of victims, symbolized by the wide red carpet that like an enormous stream of blood covers the floor of the lobby and the staircase of the Hotel Eden, to which Rosa is brought shortly before her death. This motif in turn references the huge wall decoration with a white date against a background of red carnations in front of which August Bebel stands at the Social Democrats' New Year's Eve celebration in 1899, welcoming the 20th century – which will be dominated by wars and an unprecedented shedding of blood – as the fulfillment of his political ideas. This is emphasized by the red fabric that covers the podium at the conference of the Socialist International in July 1914 at which the Social Democrats make pronouncements against the war although there are already indications that they are going to support it.

A scene in *Schwestern* (*Sisters*) contains a similar ambiguity. Shortly before Anna's suicide, the two sisters are driving along a country road on their way to see their mother. Anna, who is wearing a red coat, speaks enthusiastically about the magical powers of trees and, carried away by her feelings, gets out of the car in order to walk along the highway, to which Maria at first

78. Martha among Ana's marionettes (*L'Africaine / The African Woman*).

The color red: love, passion, fire, blood, death

79, 80. *Das Versprechen* (*The Promise*): Sophie in in a light red dress at her 1968 reunion with Konrad in Prague, and in a dark red coat surrounded by the crowd at the opening of the Wall in 1989.
81. Rosa Luxemburg: the red rose as a symbol of unfulfilled longing (with Karin Baal as Mathilde Jacob). (Photo: Margarethe von Trotta and Gudrun Ensslin, *Rosa Luxemburg. Das Buch zum Film*, Nördlingen 1986.)
82. Bank robber and hostage (Katharina Thalbach) (*Das zweite Erwachen der Christa Klages / The Second Awakening of Christa Klages*). (Photo: Westdeutscher Rundfunk.)
83. *Schwestern* (*Sisters*): The red coat as a symbol of menacing danger and a premonition of death.

reacts with irritation. Then she follows her in the car and seemingly playfully pretends she is trying to run over her. Here, red symbolizes not only death and subliminal aggression, but also passion and yearning for life. In Margarethe von Trotta's work, the two aspects are not far from each other. Another example can be found in *Heller Wahn* (*Sheer Madness*), where the two scenes in which Ruth appears dressed all in red represent moments when she gives the impression of being happy and full of vitality; however, the scenes are immediately followed by calamity – her suicide attempt and the outbreak of rivalry between Olga and Franz in Provence. In *Il lungo silenzio* (*The Long Silence*) the color red also accentuates the contradiction between the longing for a normal, happy life and the omnipresent threat. When Marco and Francesco take Carla out to eat to distract her from her worries, she wears a red dress, and to top it all the predominant color of the restaurant's decor is red. These elements underline the intrinsic meaning of the scene, in which the danger becomes all the more tangible in view of the many security precautions and the panic-stricken flight of the other guests.

The mise en scène of the inward story

The way the scenes are resolved is always meant to tell not only outward happenings but the inward, hidden story as well. Highly dramatic events take place in Trotta's films. But in contrast to many other film directors where these events are the high point of the plot, Margarethe von Trotta deliberately avoids using them to build tension. Rather, they are shown, if at all, only in snapshots, or else they are made to stand out against the plot as flashbacks (the bank robbery in *Das zweite Erwachen der Christa Klages* (*The Second Awakening of Christa Klages*), the betrayal in *L'Africaine* (*The African Woman*)); as visions (Ruth's aggression in *Heller Wahn / Sheer Madness*); as nightmares (the death in *Schwestern / Sisters*, the arson attack in *Die bleierne Zeit / Marianne and Juliane*); or through the insertion of documentary material (*Rosa Luxemburg* and *Die bleierne Zeit / Marianne and Juliane*). And at the same time one's gaze is directed at the people who are experiencing the events; the feelings of bank robbers and hostages during the bank raid; horror on the faces watching the films about the atrocities of the National Socialist concentration camps or the victims of the Vietnam War; pain at the sight of the dead sister's disfigured face; Rosa Luxemburg's tears about the victims of the war at the sight of a buffalo beaten until it is bloody; helplessness and vulnerability in the many scenes of arrest and interrogation; or mute rage and despair in the face of death.

Feelings and moods overlay the events and often take center stage. Much of this is a product of the moment, for because of limited funding that made shooting in the studio prohibitively expensive, Margarethe von Trotta, especially in her early films, was forced to work at original locations or in rented apartments furnished according to her instructions. This caused a number of limitations in lighting, sound, and camera work that inevitably affected the structure of the work.

On the other hand, however, it allowed the director to work with the existing locale and to use her own inspiration and sensitivity in order to find the appropriate resolution for the scenes.

In outdoor shots, a great deal is left up to chance. Weather conditions and light can be predicted only to a limited extent or may change, and shooting must go on even if weather does not meet the expectations of the director, since every lost day costs a lot of money. Margarethe von Trotta regards one very expressive scene in *Il lungo silenzio* (*The Long Silence*) as a piece of great good fortune since the weather was exactly right for the scene: It shows Carla and Tommasco after the latter's resignation walking by the sea, two lonely figures bracing themselves against the wind. The weather is exactly right for the scene. The overcast sky, the strong wind, and hence the laborious progress arm in arm convey the image of two people fighting a losing battle who nevertheless refuse to give up. In the book accompanying *Das zweite Erwachen der Christa Klages* (*The Second Awakening of Christa Klages*) the director recalls how she shot the scenes in Portugal almost like a documentary without rehearsals or repetitions, since she had little time, and shooting depended on the peasants' workday. Her sure feel for the right frame is shown particularly in situations she cannot control.

When she constructs a frame, her main interest is in bringing her characters into relation with their surroundings and other people in a way that at the same time says something about their state of mind. In Trotta's films medium and full shots of individuals or groups of people are the rule, as well as close-ups and blow-ups that in most cases show faces and occasionally hands with objects, for instance, in *Schwestern* (*Sisters*): Anna's hand with the blurred Polaroid picture she takes of herself shortly before her death, or Maria's hands as they prepare the coffee tray for her boss or sharpen pencils. Other motifs are rare, however. In moments of intense strain and subliminal emotions, the director directs attention to people's faces. When long shots are used, these serve – above and beyond their usual function of localization and orientation in space – as a means of distancing from an event, but also of secret observation, of emphasizing a crowd in which the individual is lost, and often to convey a special mood. Frequently they emphasize how forlorn people feel in a space. This is especially clear in *Rosa Luxemburg*, when the protagonist, a small, lonely figure, goes down the steps of the Reichstag after the war credits were approved, or when she walks alone in the prison yard. Another striking example is the scene in *Das zweite Erwachen der Christa Klages* (*The Second Awakening of Christa Klages*), when Christa and Wolfgang hike through a green landscape into a valley blocked by the concrete buildings of a housing development. Maria in *Schwestern* (*Sisters*) looks equally forlorn as she stands up to her knees in water with a rainy, North German landscape in the background and looks across the river, a frame that in structure and mood resembles the lonely walk along the river of the Maria character in *Paura e amore* (*Love and Fear*). In the beginning scene of *Il lungo silenzio* (*The Long Silence*), the long shot unmasks the apparent idyl as captivity. A medium shot shows Carla and Marco during a walk on the beach as they merrily run from the waves and talk and laugh together; the camera slowly shifts its position upward and reveals that they are surrounded by bodyguards, who soon urge them to go back to the house.

Particularly in interior shots, which make up the greatest part of her films, the director often conveys the sense that space is restricted by framing in the foreground in the form of beams, doors, windows, openings in walls, or columns, and directs attention to the action of persons in the middle distance. She also predominantly uses closed frames that allow viewers to forget the space outside the frame. Even in scenes in which many people appear – for instance, at the opening of the Berlin Wall, or the Social Democrats' New Year's Eve ball in 1899, she throws into relief clearly defined groups that are the center of the frame. While her film characters frequently enter a frame, they step out of it extremely rarely. If they leave the scene, the director usually makes a cut. Occasionally framing is also used to represent simultaneous actions: here, a second focal plane is created in the background; a particularly striking example occurs in *Heller Wahn* (*Sheer Madness*), where in one scene Franz and Olga are sitting conversing in the foreground, while in the background Ruth is shown through a gap in the wall preparing supper. There is a similar frame structure when Ruth visits Olga's apartment: Dieter comes to see Olga and goes into the kitchen with her. While the two talk, Ruth watches them through the door of the adjoining room until Dieter finally closes the door. In a later scene Franz stands in the doorway to the living room and sullenly watches Ruth and Olga's loving goodbyes at the front door. In *Paura e amore* (*Love and Fear*) Massimo is shown in the foreground as he sits brooding in the dark living room, while in the room behind him Velia vainly tries to talk Sandra into joining them. Margarethe von Trotta uses the same frame arrangement in *Il lungo silenzio* (*The Long Silence*) when she accentuates the contrast between male and female behavior: After returning from the

Distance as an expression of tensions

84, 85. Martha and Ana in *L'Africaine* (*The African Woman*).
86. Carla (Carla Gravina) and Tommasco (Giuliano Montaldo) in *Il lungo silenzio* (*The Long Silence*) during a walk on the beach.
87. Rosa Luxemburg being interrogated.
88. Marianne and Juliane's reunion at the museum (*Die bleierne Zeit / Marianne and Juliane*).

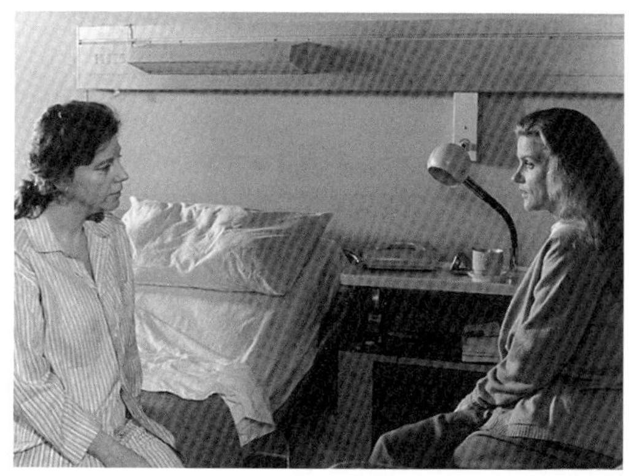

vacation Carla sits in an easy chair in the foreground calling her mother while Marco walks up and down in the room behind her talking to a colleague on the phone.

Space is deliberately used to emphasize relationships between people, yet another distinctive feature of Margarethe von Trotta's directing style. Closeness and intimacy are always expressed as physical closeness, while emotional distance and alienation are reflected by spatial distance. There is a particularly clear example of this technique in *L'Africaine* (*The African Woman*): more than by words, the inner development of the relationship between the two women finds expression in the way they approach or distance themselves from each other physically. When they first meet at the hospital, Martha at first refuses to come even physically close to Ana by withdrawing into the farthest corner of the room. Without responding to the other woman's attempts to communicate, she merely enquires briefly after her health and then gets ready to go and speak to the physician. Ana holds her back and begs her to have some understanding for her past behavior, whereupon Martha reluctantly stays and again takes her seat on the other side of the room, while her bitterness about Ana's betrayal of their friendship bursts forth. During the following visit she is more approachable. She finds Ana asleep, sits down on the bed next to Ana's and, on the night table, discovers the books on esotericism, which she looks at thoughtfully for a long time. After Ana wakes up, Martha plumps up her pillows and smooths her blanket. But when Ana wants to speak with her about the past, she refuses, and immediately creates a barrier between herself and her friend by moving to the foot of the bed. Ana asks her to forgive her. Martha gives an evasive answer, but she does sit down on the edge of the bed next to her, thus signaling that she is willing to come closer to her. At their next meeting there is less chill in the air: The two of them sit facing each other on two hospital beds in Ana's room. Ana smokes a cigarette, then sits down next to Martha and asks her to finish smoking it. Martha declines with a smile; when Ana urges her, she takes the cigarette and acts as if she were taking a drag. The doctors come into the room on their rounds and rebuke Martha for smoking in Ana's presence. Martha leaves without telling on her friend.

Spatial distance and closeness as an expression of interpersonal dynamics have special significance in the reconciliation scene at the end of the film. Jan has arranged a meeting between the two friends. He seats them at opposite ends of his sofa, puts on a record, and asks them to listen. Ana sits there tense and chilly; Martha half faces her, and at first appears at a loss. Finally she looks at her friend and apologizes to her. Ana struggles with her feelings, then turns to Martha, and both embrace. In this way the bridging of spatial distance becomes a symbol for increasing emotional closeness. Here, Margarethe von Trotta transfers the element of equilibrium – the balance of happiness, one of the fundamental ideas of all her films – to the composition of the frame. She translates the balance of forces by constructing a symmetrical, harmonious frame, often placing the characters side by side in space, a technique found in her other films as well. As in the reconciliation scene described above, this juxtaposition is not necessarily free of tensions, but stands for a stalemate situation, for instance, in *Das zweite Erwachen der Christa Klages* (*The Second Awakening of Christa Klages*), where Werner and Christa sit side by side on Ingrid's roof terrace at some distance from each other and without looking at each other after Christa has surprised him and Ingrid embracing, as he surprised her and Hans before. However, linked with closeness, this way of positioning the characters is frequently an expression of peace and harmony, for example, when Ingrid and Christa lie close to each other on camp beds in the summer house holding hands, or Christa cuts tomatoes on the table in her shack in Portugal, while next to her Ingrid washes herself in a basin, or when in *Schwestern* (*Sisters*) Miriam and Maria walk along the dike next to each other after Miriam has, so to speak, pulled her out of the water, or when in *Heller Wahn* (*Sheer Madness*) Ruth and Olga read side by side at a table in the library or sit on the couch in Ruth's living room in intimate conversation.

The antithesis to such an optical balance of spatial juxtaposition is created by the dynamics of disequilibrium, the collision of opposites, but also of power and dependency relations. Occasionally these are expressed in a spatial constellation that forces the weak to look up to the stronger, as Juliane's vision in *Die bleierne Zeit* (*Marianne and Juliane*) shows especially clearly. Here the powerful, punishing father hovers menacingly in the pulpit above the two little girls, and they stare up at him in terror, an image that refers to an earlier scene where they stand hand in hand in front of the gruesome painting of the crucifixion in their parents' stairwell and look up at it full of fear. Scenes of this type are found mainly in *Schwestern* (*Sisters*) and *Heller Wahn* (*Sheer Madness*), the two films in which the central theme is mutual personal dependency, for instance, when Maria, after offering to pay for Miriam's language school, walks up and down in the room and dictates while Miriam sits at the typewriter typing. Similarly Maurice literally lowers himself before Maria when he kneels in front of her and begs her to meet with him. There are similar spatial constellations in *Heller Wahn* (*Sheer Madness*) between Franz and Ruth, when he solicitously treats her like a child – for example, after telling her that the exhibition of her paintings cannot take place, or when she returns from the hospital after her suicide attempt. As a reaction she imagines in her vision of suicide that it is she who rises above him, if only by hanging herself from a rafter.

Differing points of view are frequently emphasized by creating spatial front lines where the characters face each other. During an argument between Christa and Hans in *Das zweite Erwachen der Christa Klages* (*The Second Awakening of Christa Klages*) their harmonious juxtaposition breaks up at the moment of discord; the figures move in different directions: Happy to see each other, they at first walk side by side along the platform of the country railroad station where they have met. Hans upbraids Christa, she is indignant, whereupon he turns around and goes in the opposite direction, while she stops walking. Suddenly both of them simultaneously change their mind, turn around, move toward each other, and embrace. The argument between Velia and Maria in *Paura e amore* (*Love and Fear*) is portrayed following the same principle: The three sisters come toward the camera side by side along the covered walk of a convent. Maria stops, leaves the line, and faces Velia and Sandra as she tells them she has fallen in love with Massimo. Velia is filled with consternation. She begins to walk faster ahead of her sisters, who follow her side by side, more and more slowly. Maria catches up with her and keeps talking, whereupon Velia flies into such a rage that she slaps Maria and goes on walking even faster. Maria overtakes her and accuses her of being jealous, at which Velia rushes at her and the two of them come to blows. Sandra separates them and stands hesitating as the two others go off in opposite directions. The dynamics of the scene are heightened by focus and camera movement: at first, in a full shot, the entire group constantly remains in the frame. When the group moves forward, the camera travels in front of it, while in the end the angry faces of Velia and Maria in medium shots are cut against each other, each time with the other's figure moving away in the background.

Montage is an important technique for representing contrasts, whether in the form of verbal confrontation between opposing viewpoints or by placing different spheres of life and characters face to face. During the conversation between Sophie and Konrad at the Olympiastadion in Berlin, in *Das Versprechen* (*The Promise*), the director creates the impression of spatial distance and closeness by changing the position of the camera and the view. At the beginning of the scene there is a long full shot that shows a side view of the couple at a table in the stadium's cafeteria and emphasizes the distance between them. This is followed by close-ups of their faces that move them closer together and create an intimate atmosphere. Very often in conversation scenes differences of opinion and contradictions between the protagonists are stressed by means of the classic shot-reverse shot technique of the Hollywood dialogue style. A typical example is a long dialogue scene from *Il lungo silenzio* (*The Long Silence*) that demonstrates the conflicting nature of emotions: Marco gets an anonymous phone call, Carla enters the room, and he tells her somebody dialled a wrong number. She seems upset and frightened, and accuses him of lying to her. When he approaches her in order to appease her, the frame changes from the preceding individual shots cut in quick succession to a more neutral two-shot, and then returns to the shot-reverse shot technique as he moves away from her and she asks him how he would react if she were threatened. Now, once more in a two-shot, he is shown approaching her full of alarm, she reassures him, but then, still upset, draws back. The camera pans after her, he enters the frame and tells her he would not want to have to feel guilty. She reminds him of the normal life they once had, and he tries to cheer her up, she again draws back, he follows her, at last she cannot help laughing and they embrace. The frame once more switches to the shot-reverse shot technique when he moves away from her and asks her to move to her mother's house until the investigations have been completed, and she answers that he won't get rid of her that way. Finally a two-shot shows her walking toward him and embracing him from the back. Here both the movements of the actors in space and the shots and montage underscore the characters' mood swings and the dynamics between them.

Another important technique is the contrasting of differing life situations, characters, or attitudes by means of parallel action. Particularly in *Schwestern* (*Sisters*) and *Heller Wahn* (*Sheer Madness*) this principle is used throughout in order to contrast – often by means of jump cuts – the lives of the two women protagonists. We find the same technique in *Das Versprechen* (*The Promise*), here in order to convey the difference between life in East and in West Berlin; in *Die bleierne Zeit* (*Marianne and Juliane*) it is used to describe the different directions taken by the sisters; finally, in *Rosa Luxemburg*, it brings out the contrast between the public and the private

Rosa. In the same way the different points of view of the two women in *Winterkind* (»Winter Child«) are revealed by comparing their behavior and their living conditions. Before the action proper begins, the lengthy opening credits first show Daniel's relationship to Elke and to his friend Jonathan, and then go on to show Jelena's arrival and the fact that she knows Ana. This confrontation is continued especially in the first part of the film: Jelena's desperate search for her son, Daniel's relationship to Elke, and the looming conflict because of Jonathan are placed side by side. After Jelena has met Michael again, the parallels mainly emphasize the development of the relationship between the two, and that between Elke and her son, which is increasingly disrupted because of Daniel's friendship with Jonathan.

Elsewhere montage is used to establish connections. In *L'Africaine* (*The African Woman*) the linking of scenes where Ana and Jan simultaneously perform their spiritual ceremonies creates the impression that a magical bond, as it were, exists between the two: The old man gazes intently into a crystal ball that reflects a candle flame. The next frame shows Ana, who takes a burning candle from the shelf in front of the bathroom mirror in her hospital room, places it in a bowl of water, and looks into the flame, whereupon the old man in front of his crystal ball again becomes visible. The candle motif is taken up again when, in a later scene, Jan visits Ana in the hospital and tells her about the close connection between health and inner harmony. There are similar references, though less clear ones, in other Trotta films: Thus, in *Heller Wahn* (*Sheer Madness*), Ruth vainly tries to overcome her fear of making a phone call and to call Olga, and in the next scene Olga listens to her answering machine and finds only messages for her lover; or, in *Paura e amore* (*Love and Fear*), a frame of the wooded riverbank cuts to a film about the dying of the forests, which introduces the next scene.

In the flashbacks in *Die bleierne Zeit* (*Mariane and Juliane*) and *Rosa Luxemburg* Margarethe von Trotta establishes associations through montage that add in important ways to what the film is trying to convey. In *Die bleierne Zeit* (*Marianne and Juliane*) the cups of cocoa on the café table create a transition to the breakfast table in the parents' house, where during the father's long benediction a skin forms on the cocoa. As Juliane looks into the prison yard through a hole in the windowpane of the prison waiting room, she remembers her childhood, when she and her sister competed with each other doing handstands by the cemetery wall. Her searching look across the endless rows of windows in the façade of the yard conveys the loneliness Marianne must be feeling, and is underscored by the flashback that follows, to the sisters' classroom where Marianne recites a Rilke poem which includes the following line: »Wer jetzt allein ist, wird es lange bleiben ...« (»Whoever is alone now, will remain so for a long time.«) A mother and two little girls on the opposite platform who are blocked from view by a passing train arouse memories in Juliane of nightly air-raid warnings during World War II. Margarethe von Trotta uses the same technique in the first two-thirds of *Rosa Luxemburg*; starting with Rosa's statements in her letters, she creates series of associations in which various aspects and stages of her life are conceptually summarized.

By the subtle use of all organizational techniques accents are shifted and an inner development is made visible. One graphic example is the prison visits in *Die bleierne Zeit* (*Marianne and Juliane*) which, except for the sisters' last meeting, have the same locale and the same external situation. During Juliane's first visit, the accent is on the irksome and humiliating procedure of searches and inspections, which Juliane's frustration when her sister refuses to see her makes even harder to bear. After she writes to Marianne, reminding her of their childhood together, she makes one more attempt to see her sister. At this meeting, both sisters weigh the elements that connect them and separate them: A woman guard opens the door to the visitors' room; Marianne stands at the opposite side of the room in a doorway. Juliane enters the room and stands facing her. The expression on her face wavers between distrust and uncertainty. Marianne begins to smile and slowly walks toward her, Juliane takes a few hesitant steps. She now looks watchful and tense. The two embrace, Marianne still smiling, Juliane less than pleased. The guard tells them to sit down, the two slowly disengage themselves and go to the table. Marianne is told to to take the seat on the opposite side. They sit looking at each other, with the door to the cell block in the background. Marianne stretches out her hand toward Juliane and reminds her of the hated waists (=bodices with garters) they wore when they were children. Juliane hesitantly places her hand in her sister's. Suddenly the mood changes. The camera focuses squarely on Marianne's face, which loses its soft expression as she whispers to Juliane that she should visit Karl as well. Juliane refuses, and finally accuses her sister that she and her friends with their bombs destroyed all the small successes of Juliane's work. During her outburst the frame changes in quick succession from her face to Marianne's and back, while an interspersed frame

89–93. Visits at the prison in *Die bleierne Zeit* (*Marianne and Juliane*).

shows the face of the guard. Marianne at first reacts indignantly, then with embarrassment. There is another shot from the side across the table as Juliane breaks off and starts crying. Marianne reminds her of her letter, her sister gets up, tells her in tears that she can't handle it today, puts the package of cigarettes she brought on the table and walks to the door. A long oblique shot from above shows Marianne alone at the table. Finally she slowly stretches out her hand and takes the cigarettes, still looking at the door.

During the next visit Marianne describes conditions in solitary confinement. A sharp cut from the previous scene, which shows the two sisters at fifteen crying in the bathroom after watching a film about National Socialist concentration camps, to the prison's visitors' room establishes a connection between the fascist period and Marianne's present situation. She is taking part in a hunger strike, her face looks careworn, and the cold white light of the visitors' room accentuates her pallor. The sequence begins with long close-up shots of the faces of the two sisters looking at each other in silence. Juliane is worried about the way her sister looks and rebukes her for wilfully undermining her health. At this, quickly and as though harassed, occasionally searching for words, Marianne begins to talk about conditions in the prison. As she speaks, the frame changes in slow rhythm from her face to Juliane's, whose expression becomes more and more horrified. The scene is interspersed with short frames showing the two women guards and the legal officials who are recording the conversation. Toward the end of Marianne's description, a medium shot similar to the one on the first visit shows both women in profile at the table. However, now the background is formed by the windows in front of which the guards are sitting, and the two sisters have changed sides. When visiting time is over, the prison officials get up, Juliane and Marianne step behind the table and embrace, Marianne suggests they should switch sweaters, the guard tries to intervene, but the two sisters forestall her. They embrace one more time. In the doorway Juliane looks back at her sister with a worried smile before the door closes behind her.

The subsequent meeting between them shows a fundamental change in the sisters' relationship. It is true that their differences of opinion erupt once more: Marianne accuses Juliane of self-deception, Juliane retorts that Marianne found detailed work too laborious, and that's why she is in jail, where she's no use to anybody. Yet basically the mood between the sisters reveals a tacit alliance against the representatives of the state. When a guard demands that Marianne hand over the perfumed handkerchief Juliane gave her when she said hello, Marianne throws it at her feet, the guard picks it up, whereupon Juliane defiantly demands it back, and then gives her sister a triumphant smile. The way the scene is presented in the film lays stress on the element of imprisonment. It begins with a frame showing Marianne being led handcuffed along a corridor past barred cells: the echoing footsteps, the rattling keys, a view of the door of the visitors' room opening all evoke the fact that this is a prison. What is more, the spatial distance between the sisters has increased, since this time they are seated at the farthest ends of the table, and the four people guarding them have moved so close that it seems as though they, too, are at the table with the sisters. Because of the lateral angle of the shot the watchdogs are constantly visible in the alternating close-ups of Juliane and Marianne, which accentuates the fact that their conversation is being closely watched. The distance between the sisters is canceled when after the incident with the handkerchief there is a change to blowups that eliminate the surroundings and create a sphere of intimacy as the sequence concludes.

There is another complete change of mood in the next visit scene. In a single long full two-shot whose background is the window of the visitors' room, we see a violent argument occasioned by an article Juliane has written about her sister. The scenery is flooded with bright, white light that makes the green of the walls and the table appear gray and underscores the hostile attitude of the two protagonists. This time there is no loving embrace in greeting, and the two do not even sit down. As Juliane enters the room, Marianne screams at her that she has sold her down the river, and besides she, Marianne, cannot be understood in terms of her personal history. Juliane defends herself: She says that by telling Marianne's personal history she tried to arouse sympathy for her, and finally flings in her face the accusation that during the Nazi period she would have joined the »Bund Deutscher Mädel« (»National Socialist organization for girls«), whereupon Marianne slaps her.

Juliane's last visit takes place in a new prison with tighter security measures. The two sisters are separated by a glass pane and have to talk through microphones. Normal communication has become impossible. The glass makes Marianne's features appear blurred, finally the sound system breaks down, and the conversation ends after a few sentences. Compared to the inhumanity of the prison regime, the sisters' differences of opinion pale into insignificance. The situation that results explains Juliane's behavior after Marianne's death.

Forlorn in space during the daily walk in the prison yard

94. Marianne in *Die bleierne Zeit (Marianne and Juliane*). (Photo: Filmverlag der Autoren.)
95. Rosa Luxemburg.

Images that convey mood

Although external events in Trotta's films are largely communicated by dialogue, pictures often tell more than all the words combined. In *Schwestern* (*Sisters*), where interest is centered on the inner story, Maria's daily return from work serves to sketch the relationship between the two sisters. When she climbs the stairs to her apartment, her slow steps already indicate the trouble she expects inside the apartment door, where her sister leaves all responsibility to her, has once again done none of the household chores, and on top of all that accuses her of coming home so late. The image of Anna swaying to her favorite music lost to the world or standing behind the greenish glass of her terrarium and watching the iguanas illustrates her longing for death, and the tensions between Maria and Miriam are made clear more than by any discussion when Maria circles around her friend with a book in her hand and gives her a vocab quiz, while Miriam sits tense on a chair and nervously tries to come up with the right answers. When at the end of the film Miriam packs her things and moves out, Maria sits on a radiator off to one side of the room and watches silently – an image that conveys wordlessly that she feels beaten, lonely, and left out.

Almost without dialogue, the party scene in *L'Africaine* (*The African Woman*) in honor of Ana's discharge from the hospital clearly shows the relationship between the three protagonists: Ana puts on a record, Martha watches her from the sofa and smiles as her friend moves toward her in the rhythm of the music and asks her if she remembers. The two smile at each other. Suddenly Ana has an idea. She runs to Victor, asks him to dance with Martha and drags him to the dance floor. Then she gets the reluctant Martha. The two begin to move to the music and surreptitiously observe Ana, who watches with an encouraging smile. After a while she approaches them. Martha steps back and leaves Victor to her. With a sad face she gazes at the two of them and then slowly withdraws to the dark recess of the bow window. The shadow of the dancing couple follows her. On the other side of the yard, Jan pushes the curtain to one side and acknowledges her presence with a smile.

Only a few images in *Paura e amore* (*Love and Fear*) tell of the moment when Maria realizes that Massimo has turned away from her. Maria is waiting for him at the country house as arranged. She has fallen asleep on the bed. Suddenly she awakes with a start, runs to the door, and looks out into the night. For a moment she remains there and then slowly walks back into the room, leans on the bed, and begins to cry. Velia's decision to give up all thoughts of being in a love relationship with a man is also condensed into images by the director: When it has become clear to Velia that Massimo is no longer interested in her, she happens to see him on the opposite side of the street one day. He looks in her direction, hesitates for a moment, and then quickly walks into a building to avoid meeting her, while Velia, agitated, gazes after him. She follows him in order to take him to task and finds herself in a room full of historical paintings showing men of earlier epochs. Suddenly she pauses, her eyes wander around the room. Then, discouraged, she stares straight ahead. Not until later does she voice the insight that came to her at this moment – that looking for happiness with a man is futile; when Marco declares his love for her, she answers, »What's the use?«

In *Winterkind* (»Winter Child«), Jelena's arrival in Cologne conveys far more than the information that a traveler has arrived: A train rolls over a bridge and into the station. Carrying a suitcase, Jelena slowly, wearily crosses the station hall. She leaves the station by a glass door and there shows a man a piece of paper with an address to get directions. Then she stops and looks up in astonishment at the Cologne Cathedral, which towers like a giant above her. These images reflect her exhaustion, her sense of being a stranger, and forlornness.

Scenes that describe a person's state of mind are found in every Trotta film: With its black doors and hunting trophies, the hallway of the country inn that Christa Klages crosses after throwing a glass of water in Wolfgang's face because he has made fun of her newly dyed blond hair represents solid German bourgeois values. At the same time it underscores the fact that she has moved far away from her former life. In a later scene she goes into the forest to scream her rage and despair out of herself, a motif that is used again in *Il lungo silenzio* (*The Long Silence*). Marianne's quick, resolute pace as she moves in a circle like a captive animal during the prisoners' yard exercise in *Die bleierne Zeit* (*Marianne and Juliane*) describes her emotional state: she is full of enraged despair, refuses to admit defeat, and feels trapped, hopeless, and lonely. Similarly the prison scenes in *Rosa Luxemburg* convey secret thoughts, feelings, and moods: the precariousness of her inner equilibrium, her hidden fears, her happiness about a summer's day, her wistfulness and sadness, and particularly the serene patience that defines her basic attitude.

Reserved and chilly, Martha in *L'Africaine* (*The African Woman*) speaks little about what is going on within her, yet her lonely walks at night through Paris, her facial expression as she watches two lovers in the bus, her wondering looks out of the car window at the city's streets after her arrival express her sense of isolation, of being a stranger, and her long trek through the corridors of the hospital demonstrates how much effort it took for her to visit Ana. In *Il lungo silenzio* (*The Long Silence*) sensual images communicate what Carla and Marco try to hide from each other: The silence of the apartment when she waits for him at night, the way she starts at each unexpected noise, her lonely meal, during which she reads the paper and is suddenly jolted by the ringing of the telephone, the way she peers through the narrow crack in the shutters at the escort that takes Marco to work in the morning all betray her tension and worry. In *Das Versprechen* (*The Promise*), the frames of Konrad watching the departing train that crosses the Spree River on its journey from East to West Berlin; his wistful face when during guard duty by the Wall he catches sight of a young woman on the other side through his binoculars; the scene of Sophie on a swing in the dark in her aunt's garden tell of unfulfilled longing; the sight of Sophie in a red evening dress sobbing uncontrollably as she lies in the dark showroom of the fashion salon, and of Konrad sitting in his bed in the army dormitory and crying after all his attempts to escape have failed speak of despair and hopelessness. When Sophie realizes she is pregnant, the motif of the train as a connection between East and West becomes a symbol of her desperate efforts to be reunited with her lover. The long shot of her tear-drenched face during her last trip underscores the fact that, as she tells him in her final letter, she no longer has the strength to live in uncertainty. When, after saying goodbye to Konrad on his 1981 visit in West Berlin, Sophie goes to her apartment door and listens to his steps on the stairs, while he stops on the landing and looks back, we understand that in spite of the long separation they still love each other. The blowup shot of the carryall Harald has left on the landing in front of Sophie's apartment communicates his decision not to accept his deportation from the GDR. In two short scenes in *Winterkind* (»Winter Child«), Margarethe von Trotta condenses Elke's inner agitation and despair when she becomes aware that her life is built on illusions. After Elke takes her father to task about his time in Russia, she runs out of the house and jumps into her car. When she backs up, the bumper collides with a stack of wood and knocks it over. In the next scene she stands on a bridge staring into the river. A ship passes below and hides the water from her view. In a similar way, the director illustrates Jelena's frame of mind when she shows her sitting alone and sad in a bar, forlornly watching two women singers. The singers prowl around her caterwauling a song that is in complete contrast to her mood, sounds like mockery, and evokes the preceding scene, where Daniel said goodbye to Jonathan and promised that he would take care of the old man's cat.

The landscape shots occasionally included in Trotta's scenes are also pure evocations of mood: A rainy marsh landscape in *Schwestern* (*Sisters*) mirrors Maria's sadness and shock when she flees to Fritz after Anna's death. The clouds of smoke over the rugged slopes of Mount Etna in *Die bleierne Zeit* (*Marianne and Juliane*) presage the tragic events that will change Juliane's life. Like the Portuguese landscapes in *Das zweite Erwachen der Christa Klages* (*The Second Awakening of Christa Klages*), the panorama of the vineyard that surrounds the Provençal country house in *Heller Wahn* (*Sheer Madness*) conveys an image of peace and tranquillity. In *Rosa Luxemburg* the yellow color of the flowering fields of rape underscores Rosa's joyous expectation and desire for action when, after being released from prison in 1906, she travels by train from Warsaw to Berlin; the idyl of Lake Garda underscores the casual and cheerful vacation with Luise Kautsky, while gray overcast skies express moments of depression and evil forebodings during her prison term. A love scene between Velia and Massimo in *Paura e amore* (*Love and Fear*) is introduced by a long pan across the water of the river and the gravel beach, and there is a view of the misty landscape and the willow-bordered driveway of Massimo's country house both at the beginning and at the end of his relationship with Maria, conveying the melancholy that surrounds it. The dim light of the full moon in the hazy sky emphasizes Maria's mood as she waits for Massimo in vain. The peace and harmony of the Celtic holy well and the Breton summer landscape in *L'Africaine* (*The African Woman*) become a symbol of the peace Ana seeks there.

Cinema as a Gesamtkunstwerk – music, literature, painting

In the films of Margarethe von Trotta music underscores moods or sometimes creates them from the ground up, for its effect is disturbing, dramatic, irritating, menacing, meditative, contemplative, relaxing, or lively. Music lends pathos or heightens the drama. It conveys the feelings of the

96, 97. Rosa Luxemburg (Barbara Sukowa) in summer and in winter in her little garden at the Wronke prison.
98. Music as a direct commentary on the action: Konstantin Wecker appearing at the club (*Schwestern / Sisters*).

protagonists, their joy and euphoria, their affection and tenderness, their merriment and contentment. In the same way, the characters' sadness and melancholy, their nostalgia and unfulfilled longings, their disappointment and fear are expressed in the music. Also, characters are assigned musical motifs that accompany them throughout the film and vary according to their state of mind. Occasionally a musical motif also characterizes certain occurrences, like the encounters between Sophie and Konrad in *Das Versprechen* (*The Promise*), or Carla's and Marco's happy moments in *Il lungo silenzio* (*The Long Silence*). It functions to establish connections, to trigger memories, and to explain emotions, for instance, when Carla, after her husband's death, unpacks a box of his personal effects from his office, and we hear their theme music. For *Dunkle Tage* (»Dark Days«) the filmmaker commissioned a musical score whose content is suggested by the piano-playing that comes from the neighbor's apartment and by Fabian's music studies. While these motifs accompany the brighter moments of the plot, African drum music is associated with the mother's addiction and the children's belief in ghosts. Occasionally a song serves as a leitmotif for a person or an event. Anna's favorite song in *Schwestern* (*Sisters*) is Dido's lament »When I Am Laid in Earth«, from *Dido and Aeneas*, whose text and music have a direct relationship to her longing for death and come to symbolize her suicide. At their first meeting in Provence, when Ruth and Olga are sitting in an outdoor café, the song »In cerca di te«, sung by Gabriella Ferri, is heard in the background. Henceforth it represents the two women's friendship. Sophie and Konrad's musical leitmotif is the blues song »Everywhere You Are«, to the sound of which they dance in a close embrace at the party in the beginning scene. And in *L'Africaine* (*The African Woman*), an Italian hit tune reminds the friends of happy times they have shared.

Repeatedly music becomes the means for people to come closer to each other, to relax, to make peace. In *Das zweite Erwachen der Christa Klages* (*The Second Awakening of Christa Klages*), it is a cantata by Johann Sebastian Bach – sung by Janet Baker, the filmmaker's favorite singer, whose recordings she also uses in *Schwestern* (*Sisters*) and *Die bleierne Zeit* (*Marianne and Juliane*) – that allows Christa and Hans to get closer to each other. The music the family members make together gives the final scene of *Paura e amore* (*Love and Fear*) a conciliatory character in spite of the unresolved conflicts. In *Heller Wahn* (*Sheer Madness*), Olga asks her friend Alexej to play something for her on the piano in order to rouse him from his depression, and there is a similar motif in *Rosa Luxemburg*. Music as a symbol of harmony is used particularly explicitly in *L'Africaine* (*The African Woman*), where Ana listens to music in order to calm down after she has waited in vain for Martha's visit, and where Jan plays a piece from Christoph Willibald Gluck's *Orpheus and Eurydice* for the two women in the reconciliation scene – a scene about Orpheus's search for Eurydice in the underworld and his desire to bring a dead woman back to life, an idea directly related to Ana's belief that she can be healed only through reconciliation with Martha.

Elsewhere, too, the function of music and literature is to comment directly on the action and to extend its significance. Juliane's vision when she breaks down after her sister's death is underscored by an aria from George Frederick Handel's *Lucrezia*, describing how after Lucrezia's forced suicide the blood flows from her veins and she demands vengeance. In *Schwestern* (*Sisters*), the songs of Konstantin Wecker sum up the situation and feelings of white-collar workers like Miriam when he sings: »Freiheit, das heißt doch: für die, die dich lenken, frei bist du nur, wenn du tust, was sie denken« (»Freedom? Of course, that's for the ones in charge – you're only free when you do what they think«), a line that is quoted in *Dunkle Tage* (»Dark Days«) during the parents' conversation about the mother's job. Another song from *Schwestern* (*Sisters*) says, »Dieser Tag wird sicher auch nicht neuer, und man nimmt das Leben wieder mal in Kauf.« (»This day will certainly not get newer, and once again you must put up with life.«) The mother's state of mind is elucidated by her reading of the poems of Nikolaus Lenau, whose work is permeated with melancholy, Weltschmerz, weariness, and forebodings of death, and who was mentally ill when he died. Poetry is important in all of Trotta's films up to the mid-1980s. In *Das zweite Erwachen der Christa Klages* (*The Second Awakening of Christa Klages*), Hans gives Christa a volume of Yeats's poems as a goodbye present; from now on it will accompany her on her flight. When, at the end, she locks herself alone into an empty apartment, she sits in front of a wall she has filled with quotations, and a Yeats poem comments on her depression. A gaily romantic poem to night by Eduard Mörike in *Rosa Luxemburg* accentuates the emotional, dreamy side of the revolutionary that forms a bond between her and Kostja Zetkin. When, in *Die bleierne Zeit* (*Marianne and Juliane*), Marianne recites in class the Rilke poem quoted previously, rebellious Juliane responds by demanding to read Bertolt Brecht's »Ballade von der Judenhure Marie Sanders« (»Ballad of the Jews' Whore Marie Sanders«), thus setting rationality against soulfulness.

There is another reference to the poet in *Il lungo silenzio* (*The Long Silence*), when Carla says that to her Marco is a hero, and her mother answers, borrowing from Brecht: »I don't think much of heroes, or of times that need heroes.« In *Das zweite Erwachen der Christa Klages* (*The Second Awakening of Christa Klages*), Margarethe von Trotta also uses a Brecht work to explain Christa's motivation. Inspired by her views, the minister Hans points out a parallel between her actions and those of the mute Kathrin in Brecht's *Mother Courage* who, immediately before the enemies attack the town, beats the drum to warn the inhabitants instead of praying as she was advised to do. By focusing on the virtue of active love for other people, Hans corroborates the positive aspect of Christa's stance. This motif is taken up again later when Christa gives her daughter a drum and watches her standing in front of the daycare center beating on it.

Heller Wahn (*Sheer Madness*) is shaped by motifs taken from the literature and graphic arts of the Romantic period. A leitmotif here is the painting *Woman at the Window* by Caspar David Friedrich, which is directly associated with the figure of Ruth. Ruth paints a black and white copy of it in a museum, and as she does so, for a moment in front of the window, she assumes the same position as that shown in the picture. This motif runs through the entire film, starting with the beginning scene where Ruth stands at a barred window looking out into the rain. The emphasis on the strong contrast between the dark foreground and the bright wide background – this painter's most salient characteristic – is repeated in the two female figures, but also enters into the way frames are structured. Especially the landscape shots in Provence absorb the mood of Friedrich's paintings when the observer's eye focuses through the shadowy gateway or the dark trees in the foreground on the landscape that lies beyond, but even the framing of the center of the picture, described above, follows this pattern. An additional Romantic element is the story of two friends of the early Romantic school, Bettina Brentano and Karoline von Günderrode. This story, motivated in the drama by a lecture Olga gives at the university, creates a parallel to the friendship between Olga and Ruth and adds certain aspects to it, for instance when Günderrode's depressions, which ended in her suicide, are linked to the fact that she is a woman, yet has »desires like a man, without a man's strength«, as Olga quotes from one of Günderrode's letters. Later Ruth reads a passage from the poet's work *Der Schatten eines Traumes* (*The Shadow of a Dream*): »Der Friede, mit solchen Opfern erkauft, war nur zu teuer, und ich konnte den Gedanken nicht ertragen, mich teilweise zu vernichten, um mich teilweise desto besser erhalten zu können.« (»Only, considering the sacrifices, peace was bought at too high a price, and I could no longer bear the thought of partially destroying myself the better to be able to keep myself partially alive.«) Here the idea of suicide as liberation, which also appears in Ruth's visions, is put into words. In one of her lectures Olga portrays the point of view of Bettina Brentano, the friend who was left behind alone: »Es kränkt mich und ich mache ihr Vorwürfe, wie ich ihr damals in Träumen machte, daß sie die schöne Erde verlassen hat. Ja, sie hat's bös mit mir gemacht, sie ist mir geflüchtet, gerade wie ich mit ihr teilen wollte alle Genüsse.« (»I feel hurt, and I reproach her, as I did in dreams at the time, for leaving this beautiful earth. Yes, it was wicked of her to do this to me, she fled from me just as I was hoping to share all pleasures with her.«)

Similarly, in *Paura e amore* (*Love and Fear*), Velia's lecture about medieval Christian women mystics serves to put into words in encoded form the things that concern her deeply – renouncing an imperfect relationship with a man, and her ensuing loneliness. In one scene she reads a long passage about love that here takes on an idealized, divine dimension and comes to be associated with solitude. It goes as follows: »Eines Tages in der Fastenzeit erschien es mir, als wär ich ausgetrocknet und ohne Andacht. Da bat ich Gott, er möge mir von sich geben, dieweil ich alles Guten ledig sei. Und da wurden mir die Augen meiner Seele aufgetan, und ich sah die Liebe, die auf mich zukam. ... Und als die Liebe mich berührte, sah ich alles mit den Augen der Seele, die mehr enthüllen, als die Augen des Körpers. ... Und ich wollte keine andere Kreatur weder sehen, noch hören, noch verspüren.« (»One day during Lent it seemed to me as though I was parched and without devotion. Then I prayed to God that he should give me of himself since I was empty of all that is good. And then the eyes of my soul were opened, and I saw love coming toward me. ... And when love touched me, I saw everything with the eyes of the soul, which reveal more than the eyes of the body. ... And I wanted neither to see, nor hear, nor feel any other creature.«) During her visit to the convent, there is a discussion about the torment of loneliness, in the course of which Velia speaks of how those women mystics practiced mortification of the flesh, which they understood as love, in order to overcome their loneliness.

The differentiated use of music and literature points to the cultural interest of the director. This is also true of the paintings and sculptures used in the films, which in some cases underscore moods, in others provide added detail to the characterization of figures and situations, while oc-

99. The leitmotif of *Heller Wahn* (*Sheer Madness*): Ruth in front of Caspar David Friedrich's painting *Woman in the Window*.
100. Margarethe von Trotta with Jutta Lampe and Barbara Sukowa during the making of *Die bleierne Zeit* (*Marianne and Juliane*), 1981. (Photo: Filmverlag der Autoren.)

casionally they can also be elements of the plot. They also throw light on Margarethe von Trotta's predilections. The paintings from *Mit fünfzig küssen Männer anders* (»At Fifty Men Kiss Differently«), for example, are by Angelika von Schwedes, a painter of whom the filmmaker thinks very highly and who, like the protagonist of the film, changed her style of painting at a particular point in her career.

By deliberately exploiting the special characteristic of the medium – its ability to subsume all other artistic genres within it – film here becomes a way of creating a multilayered work of art – a Gesamtkunstwerk.

Actors

The effect of Trotta's films is based to a great extent on the skill of the actors. The filmmaker herself has described the art of directing actors as one of her best qualities, and her directing has been praised again and again by actors who have worked with her and by film critics. Agnes Fink, speaking about her, says: »Who but Margarethe has looked into the hearts and minds of women as intensively? What happens in her films is unbelievable. When I think of her film *Die bleierne Zeit* (*Marianne and Juliane*) – what the two actors Jutta Lampe and Barbara Sukowa achieved working with Margarethe – all I can say is that what they did was unique.«[16] There is general consensus that she concentrates completely on the work with the actors so as to clarify each scene down to the last detail, and to make it possible for the cast to exteriorize psychological processes. Here her own experience as an actor comes in useful, but also her sensitivity and special ability to empathize with others, by means of which she builds up trust, the factor she herself considers to be crucial for the unimpeded development of her cast. The result is that an inner tension is built up between the characters. Frequently it arises almost unnoticed, and is initially expressed only with restraint, only to escalate into an emotional outburst at the end.

This takes actors who are particularly skilled in making visible nuances while at the same time being able to portray strong emotions plausibly. Therefore Margarethe von Trotta considers it important to cast actors who are versatile in expressing themselves, and who can also relate to their part emotionally and identify with it. For the leading parts in her early films, like other filmmakers of the New German Cinema, she used mainly women character actors whom she knew from the theater and who often had little or no film experience. Repeatedly she worked with Jutta Lampe and Barbara Sukowa, two names that are inextricably linked with Trotta's films.

Like Tina Engel and Angela Winkler, Jutta Lampe had for a long time belonged to the ensemble of the Berliner Schaubühne, which had its origins in the spirit of the movement of '68 and which had gained high artistic prestige. When Margarethe von Trotta offered her the part of Maria in *Schwestern* (*Sisters*), Jutta Lampe agreed only hesitantly, since she had hardly any film experience and feared her work would deteriorate. Besides, she felt that as far as the type went, she

felt closer to the part of Anna, the sensitive, emotional sister. Finally, however, she allowed herself to be persuaded by the director, and gave a star performance that brought her the 1980 Filmband in Gold (»Filmstrip in Gold«) of the Bundesfilmpreis (»Federal German Film Award«). Playing the strong, rational sister, she lends the character an inner contradiction that allows the audience to understand her moments of weakness and vulnerability. In the part of Juliane (*Die bleierne Zeit / Marianne and Juliane*), she again portrays a strong personality firmly rooted in life, the cracks in whose character she is able to portray convincingly. For this role, she received the Golden Phoenix at the 1981 Venice International Film Festival.

Barbara Sukowa, too, was trained as a stage performer. From 1968 until 1969, she studied at the famous Max Reinhardt Seminar in Berlin, and after that gathered stage experience at the Berliner Schaubühne, in Darmstadt, Bremen, Frankfurt on the Main, Hamburg, and at the Salzburg Festival before she began to accept film parts. She became well-known for the role of Mieze in the series *Berlin Alexanderplatz*, made for television by Faßbinder in 1979–1980. In 1981, Margarethe von Trotta first engaged her, for the part of Marianne in *Die bleierne Zeit* (*Marianne and Juliane*). Since she is the type of personality that has a great deal of charisma and presence, she was able to separate the figure of Marianne from the stereotype of the fanatical terrorist and to make the motives for her actions more transparent by allowing despair and powerlessness to show through her harshness against herself and others and her refusal to compromise. This part was her international breakthrough and, in 1982, won her the Golden Phoenix at the Venice Film Festival and the Federal German Film Award. Another brilliant performance was her interpretation of Rosa Luxemburg, a part that Margarethe von Trotta offered to her because, after a lengthy search for an actress who closely resembled the historical Rosa, the director became convinced that charisma, intelligence, temperament, warmth, and above all the ability to identify with the personality of Rosa Luxemburg were crucial – qualities she knew in Barbara Sukowa, for the actress lives her parts and plumbs their very depths. As she had already done in *Die bleierne Zeit* (*Marianne and Juliane*), when, the night before the scene where Marianne is in the middle of a hunger strike, she did not sleep so as to look pale and haggard, she also completely identified with the part of Rosa Luxemburg. Even when no shooting was going on, she adopted Rosa's idiosyncrasies, her limp due to a hip injury and the rolled »r« of her Polish accent. At the same time she began an intensive study of the person and her writings and letters in order to be able to understand Rosa Luxemburg's political goals and private longings. The result is an extremely sensitive, multilayered portrait of the revolutionary, which was honored in 1986 with the Actors' Award of the Cannes Film Festival and the Filmband in Gold (»Filmstrip in Gold«) of the Federal German Film Award. In 1990, Sukowa worked together with Margarethe von Trotta once again, in *L'Africaine* (*The African Woman*), this time in the role of Martha, again an aloof, strong, and uncompromising personality whose tough surface develops cracks and becomes conciliatory as she has to confront the betrayal of her former partner and her best woman friend.

Tina Engel, Sylvia Reize, Angela Winkler, Hanna Schygulla, Eva Mattes, Katharina Thalbach, Rüdiger Vogler, Daniel Olbrychski, Heinz Bennent, Otto Sander are names that are considered the trademarks of New German Cinema. For Tina Engel the role of the title character in *Das zweite Erwachen der Christa Klages* (*The Second Awakening of Christa Klages*) was her first film part, for which she won the Filmband in Gold (»Filmstrip in Gold«) of the 1978 Federal German Film Award. Because of their good collaboration, Margarethe von Trotta had originally intended to make her second film with Engel in the title role as well, but in the process of writing the screenplay, the character moved further and further away from the direct, practical, independent type of woman she portrays.

Not until 1995 did they again collaborate when Tina Engel played the role of Sophie's aunt in *Das Versprechen* (*The Promise*). Sylvia Reize – Ingrid in *Das zweite Erwachen der Christa Klages* (*The Second Awakening of Christa Klages*) – is also first and foremost a stage performer, even though prior to this she had already become known through her appearance in Erwin Keusch's film *Das Brot des Bäckers*, (»The Baker's Bread«), 1976. The first time Margarethe von Trotta worked with Angela Winkler was in *Die verlorene Ehre der Katharina Blum* (*The Lost Honor of Katharina Blum*), for which the performer drew outstanding reviews for her portrayal of the title role and received the Filmband in Gold (»Filmstrip in Gold«) of the 1976 German Film Award. Previously she had given an outstanding performance as the servant girl Hannelore in Peter Fleischmann's *Jagdszenen in Niederbayern* (»Hunting Scenes in Lower Bavaria«), for which the latter received the 1969 Federal German Film Award. She later worked, among others, with Reinhard Hauff, Ingemo Engström, Herbert Achternbusch, and repeatedly with Volker Schlöndorff in such films as *Deutschland im Herbst* (*Germany in Autumn*), 1978, *Die Blechtrommel* (*The Tin Drum*),

101. Margarethe von Trotta, Tina Engel and Peter Schneider during the filming of *Das zweite Erwachen der Christa Klages* (*The Second Awakening of Christa Klages*), 1977. (Photo: Berneis & Pecholt.)
102. With Hanna Schygulla, 1982.
103. With Heinz Bennent while working on *Schwestern* (*Sisters*), 1979.
104. The »three sisters« from *Paura e Amore* (*Love and Fear*): Greta Scacchi, Fanny Ardant and Sandra Golino, 1987.
105. The lead actors in *L'Africaine* (*The African Woman*): Stefania Sandrelli, Sami Frey, Barbara Sukowa, 1990.
106. Jacques Perrin (leading actor) during the filming of *Il lungo silenzio* (*The Long Silence*).
107. Margarethe von Trotta during the shooting of *Schwestern* (*Sisters*), 1979.

1979, and *Krieg und Frieden* (*War and Peace*), 1983, a joint film made by Alexander Kluge, Volker Schlöndorff, Stefan Aust, and Axel Engstfeld, with a screenplay by Heinrich Böll. Hanna Schygulla, with whom Margarethe von Trotta had worked as an actor as early as 1970 under the direction of Faßbinder in *Götter der Pest (Gods of the Plague)*, and who took the part of Olga in *Heller Wahn* (*Sheer Madness*) in 1983, had become an international star in the 1970s because of her roles in Faßbinder's films. She also played under the direction of Reinhard Hauff and Volker Schlöndorff. Since the early 1980s, she has been working predominantly in France, and like Margarethe von Trotta lives in Paris, where she again worked with the director in Jean Claude Carrière's play *La sainte femme*, which premiered on May 3, 1999. Agnes Fink, who played the part of the mother in both *Schwestern* (*Sisters*) and *Die bleierne Zeit* (*Marianne and Juliane*), is one of the great names in German postwar theater, and also became well-known because of her film and television roles. Katharina Thalbach had already had a long theater and film career in the GDR when she moved to West Berlin in the mid-1970s and accepted the part of Lena in *Das zweite Erwachen der Christa Klages* (*The Second Awakening of Christa Klages*), her first film role in the West. Since then she has been a very busy film, television, and stage performer, whose credits include *Die Blechtrommel* (*The Tin Drum*). Also in the cast of *Die Blechtrommel* (*The Tin Drum*) was the Polish actor Daniel Olbrychski, whom Margarethe von Trotta signed on in 1985 for the part of Leo Jogiches in *Rosa Luxemburg*. Rüdiger Vogler became famous mainly through his work with Wim Wenders. Through his roles in *Falsche Bewegung* (*False Movement*), 1974, *Alice in den Städten* (»Alice in the Cities«), 1975, and *Im Lauf der Zeit* (*Kings of the Road*), 1976, he developed into the quintessential Wenders persona. Eva Mattes, with whom Margarethe von Trotta made the episode *Eva* in the collaborative film *Felix* and with whom she later again worked in *Das Versprechen* (*The Promise*), where Mattes plays the pastor Barbara, is considered to be a full-blooded actor of extraordinary intensity. She worked, among others, with Faßbinder, Werner Herzog, and Helma Sanders-Brahms. Heinz Bennent was well-known as a renowned stage and television character actor when he first worked with Volker Schlöndorff and Margarethe von Trotta in *Die verlorene Ehre der Katharina Blum* (*The Lost Honor of Katharina Blum*), 1975. Thereafter he had a number of guest appearances in films categorized as representing the New German Cinema – *Deutschland im Herbst (Germany in Autumn)*, *Die Blechtrommel* (*The Tin Drum*), *Krieg und Frieden* (*War and Peace*), as well as in the role of Münzinger in *Schwestern* (*Sisters*). The same is true of Otto Sander, who portrays Karl Liebknecht in *Rosa Luxemburg* and Dr. Lorenz in *Das Versprechen* (*The Promise*). Peter Striebeck, too, was already a famous and experienced stage and television actor when he accepted the part of Franz in *Heller Wahn* (*Sheer Madness*).

The feminist demand for authenticity was one reason why, in her first films, Margarethe von Trotta decided to work in part with performers who were not trained actors. Thus, for instance, the writer Peter Schneider played the minister Hans in *Das zweite Erwachen der Christa Klages* (*The Second Awakening of Christa Klages*), and the songwriter Konstantin Wecker took the part of the accountant and singer Robert in *Schwestern* (*Sisters*). Since that time, the latter has repeatedly appeared as a performer – for example, in Marianne Rosenbaum's *Peppermint-Frieden* (»Peppermint Peace»), 1983, and recently in the two Trotta films *Mit fünfzig küssen Männer anders* (»At Fifty Men Kiss Differently«) and *Dunkle Tage* (»Dark Days«). Again for reasons of authenticity, but also because of her limited budget, the filmmaker, especially for smaller subordinate - parts, used nonprofessionals who played themselves. Since the result was not always satisfactory, however, she soon stopped doing so.

For the main parts in the three films Margarethe von Trotta made in Italy and France, she primarily signed on internationally known actors whose names are associated with European cinema: For the role of Velia in *Paura e amore* (*Love and Fear*) she engaged Fanny Ardant, the life partner of François Truffaut, a performer with extraordinarily strong charisma, while Greta Scacchi, an English performer of Italian descent who was shortly thereafter discovered by Hollywood, played the part of Maria.The part of Sandra was performed by the then 22-year-old Valeria Golino, who had had her first film roles at the early age of 17, and had received the Actors Award at the 1986 Venice Film Festival for her work in *Storia d'amore* (screenplay and direction: Francesco Maselli). Beside Barbara Sukowa as Martha, *L'Africaine* (*The African Woman*) included such performers as the French actor Samy Frey, who began his career in films by Henri-Georges Clouzot (*La vérité / The Truth*, 1961) and Jean-Luc Godard (*Bande à part / Band of Outsiders*, 1964) and has a long list of international films to his credit, as well as Sandra Sandrelli, who became internationally well-known primarily through her work with Ettore Scola (e. g., *La terrazza / The Terrace*, 1980) and Bernardo Bertolucci (e. g., *Novecento / Nineteen Hundred*, made in 1976).

The principal roles of investigating magistrate Marco Canova and his wife, Carla Aldrovandi, in *Il lungo silenzio* (*The Long Silence*) were played by the French actor and producer Jacques Perrin, who is associated with well-known directors like Agnès Varda, Pierre Schoendorffer, Jean-Jacques Annaud, Giuseppe Tornatore, and especially Costa Gavras; and by the Italian Carla Gravina, who had already begun her film career at 16 with Dino De Laurentis, but was then boycotted by film and television for many years because she had an illegitimate child at 19, whereupon she devoted herself to the theater. Later she acted in films that included *La terrazza* by Ettore Scola, who won the Golden Palm at Cannes in 1980 for the best film. For the role of the mother, Margarethe von Trotta signed on Alida Valli, who had gained fame in the 1950s with Antonioni's *Il grido* (*The Cry*) and Visconti's *Senso* (*The Wanton Countess*), 1953/54, and had since then acted in countless films.

An actor who is of special significance for Margarethe von Trotta and whom she calls her mascot was Jan Biczycki, who, between 1985 and 1991, worked with the director in three films: He played August Bebel in *Rosa Luxemburg*, Cecchini, the old family friend, in *Paura e amore* (*Love and Fear*), and Jan in *L'Africaine* (*The African Woman*), and he typically portrays the serene, worldly-wise, and cultured elderly gentleman.

For the principal male parts in *Das Versprechen* (*The Promise*) and *Winterkind* (»Winter Child«), the director engaged Konrad Zirner, an actor known mainly for his television parts, but also for his acting in recent German films like *Stadtgespräch* (*Talk of the Town*), 1995, or *Die Apothekerin* (*The Pharmacist*), 1997, who had already worked with Volker Schlöndorff in *Homo Faber* (*Voyager*), 1991, but is also very active as a stage performer. He typically portrays the rather sensitive, introverted, »weak« man Margarethe von Trotta has preferred to show particularly in her last films, where the male roles have been relatively important. For the principal female roles in *Das Versprechen* (*The Promise*), she signed on Meret Becker, known for her acting in some of the most successful German films of the 1990s and for her television roles, for the part of the younger Sophie; and Corinna Harfouch, one of the most noted female actors in the former GDR and now one of the best-known film and television performers in reunified Germany, for the part of the older Sophie. For *Winterkind* (»Winter Child«), in Lena Stolze and Susanna Simon, she found two extraordinarily expressive and sensitive actors for the principal female parts; they were able to make their characters' actions appear psychologically credible, and it was their acting that kept the plot from lapsing into kitsch, an achievement for which Margarethe von Trotta was largely responsible, as the periodical *Der Spiegel* remarked in its advance review: »It is to film director Margarethe von Trotta's credit that for long stretches at a time she makes viewers forget the material, which smacks of a cheap romance, and, thanks to the meticulous performances of the actors, builds up psychological tension.«[17]

The principal performers of her last two productions for television are among the most prominent and famous German TV actors. In *Mit fünfzig küssen Männer anders* (»At Fifty Men Kiss Differently«) the cast includes not only Senta Berger, whose filmography lists more than 100 films in over 40 years and who is one of a small number of internationally known German-speaking women actors, but also Ulrich Pleitgen, Eleonore Weisgerber, Gerd Warmeling, and Hans-Peter Hallwachs, actors who have decades of all-round film and television experience, and who manage to strike the right note in this »sophisticated comedy.« *Dunkle Tage* (»Dark Days«), because of the succinct way the story is told, is alive like no other Trotta film thanks to the unusual skill of the actors. Suzanne von Borsody as the mother manages to convey her personality changes convincingly and to make her into a character that arouses more sympathy than repugnance. Her fine performance is equalled by that of the actors in the parts of Felicitas and Max – who as children are played by Helen Dehorn and Cornelius Lehmann, and as teenagers by Stefanie Stoppenbeck and Siggi Kautz. The proof is the unusually sophisticated and expressive portrayal of Felicitas and Max as children. As in *Winterkind* (»Winter Child«), where ten-year-old Benjamin Kaatz portrays the character of Daniel, Margarethe von Trotta once again impressively demonstrates in this film her capability for doing theatrical work with children.

Woman as an image in *Lulu*

108–110. Susan Roberts as a redheaded Lulu in front of the portrait of Lulu from Wilhelm Pabst's film, as a blonde femme fatale with Dr. Schön, as an aging woman before a portrait from her youth. (Photos: A. T. Schaefer.)

4. Elements of Margarethe von Trotta's cinematic language

The destruction of the traditional image of women

In most of the director's films her central concern is to search for a new image of women. For her this is a crucial element of a new female aesthetics. First of all she is interested in destroying – both in a real and figurative sense – the image of women that shapes public consciousness and affects the way women see themselves. Influenced by feminist ideas, she has realized that the traditional portrayal of women in cinema as vamps and mothers, plus all the variants thereof, are male projections that have little to do with reality.

Ruth in *Heller Wahn* (*Sheer Madness*) says in a conversation with Olga: »He believes that his image of me is identical with my secret desires.« In her production of Alban Berg's opera *Lulu* in July 1997 at the Stuttgart Staatstheater Margarethe von Trotta focuses on this idea. In Berg's libretto Lulu is introduced as a serpent, Eve, the archetypally feminine, menacing, evil, dangerous – pure, naked instinct that leads men to destruction if they submit to it. Each man creates his own image of Lulu and even renames her himself: In the beginning she is Nelly, a child-woman, the wife of an aged senior medical officer whom her infidelity sends to his grave. For her second husband, an artist, she becomes Eve and is transformed into his muse, his model, and profitable source of income. After the painter's suicide, with the help of Alwa, the son of her long-time lover Dr. Schön, who arranged her first two marriages, she begins a career as a revue star, and later marries Dr. Schön, who calls her Mignon. But originally she was a prostitute and thief, and was called Lulu, a name she reverts to when she goes back on the streets and is killed. In the Stuttgart version Margarethe von Trotta makes her into a tragic figure who sacrifices her individuality to men's ideas of her, into an object they use only to throw it aside when they have no further use for it. In the prologue, the stage director places her in a cage that is open in front; white streaks of light fall across her figure which is profiled in front of the dark background of the stage; before the cage sits Alwa with his back to the audience watching her with fascination, an image that gets to the heart of Lulu's nature: a wild animal in captivity, menacing, unpredictable, yet also fascinating in its exotic beauty, a snake that sheds its skin in order to adapt to its surroundings and to survive. Margarethe von Trotta accentuates Lulu's object status by showing her in a large number of roles and disguises, thus making it clear that Lulu has many faces, behind which her true identity disappears. In the beginning she presents herself youthfully naïve in a pierrot costume, her hair in a black pageboy, as the painter's model – a getup reminiscent of the Lulu in Willi Pabst's film. As the wife of the painter she appears as a redheaded muse in green and gold lounging pajamas, catlike and sensual. In the luxurious black velvet revue costume, the gold-colored transparent skirt, her hair concealed under a golden turban, she is the celebrated dancer receiving her admirers in the theater dressing room. In Dr. Schön's house, in her white minidress and simple hairstyle, she looks like a prostitute, just as she does in the final scene, where she works as a prostitute; at first she is girlie-like and almost natural, but when, behind her husband's back, she holds court in her bourgeois salon for her lovers and for the outcasts of society, she changes roles and becomes a femme fatale disguised as a lady, wearing a white ball gown with a deep décolleté, and a straw-colored wig. After murdering Dr. Schön she succeeds in escaping from jail by switching identities with her lesbian friend Countess Geschwitz, and wearing the latter's black mourning. Later she lives under a false name in Paris, where she and Alwa run a gambling salon in the demimonde milieu of speculators and prostitutes, and where she tries with her appearance to bring back to life the glamor of former times, but the glaring orange of her Hindu-style evening dress with its gold-colored bustier gives her a touch of vulgarity and can hide neither the fact that she has come down in the world nor that her beauty is gradually fading.

The men are no longer attracted by her sex appeal, but only by her money. Because of her past she gets in the clutches of blackmailers and is able to escape being turned over to the police only by exchanging her clothes for a bellboy's uniform. By changing the external appearance, Margarethe von Trotta turns the loss of personal identity outward: Lulu's dressing up is unmasked as part of a role she resists by putting away the wigs and taking off the disguises. Thus, for brief moments, the real Lulu, an almost sexless creature, makes her appearance when she snatches the black wig from her head after the medical officer's death and shortly thereafter shows up in a simple close-fitting black dress that is not associated with any of her men, or when, after the painter's suicide, she leaves the house in a dark raincoat, her hair combed back smooth, unconcerned and indifferent to what is happening around her, like an actress at the end of the performance. In the end she returns to her original role, that of the streetwalker, and appears without any disguise from this point on, in a white minidress with black net stockings, high-heeled ankle boots, sans wig, bereft of glamor, reduced to the things that constituted her existence all this time: sex and money.

In the Alban Berg opera, Lulu is an artificial creature: As Eve in the Bible was made from Adam's rib, Lulu was created in the minds of men. Margarethe von Trotta, on the other hand, shows her as a real woman, and as such she represents the extreme form of a destiny she shares with the majority of women. This becomes obvious when in act 3 the women guests of the gambling salon appear in Lulu's costumes from previous scenes. A young girl – who, according to the script of this scene, is the center of the men's interest along with the purchase of stocks – is wearing the pierrot costume from act 1. As she stops in front of the portrait of Lulu that could just as well be her own and gives it a long, admiring look, she becomes the embodiment of the child-woman Lulu once was. In Margarethe von Trotta's version, this picture, which according to the stage directions accompanies the entire action, is the portrait of the Lulu from Pabst's film that has become the model for this character and has frequently been reproduced in other stagings of the opera. Used here as a symbol for Lulu's objectification, it always hangs in the background larger than life whenever Lulu submits to male notions of who she is as a person. During her marriage to the artist, the latter makes multiple copies of her portrait and thus becomes a rich man. Later, when Lulu is put on trial for murdering her third husband, the back of the picture is used as a surface on which the tabloid headlines are projected. When she is murdered by Jack the Ripper in the final scene, the portrait is on the floor, and the murderer wipes his bloody hands on it. When Lulu shoots Dr. Schön in act 2, the first bullets enter this canvas. She kills the man and at the same time destroys the image he has created of her. The parallel to the final vision in *Heller Wahn* (*Sheer Madness*), which recalls *Die verlorene Ehre der Katharina Blum* (*The Lost Honor of Katharina Blum*), is obvious. In all three cases there is rebellion against the image of woman that has sprung up in men's minds. The killing of the man, whether he is the husband or the unscrupulous journalist, becomes a metaphor for resistance against the prevailing image of women and for its destruction. Margarethe von Trotta's Lulu is a woman who submits to men's desires in order to survive, but secretly resists her submission. Her infidelity, the breaking of taboos, her intrigues, the way she uses her sexuality to obtain power over others, her exploitation of those who love her, are not due to her craving for destruction, but are on the one hand the expression of a personality deformed by restraints, while on the other hand they are signs of a struggle to exist as an independent person. During her argument with Dr. Schön she goes up the stairs in order to literally rise above him, but he drags her down again. In *Heller Wahn* (*Sheer Madness*) there is a similar scene: Franz makes a scene in front of Ruth because she has come home late after meeting with Olga. She protests and at the same time goes up the steps of a staircase until she stands above him. He follows her and pacifies her protest with an embrace: Oppressive demonstrations of love in this instance and violence in the other are a means of maintaining dependency.

Violations of the feminine ideal of beauty

111. Marianne's body in the coffin (*Die bleierne Zeit / Marianne and Juliane*).
112. Rosa Luxemburg moments before she is murdered.
113. Christa Klages (*Das zweite Erwachen der Christa Klages / The Second Awakening of Christa Klages*). (Photo: Filmverlag der Autoren.)

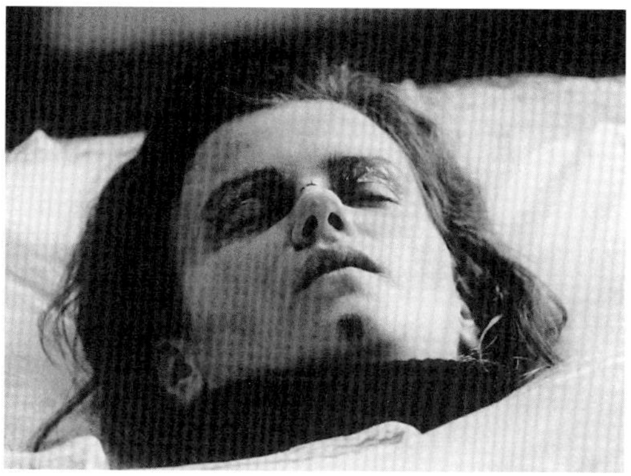

The search for a new female identity

The resistance against male fantasies that Margarethe von Trotta shows in her staging of *Lulu* is repeated in her films. Her female characters protest against meeting the expectations of their partners and conforming to the pressures of male-dominated society. Similarly, the filmmaker herself opposes the image of women generally disseminated in men's films, in the media, and in advertising. She makes a conscious effort to represent women in her films in a way that has nothing to do with the habitual way Hollywood views them. For example, she deviates from the traditional ideal of beauty, and from the prevalent practice of beautifying women in the cinema by costume, makeup, lighting, and focus. She does not produce idols, but female personalities. A clear example is the difference between the appearance of Barbara Sukowa and Hanna Schygulla in Faßbinder films like *Lola*, 1981, or *Lili Marleen*, 1980, and their roles in *Die bleierne Zeit* (*Marianne and Juliane*) or *Heller Wahn* (*Sheer Madness*). Costumes and makeup accentuate their natural appearance; the unflattering aspects are not glossed over. Not infrequently there is the courage to be ugly if the role demands it, for example when Gudrun Gabriel, the Anna in *Schwestern* (*Sisters*), appears to her sister in a vision, her face covered with white makeup like that of a corpse; when Barbara Sukowa as Marianne in *Die bleierne Zeit* (*Marianne and Juliane*) lies in the coffin with a horribly disfigured face; or when, as Rosa Luxemburg, Barbara Sukowa becomes a pale and haggard shadow of herself; and especially in *Dunkle Tage* (»Dark Days«), where the growing self-destruction of the mother (Suzanne von Borsody) results in her physical deterioration and the neglect of her own appearance. The issue of women's resistance against current ideas of beauty is brought up in *Das zweite Erwachen der Christa Klages* (*The Second Awakening of Christa Klages*): Christa watches Ingrid getting undressed and says, »You're beautiful.« But Ingrid disparagingly touches her thighs, which are not exactly thin, and answers, »Look at my thighs, will you.« Whereupon Christa replies, »So what? I've got them, too.« All this testifies to the fact that women have a new sense of self-confidence, expressed as resistance against conforming to prevailing male fantasies. But at the same time Margarethe von Trotta also refuses to create a new ideal image of women, as has been done by some parts of the women's movement. The women in her films resist all stereotypes, both in regard to appearance and to character, and in the final analysis each woman fights for the right to develop as an individual, with all the strengths and weaknesses that implies.

Couples in relationship

It is no accident that even in her first film *Das zweite Erwachen der Christa Klages* (*The Second Awakening of Christa Klages*), Margarethe von Trotta makes relationships between men and women her focal point, and examines women's living conditions and behaviors in the light of those relationships. For her, emancipation in general, and the emancipation of women in particular, means above all liberation from behavior patterns that have been internalized as a result of social conventions and the expectations of other people. The search for a new identity must thus inevitably be based on the study of interpersonal relationships and of the traditional role of women. This is why the frequently made assertion that there are practically no men in Margarethe von Trotta's films has no basis in truth. However, she does view men from a woman's perspective, and that perspective is merciless, reserved, disillusioned, and sometimes ironic. The portrayal of couple relationships serves to take a close look at societal role allocation and its compulsive character.

It becomes clear that relationships between the sexes are shaped by expectations opposite to those professed by the social role. Frequently men in Trotta's movies – as so often in real life – look for a mother substitute in their female partners (Wolfgang in *Das zweite Erwachen der Christa Klages / The Second Awakening of Christa Klages*, Alexej, Dieter in *Heller Wahn / Sheer Madness*), a mother for their children (Wolfgang and Werner in *Die bleierne Zeit / Marianne and Juliane*, Sandra's male friend in *Paura e amore / Love and Fear*), or a dependent little woman who is unable to cope with life, someone they can feel superior to and who will also make a cheap housekeeper, cleaning woman, and cook (Ingrid's husband in *Das zweite Erwachen der Christa Klages / The Second Awakening of Christa Klages*, Franz in *Heller Wahn / Sheer Madness*), Massimo in *Paura e amore / Love and Fear*). It is not only recognized that women are weak, emotional, and impulsive, it is also expected of them. And insofar as they identify with the existing role allocation and try to meet the man's expectations, they sacrifice their own individuality and bury their own desires. In return, they expect that men should act strong and superior and be successful. A particularly cogent example is the way the sensitive Roberto in *Paura e amore* (*Love and Fear*), instead of becoming a musician, is pressured to follow a career in banking, and even Werner in *Das zweite Erwachen der Christa Klages* (*The Second Awakening of Christa Klages*), actually a fairly weak man, likes to act macho with Christa, although she has the stronger character. The other side of the coin is women's dependency and their submission to the needs of the man. Ingrid (*Das zweite Erwachen der Christa Klages / The Second Awakening of Christa Klages*), asked why she got married, responds, »He always knows what he wants. And he wanted me.« Though she has lost her dreams, in the long run she sees marriage as an institution that supplies her material needs, and that is why she has to put up with her husband's accusations that she entertains her friends on his money. And in *Heller Wahn* (*Sheer Madness*), when Ruth complains Franz doesn't spend any time with her, he replies, »I hope you're not trying to hold it against me that I make money.« Maria, in *Schwestern* (*Sisters*), uses a very similar argument when she says, »If I didn't work so much, you wouldn't be able to go to school.« All of them, including Maria, who has adopted the masculine mentality, get their sense of identity from their professional life, while for women their partner comes first. Margarethe von Trotta has Rosa Luxemburg voice this idea when Rosa tells Leo Jogiches, »And for your work you would leave any woman.« In *Das Versprechen* (*The Promise*), the director comes back to the idea when Sophie accuses Konrad that he gave her up because of his career. However, this role has its price, for since the men are expected to repress their fears and weaknesses, there is the risk that in the long run their emotions will atrophy. »And imagine always having to hear that you yourself can't love the way they do. Too little feeling, too little empathy, too little sympathy, as though your whole life revolved only around feelings, as though – damn it – there were nothing more exciting«, says Margarethe von Trotta's Felix in her episode of the film by the same title, whereupon Eva asks him, »What would that be?« And when he finally can no longer keep back his tears, he hides them bashfully, for he is unable to admit that his wife has left him. Of course, there are also men in Margarethe von Trotta's films who reject the idea that they are insensitive and cold. In *L'Africaine* (*The African Woman*) Victor accuses Martha during an argument that she thinks she is the only one who is really able to love. During a fight between Olga and Franz in the final part of *Heller Wahn* (*Sheer Madness*), she shouts, »Your concern for her is only worry about yourself ... Why, she could outshine you.« And he retorts, »You and your snobbishness, always so intellectual and sensitive! Karoline von Günderrode! As if women were the only ones who have souls.« The positive traits of Trotta's male characters emerge to the extent that they manage to go beyond the boundaries of their role. They prove their worth or fail on the basis of their attitude toward women. Positive male figures like Hans in *Das zweite Erwachen der Christa Klages* (*The Second Awakening of Christa Klages*), Maurice and Robert in *Schwestern* (*Sisters*), Kostja Zetkin in *Rosa Luxemburg*, Cecchini in *Paura e amore* (*Love and Fear*), Victor in *L'Africaine* (*The African Woman*), Marco in *Il lungo silenzio* (*The Long Silence*), or Konrad in *Das Versprechen* (*The Promise*) stand out because they succeed in overcoming their macho role. They are given likable traits since they allow themselves to show their weaknesses and inner contradictions, and try to respect and love women as human beings. Of course it becomes clear that men are in the better position every time, for whatever happens they are the winners. On the other hand, when women deviate from their traditional role and show that they are strong and independent, they are punished by being deprived of love, like Olga in *Heller Wahn* (*Sheer Madness*), to whom her lover Alexej sends a farewell message that he is leaving her because she overpowers him, or Velia in *Paura e amore* (*Love and Fear*) and Martha in *L'Africaine* (*The African Woman*), who are under the illusion that an equal relationship with a man is possible, and must then realize that in the long run men do still choose the weak little woman. A couple relationship that is satisfactory for both partners remains a utopia in Trotta's films. The only truly lived, harmonious relationship, an ideal case in a way, is found in *Il lungo silenzio* (*The Long Silence*), a film whose screenplay was written by a man, and in which the conflict with social conditions overshadows everything else.

Moments of harmony do exist in Margarethe von Trotta's films, in the love scenes, whose mise en scène is determined by feminine ideals of love and sexuality. This interpretation is opposed to the abuse of the female body as a sexual object and stresses intimacy, affection, and deep bonding. Margarethe von Trotta stages one of her tenderest love scenes between Rosa Luxemburg and Kostja Zetkin: After a walk through a field of lupines Rosa and Kostja sit facing each other one night in her apartment. He reads her a poem by Mörike. There is a cut to her face, her features slowly relax as she listens and become quite soft and tender. The peaceful mood continues in the next sequence. A close-up focuses on the two embracing in bed, Rosa has loosened her hair and wrapped his head in it, while he strokes her shoulder. As they caress each other, they speak of Rosa's impending trip to a party convention in London. She pushes back her hair so that his face is visible, and begins to cover his cheeks and his neck with kisses, then sinks back on the pillow next to him and snuggles up to him.

Some of the most erotic moments in Trotta's movies occur between women without there being a sexual relationship, for instance, when in *Schwestern* (*Sisters*) Maria lies down next to Anna, who is chilled to the bone, in order to warm her with her naked body, or when Rosa Luxemburg, in prison, sits on her friend Luise Kautsky's lap and both crouch there locked in each other's arms to comfort each other. Only once in all her films up to now does the director show people actually making love – in *Das Versprechen* (*The Promise*), when Sophie and Konrad are reunited in Prague after years of separation. The representation is extremely discreet and avoids even a suggestion of voyeurism. The euphoria of the moment is conveyed by the previous scene in which, to the sound of violin music, the two lovers exuberantly run up the hotel staircase, stopping over and over again to embrace and kiss as the camera circles around them. The next shot shows both in a close embrace on the bed of the hotel room, which lies in intimate semi-darkness. The camera pans in a close-up along the curves of their bodies and finally stops at the head of the bed to observe their faces through the bars of the bedstead. At the moment of orgasm, there is a cut to a film sequence of a solar eruption, the music fades away, while the cam-

Lovers

114. Sophie and Konrad in Prague (*Das Versprechen / The Promise*). (Photo: Bioskop-Film.)
115. Juliane and Wolfgang (*Die bleierne Zeit / Marianne and Juliane*). (Photo: Filmverlag der Autoren.)
116. A father-child relationship: Ruth and Franz (*Heller Wahn / Sheer Madness*).

era pans from the screen to Lorenz, who is giving Konrad's lecture for him in the conference hall since Konrad is late because he is with Sophie.

In all her other films Margarethe von Trotta emphasizes the moments before and after love-making, and leaves the act itself up to the viewers' imagination. In *Schwestern* (*Sisters*) Maria and Maurice seem to soar above the street after sleeping with each other, an effect produced by looking down on the nocturnal street with its car headlights visible through the window behind the bed. The director manages to create a love scene full of tension and passion in *L'Africaine* (*The African Woman*), between Victor and Martha: He asks her whether all those years she did not enter into another relationship. When she says no, he embraces her and tells her he still loves her. She fends him off and asks sarcastically if he is looking for a substitute in case Ana should die, whereupon he slaps her face. For a moment she stands there paralyzed, then blindly begins to hit him. He grabs her and hurls her to the ground, where she lies sobbing while he sits on the sofa and covers his face with his hands. After a while she crawls toward him, embraces him and confesses to him that she, too, still loves him. Hesitantly at first, then more and more passionately, he responds to the embrace. In the next frame the two can be seen relaxed and in high spirits at breakfast. Both here and in *Winterkind* (»Winter Child«), love and violence are not far from each other: When Michael offers Jelena money so she will let him have their son and go back to Russia, she is shocked and hurt, and starts pummeling him. He pins her arms to keep her from hitting him; she stops and both stare at each other. Finally she takes a step back, the rage vanishes from her face. They both rush toward each other almost compulsively, simultaneously pull their sweaters over their heads, begin to embrace passionately and almost hectically, and sink on the sofa, their bodies intertwined. In the next frame Elke enters her son's bedroom, lies down next to the sleeping boy, and strokes his hair. This is followed by a short take of Jelena and Michael, who are now lying relaxed on the sofa. She speaks of a life together, but he answers that he cannot leave Elke.

As here, so in the other films of Margarethe von Trotta the dramaturgical function of the love scenes is to underline the conflict constellation. Frequently these scenes are the last few moments of peace and calm before disaster strikes. In *Schwestern* (*Sisters*) the coming together of Maria and Maurice triggers Anna's suicide. The relaxed atmosphere between Juliane and Wolfgang in *Die bleierne Zeit* (*Marianne and Juliane*) when, vacationing in Italy, they fool around with abandon one morning in bed before getting up is followed in the next scene by the news of Marianne's death. The last peaceful moments of Rosa Luxemburg's life show her romance with Kostja Zetkin, to be followed by the big confrontation with the leading Social Democrats and her struggle against war. The reconciliation between Victor and Martha in *L'Africaine* (*The African Woman*) causes the conflict between her and Ana to intensify. In *Das Versprechen* (*The Promise*), the love scenes between Sophie and Konrad in Prague are the high point of their relationship before their definitive separation. And in *Winterkind* (»Winter Child«) the rekindling of the sexual relationship with Michael motivates Jelena to demand her son from Elke and to destroy Elke's life once and for all.

The other woman as a threat

Even if the relationship to men is an important aspect in analyzing female existence, still Margarethe von Trotta seeks the starting point for a new female identity primarily in women themselves. As always in her films, here, too, the tension is in the opposites. Her central female characters, from whose point of view the story is told, are strong and independent personalities. They have an above-average education, are professionals, often have children, or play the mother's role with their younger brothers and sisters, and know what life is all about. Juxtaposed with the latter are weak, emotional, feminine women who are subject to depressions and emotionally lean on others, like the student Anna (*Schwestern / Sisters*) or housewives like Ingrid (*Das zweite Erwachen der Christa Klages / The Second Awakening of Christa Klages*), Ruth (*Heller Wahn / Sheer Madness*), Maria (*Paura e amore / Love and Fear*), or Ana (*L'Africaine / The African Woman*), but also Marianne (*Die bleierne Zeit / Marianne and Juliane*) before she joins the underground. With the exception of *Rosa Luxemburg*, this pattern appears in all her films up to *L'Africaine* (*The African Woman*), 1990. Occasionally cheerful young women also appear – women like Miriam (*Schwestern / Sisters*) or Sandra (*Paura e amore / Love and Fear*), and, with reservations, Lena (*Das zweite Erwachen der Christa Klages / The Second Awakening of Christa Klages*) and Maria (*Il lungo silenzio / The Long Silence*), who are still full of illusions and dreams and expect everything from life: In their case it is still open in which direction they will develop.

All of them strive for the balance of happiness, an idea Margarethe von Trotta first played through in *Schwestern* (*Sisters*), but which is contained in all her films. She is interested in exploring the relationship of strong and weak, emotional and rational, rebellious and conformist characters who attract each other like all opposites, are mutually dependent and need each other. Driven by curiosity, admiration, longing, but also disapproval, suspicion, and jealousy, they set out to search for the other woman. They investigate her life as Lena does that of Christa Klages, track their rival and find out her habits and interests as Martha does, spy on and observe each other like Anna and Maria, secretly dog her heels as Ruth dogs Olga's, pursue her and badger her as the mother does her daughter in *Dunkle Tage* (»Dark Days«), or force an entry into her ordered existence and call it into question as Christa does Ingrid's lifestyle, or Marianne does the road taken by Juliane, or Jelena in *Winterkind* (»Winter Child«) the apparently harmonious family life of Elke. However, if they come together, they can only attain an ill-fated equilibrium on the basis of mutual dependency, for their attempt at friendship is based on what each expects from the other – hope of rescue, as the filmmaker once put it: Maria expects that Anna should finish her studies and have a career, Anna looks for affection and support, Miriam expects Maria to liberate her from the open-plan office, and Maria offers that Miriam should move in with her to make up for the loss of her sister. Both Juliane and Marianne demand that the other give up her goals and adopt her own; Ruth longs for Olga to free her from the dependent relationship with her husband, while Olga gets her satisfaction from helping the other woman; and Martha secretly longs to overcome her inner hardening, while Ana hopes to be healed.

The relationships between these women are dominated by tensions and conflicts that are potentially destructive. They are interspersed with frames of secret observation and pursuit, for which the classic techniques of the thriller and »film noir« are employed: Nerve-racking music; light and shadow effects; moments of silence when the rustling of a paper or the creaking of a door make one jump; the searching sweep along the walls; or the camera dollying into a dark forest; the ransacking of drawers and closets; the observer's view from concealment; people spying on each other; quick, hectic movements, and jump cuts, but especially the art of omission – an art that Hitchcock, one of Margarethe von Trotta's great models, developed to mastery level – create a disturbing and menacing atmosphere. In *Das zweite Erwachen der Christa Klages* (*The Second Awakening of Christa Klages*) it is not the police who force Christa to go on running all the way to Portugal and finally to the self-created prison in Munich – no, the bank clerk Lena, conventional, conformist, pursues Christa, the rebel against existing conventions, the emancipated woman. Lena rummages in Christa's life, appears at her commune, her child-care center, at her mother's house and that of her friend Ingrid. For a long time it is not clear what her intentions are. In *Winterkind* (»Winter Child«) Jelena's inquiries about her lost son, her initially se-

Confrontations with the other woman

117. Christa Klages and Lena Seidlhofer (*Das zweite Erwachen der Christa Klages / The Second Awakening of Christa Klages*). (Photo: Westdeutscher Rundfunk.)
118. Jelena and Elke (*Winterkind* /»Winter Child«). (Photo: Westdeutscher Rundfunk.)

Persecutions

119. Ruth secretly observes Olga (*Heller Wahn / Sheer Madness*). (Photo: Monika Hasse.)
120. Maria harasses Anna (*Schwestern / Sisters*).

cret intrusion in Elke's, Daniel's, and Michael's lives as they unsuspectingly go about their daily business, her repeated visits at the nursery when she takes note of every detail and her covert questions to the nursery employee and to Daniel also contain a menacing element. In *Paura e amore* (*Love and Fear*), too, there is a subliminal menace behind Velia's apparently casual, hidden glances at other women. When, during a viewing of the country house, she happens to see Maria standing alone by the fountain in the courtyard until Massimo comes and stands next to her; when, at the party in the TV studio, she watches Sabrina flirting with other men without embarrassment; or when, by chance, she observes Sabrina on the street as her lover comes to pick her up, Velia is confronted with the traditional women's role. Strong, capable, and emancipated, Velia thinks she has left this role behind her, but she has actually been flirting with it during her affair with Massimo, even though she realizes this will jeopardize the way she sees herself.

The menace becomes acute and dangerous when the weak woman begins to hound the strong one. This is also always about the confrontation of light and shadow figures, the golden girl and the pitch-covered girl, as they are called in *Heller Wahn* (*Sheer Madness*). Referring to this confrontation, the filmmaker herself spoke of the contradiction between the dark, Romantic German primeval slime and the sunny, lucid element of the South that are both inherent in her, and that come out in her films.[18] One woman lives in the limelight and is physically surrounded by light and clarity, while the other moves in a dim world of shadows that threatens to kill her. Her element is night, all that is dark, unfathomable, hidden, and supernatural, manifested in her belief in miracles, among other things. Thus Ana in *L'Africaine* (*The African Woman*) is not the only one who, because of her illness, is intensely preoccupied with esotericism and miracle cures. Ruth in *Heller Wahn* (*Sheer Madness*) also consults a fortune-teller on two occasions, and even rational, strong Carla in *Il lungo silenzio* (*The Long Silence*) plays a game where, eyes closed, she opens an arbitrary book and looks on the first sentence she happens to read as an omen, a habit Margarethe von Trotta learned about by watching her neighbor in Rome, the writer Luigi Malerba, who also wrote the book she uses in the scene. Cultural historians associate this penchant for magic, for the occult, with the archetypally feminine, the unpredictable aspect of women, which represents a danger for rationalists.

The glances from concealment with which Ruth in *Heller Wahn* (*Sheer Madness*) pursues Olga after their first encounter bode no good, and Dieter advises Olga not to deepen her acquaintance with Ruth while there is still time. But Olga disregards his warning and rushes into a crisis. The effect is far more ominous and almost spooky when in *Schwestern* (*Sisters*) Anna after her death takes possession of her sister's life. The accusation she leaves behind in her journal becomes a curse Maria cannot escape. Anna's fearful visions and nightmares come over Maria and throw her life off balance. The image of the dead sister lying on her desk with her veins slit pursues her even in sleep, but now it is she herself who lies sprawled across the desk in a puddle of blood, while Anna stands in the doorway and smiles. At the inn by the dike, when Maria carries her plate of food through the room, the door creaks open, and suddenly she sees Anna with her face deathly pale sitting at the table eating. Back in the Hamburg apartment she gazes at herself in the entryway mirror and encounters in it a variation of one of Anna's nightmares that the latter told her about earlier: Instead of her face, she sees only what appears to be the back of her head, but then the figure turns around, and her sister is looking at her. In these scenes the persecution is expressed in the form of being haunted by a dead woman, a motif that also plays an important role in *Die bleierne Zeit* (*Marianne and Juliane*), where through her death Marianne takes over her sister's life.

Here the emancipated, rational, capable, strong, motherly woman is spied upon, persecuted and menaced by the emotional dreamer, the depressed and introverted woman. Or, in other words: The dark, hidden side of the personality represented by the shadow figures attempts to dominate the conscioous, rational part. However, this is not just a clash between reason and emotion, strength and weakness, or capability and dependency, but a struggle between the will to live and the longing for death, and this is what is really dangerous about it.

This contradiction concerns Margarethe von Trotta in all her films and is expressed in a conflicting attitude toward death. On the one hand, death is a menace, while on the other hand it also has something fascinating and tempting about it, like the magic kingdom of night that the Romantic poet Novalis in his »Hymnen an die Nacht« (»Hymns to Night«) associates with death, a night drunk with love, divine, in which lies the true essence of human beings. Closely linked with this is the motif of the dissolution of the physical body. In Trotta's films, too, this is a harbinger of death: The blurry figure of Anna behind the glass walls of her terrarium in *Schwestern* (*Sisters*) and the unfocused contours of her face in a series of Polaroid pictures she takes shortly before her death, the last frame of the living Marianne in *Die bleierne Zeit* (*Marianne and Juliane*) showing the blurring features of her face behind the glass partition in the visitors' room at the high-security prison, but also the reflection in a store window of Felicitas's face in *Dunkle Tage* (»Dark Days«), before she herself begins to drink, all refer to this semantic context. Very obviously, in *Il lungo silenzio* (*The Long Silence*), the dissolution of the outward appearance is associated with death when Carla's face blurs behind the windshield of her car, which is streaming with rain, as she tries to escape her murderer.

The mise en scène and rhythm of this death scene convey the ambivalence of death: After fleeing wildly from the apartment to the office and from there to the street, where she tries in vain to start her car, Carla runs into a telephone booth and picks up the receiver. The murderer, recognizable only as a shadow in the dark and rain, approaches the booth from the side and blocks the audience's view of it. He shoots, the receiver dangles down, then Carla is seen slowly sliding down the wall of the phone booth. In contrast to the hectic rush of the preceding moments, this last, relatively long take of her face conveys a feeling of peace, and makes her death appear like a melting away. There is mortal terror in this dying, but there is also a liberating aspect – the reunion with her husband in death. This aspect frequently appears in Margarethe von Trotta's films, for instance, in the death scene in *Rosa Luxemburg*. Here, the emphasis on Rosa Luxemburg's physical and mental exhaustion, which makes her appear almost apathetic, and the concluding image of still water shows death as a liberation from the burden of the body, a note that is also struck at Marianne's death in *Die bleierne Zeit* (*Marianne and Juliane*). The mother's violent death in *Dunkle Tage* (»Dark Days«) also primarily implies a liberation from the curse that has weighed heavily on the family since the father's death as shown by the following peaceful scene where Felicitas lights candles and places them around her mother's dead body.

The representation of the death scenes never actually conveys the terror of death. Even Werner's death by shooting in the open street in *Das zweite Erwachen der Christa Klages* (*The Second Awakening of Christa Klages*) seems almost innocuous, like stumbling into death – according to the director, the portrayal was influenced by Jean Paul Belmondo's dying in *A bout de souffle*. Regardless of whether they seek death, like Anna in *Schwestern* (*Sisters*), Werner in *Die bleierne Zeit* (*Marianne and Juliane*), or Harald in *Das Versprechen* (*The Promise*) – his death, too, is basically a kind of suicide – or whether they are murdered, to those who die death presents itself more like a good friend who frees them from life's trials and tribulations and promises calm and peace. It is true that death is truly menacing for strong personalities like Christa Klages, Maria, Juliane, Olga, Rosa Luxemburg, or Carla, for because they know death firsthand, they are all caught up in the maelstrom of the longing for death, and are in danger of coming under its spell. However, this is only possible because in each strong woman, each figure of light, there exists a shadow side.

If we take seriously Margarethe von Trotta's statement that her women characters, when all is said and done, could be a single person, then light and shadow figures embody a dialectical whole and become a symbol for the will to live and the longing for death, for the physical and the spiritual, for rationality and emotion, which are part of the total personality, of the »universal« human being sought by the German Romantics. Behind this search, in the final analysis, there is always the search for oneself by penetrating into the dark, hidden aspects of one's own self, whose driving force is the longing for a harmonious fusion of these two elements.

The doppelgänger motif – mirrors and mirror images

The confrontation of two opposing figures to point out the hidden potential of an individual is related to one of the most important recurring motifs in Margarethe von Trotta's work – that of the doppelgänger. She is fascinated by the encounter with oneself as the alter ego, and this is what links her with her predecessors in literature and film: with Dostoyevsky, German Romanticism, and, in it, particularly with E. T. A. Hoffmann, whose work is permeated with doppelgänger motifs – looking at one's own reflection, exchanging roles, transformation, and disguises. Ingmar Bergman, too, makes references to E. T. A. Hoffmann's work both thematically and structurally, for example, when he gives the characters in *The Hour of the Wolf* names from Hoffmann. The doppelgänger motif also links Margarethe von Trotta with Hitchcock, in whose films the same predilection for mirror reflections and doubling is expressed, for instance, in *Vertigo*. In addition, this motif also occurs in the tradition of expressionist German cinema, of which Lotte Eisner says: »We find these eerie doubles in many German films: Caligari is at once a barker at a fair and the director of a mental asylum; Nosferatu, the vampire, is the lord of a castle and negotiates the purchase of a townhouse with an equally diabolical real-estate agent. Even weary death is a traveler who seeks to buy property near the cemetery.«[19]

This spiritual affinity is expressed in a repertoire of visual motifs that have been associated since Romanticism with loss of identity and inner conflict: the doubling and multiplication of the human reflection in mirrors, glass walls, or in water; assuming another identity through disguises and masks; and mirroring one's own existence in that of another.

In Trotta's films the mirror motif appears in a number of different variations and meanings. Associated with the many scenes where people put on makeup or get dressed, the gaze into the mirror is an expression of narcissism and vanity, as in the episodes in *Paura e amore* (*Love and Fear*) when Massimo checks his appearance in front of the entryway mirror as he calls on the sisters on Sandra's 18th birthday, or when Sabrina makes up her face in front of the dressing table in her bedroom for a meeting with her lover and, satisfied with the result, throws her mirror image a kiss.

In *Winterkind* (»Winter Child«), however, changing one's clothes also implies a love for disguise that has more to do with self-love than with self-infatuation. In one characteristic scene Ana and Jelena are trying on clothes in a boutique: Ana strikes the pose of a model before her mother and Jelena, then inspects herself from all sides in the mirror, and exclaims, »Wonderful!« Then Jelena approaches the mirror and critically scrutinizes her boring knit dress, whereupon Ana gets a suit from the display in the window and holds it up in front of her. Jelena disappears in the dressing room to put it on, and returns a little while later smiling timidly to admire herself in the mirror as the two other women make appreciative comments. Finally Ana approaches her with a lipstick and touches up her lips. In the scene that follows Jelena sits in the social worker's office at the youth welfare department in the same dress and a new coat wearing discreet makeup. Her new outfit covers up the scars left by imprisonment and poverty. The resulting outward adaptation gives her an unaccustomed air of self-confidence.

Here, changing and putting on clothes and applying makeup have to do with practicing a social role. Similarly, in one of the flashbacks from *Die bleierne Zeit* (*Marianne and Juliane*), Marianne tries on her ball dress for the graduation ball and looks at herself in the mirror from all sides, while rebellious Juliane, whom their father has forbidden to go because she refuses to wear a dress, watches with disapproval. Like the dress code at the bank mentioned in *Das zweite Erwachen der Christa Klages* (*The Second Awakening of Christa Klages*), one's outfit is part of one's self-portrayal. Typically, in *Schwestern* (*Sisters*), Miriam and Maria also meet in the bathroom on the executive floor, where they check their appearance in the mirror and touch up their lips. The scene is a direct allusion to one of the flashbacks to the childhood of the two sisters Maria and Anna, where the little girls paint their lips with screaming red lipstick, then, with puckered mouths, print a kiss on each other's cheeks, and look at themselves in a three-part mirror that multiplies their faces. Making up one's face becomes an act of putting on a mask through which one creates an external image of oneself. Behind it is the pressure to adjust to societal norms in order to be attractive, leading to the suppression of one's individuality and the cloning of the personality. »Can you imagine what it would be like if there were several of you? ... Exactly like you: your eyes, your hair, your hands. Or your characteristics: intelligence, energy ...«, Anna asks her sister and conjures up the specter of a human being as part of a conformist, amorphous mass of people, something she experiences as a real threat based on new developments in genetic engineering she has been dealing with in her studies.

Thus transformation of one's outward appearance frequently goes hand in hand with the deformation of one's personality. The perception of the world via the impenetrable, smooth, and cold surface of a mirror has a distancing effect and always has something alien about it: inner distancing among people and the alienation of individuals from themselves. In *Das zweite Erwachen der Christa Klages* (*The Second Awakening of Christa Klages*) gazing into the mirror accompanies the protagonist's growing loss of identity because of conditions during her flight. After she has dyed her hair blond and changed the style of her clothes at the parsonage with Hans's help, she looks at herself with irritation in the mirror, from which a strange face looks back at her. The next morning she again stands in front of the mirror in the room at the inn where she and Werner spent the night, inspecting herself critically. Werner comes and stands beside her, and scornfully looks at the conservative bourgeois clothes with which he is trying to disguise himself. His eyes meet Christa's in the mirror, and he tells her he preferred her hair dark. She reacts with exaggerated violence by throwing a glass of water in his face, and by this reaction she also shatters the image before them: two strangers in the mirror.

When, as in this scene, people perceive the world in the smooth, impenetrable surface of a mirror, they distance themselves from each other. Again and again arguments take place in front of a mirror – for instance, a segment of the first conversation between Victor and Martha in *L'Africaine* (*The African Woman*), for which the director had a mirror specially hung over the living-room fireplace. After a tour of the apartment, Martha goes and stands in front of the mirror, Victor approaches from the other side, and the figures of both are doubled while he informs her that Ana thinks she is ill because Martha put a spell on her, and that she considers Martha's coming to be a good omen and believes Martha is willing to forgive her and to turn the evil magic away from her. Martha is full of consternation and turns completely toward the mirror to study her face. She feels pressured and believes that Victor expects too much when he asks her to think of Ana first, and she refuses all further overtures of friendship by leaving the apartment. Here the mirror conveys the distance between the protagonists and underscores their tensions. Martha's suppressed resentment and her resistance, and Victor's guilt feelings and insecurity become obvious when she is in conversation with him as she keeps looking at his reflection, but finally turns away completely while he approaches her directly.

The mirror motif in *Winterkind* (»Winter Child«) also appears to be an expression of critical distance. Jelena is brushing her teeth in front of the bathroom mirror and tells Ana, who is sitting on the toilet close by with a white beauty mask on her face, that Michael looks even better now than he did before. Ana tells Jelena not to get any silly ideas, for after all the guy walked out on her; she asks her about Michael's wife, whereupon Jelena looks at herself attentively in the mirror and answers, »Boring.« Ana comes and stands next to her. The women's faces are visible next to each other in the mirror as Ana asks whether he has told his wife that he intends to come back to Jelena, and Jelena answers, confident of victory: »He will. Boris belongs to us, to Michael and me.«

While in these scenes the mirror is thrust like a barrier between people, on other occasions it acts as a partition between individuals and their surroundings. A variation of the motif, the reflection of Martha's face in the windowpane of a public bus, becomes a metaphor of alienation and isolation. A similar meaning is conveyed by a shot from *Winterkind* (»Winter Child«), where soon after her arrival, in Ana's apartment, Jelena absently looks out the window that reflects her blurred features. Along the same lines there is a scene in which Jelena, traveling to discover the whereabouts of her son, is waiting for Ana in a café. While there she longingly observes a mother with a small child sitting opposite her under a large mirror. Soon Ana briefly appears in the mirror as she enters the café. The scene expresses not only alienation, but also longing and hope, which are associated with Ana's image in the mirror.

In addition, however, the mirror also mercilessly makes the observers aware of reality, it forces them to take note of disagreeable or painful truths, and may have a disillusioning effect. In *L'Africaine* (*The African Woman*) Martha discovers the affair between Ana and Victor in the form of a mirror image: She unexpectedly comes home from work because she doesn't feel well, and pauses for an instant in front of the entryway mirror. When she looks up, she sees Ana and Victor dancing with their arms tightly about each other, and stares at the scene before her in stunned silence. The mirror shows her as she slowly approaches the living-room door and stops in front of it. The focus changes and shows her face reflected in yet another mirror next to the living-room door, then the camera pans to the couple in front of Martha's favorite painting in the background and brings them closer with a zoom. The motif of the wardrobe mirror is taken up again later, when Martha, after betraying Ana, wants to leave town in a hurry and leaves a note on the mirror. After the reconciliation of the two friends, in front of the same mirror, Victor finds one of Ana's dolls with a note in which they inform him that they've gone to Africa together.

In a similar context of meaning, there is the image of the broken mirror as a symbol of inner conflict and frustration. Sophie and Konrad's happiness in *Das Versprechen* (*The Promise*) literally breaks like glass: The reverberation of the tanks as they enter Prague shatters the hotel-room mirror in which their startled faces are reflected immediately afterward. After Leo in *Rosa Luxemburg* explains to Rosa that her wish for children and a normal family life is incompatible with her political work, she is so disappointed she smashes a mirror in which her face is doubled.

As here, so in *Schwestern* (*Sisters*) the mirror motif is linked to a distorted perception of oneself that goes hand in hand with a loss of self-image. This motif is reproduced by Anna's nightmare – mentioned above – in which, instead of her face, she sees only the back of her head in the mirror. It symbolizes her loss of identity and her inner conflict. The same dream later haunts Maria when after her sister's death she comes home to the empty apartment, but now, instead of the back of her head, the image of Anna appears and covers up her own. This variant makes it clear to what extent the sister, by her suicide, has taken possession of Maria's life and has

Women confront themselves

121. Martha in *L'Africaine* (*The African Woman*).
122. Maria in *Schwestern* (*Sisters*).

Women confront their future self

123, 124. Anna and the blind old woman (*Schwestern / Sisters*).
125. Ruth and her mother (Agnes Fink) in *Heller Wahn / Sheer Madness*). (Photo: Filmverlag der Autoren.)

made Maria doubt her self-image. In later scenes Maria repeats the look into the entryway mirror whenever she comes home, as though to reassure herself that the terrible vision will not reappear, for example, on the day when Miriam has found Anna's journal and the sister's legacy once again closes in on Maria and disturbs her inner equilibrium. The mirror here becomes a symbol of a split in perception, a menace that undermines Maria's idea that »only what people do in their profession and on the job shows what they are capable of and what they are worth«, as she argues in her conversation with Fritz. This conviction is vital to her, for she goes on: »If I didn't believe that, I would no longer be able to get up in the morning.«

A variation of the mirror motif as a distortion of the ego is the mirroring of one's own situation in the existence of another person. In *Das zweite Erwachen der Christa Klages* (*The Second Awakening of Christa Klages*), Christa's encounter with the warped existence of the old man in the garden colony, who obsessively copies picture postcards of his former home town of Riga in needlepoint, anticipates what lies in store for her later: the loss of her native country, loneliness, isolation, and depressions that drive her to the brink of suicide. In *Schwestern* (*Sisters*) Maria has a double in the typist pool supervisor, a narrow-minded, complacent, middle-aged woman who believes in authority, kicks those who are below her, and kowtows to those who are above her, a Cerberus who is proud of having risen to the position of supervisor of fifty women, as she is characterized in the screenplay. Meanwhile, through the two old sisters with whom Anna takes a job listed at the students' employment office, she confronts her relationship with her own sister: Theirs is an existence that is uneventful and bereft of content – two embittered old women in a love-hate relationship, one dominant and strong, the other tied to the house by her blindness, and full of fear.

In *Heller Wahn* (*Sheer Madness*) it becomes clear to Ruth where she herself might eventually wind up when she sees Olga's former schoolmate Renate, who is a patient in a mental hospital. Renate has tried to commit suicide and labors under the illusion that she must go to a high mountain and proclaim the Biblical prophecy of the flood, to which nobody listens. Like Ruth, she paints black and white pictures of this mountain, and at their first meeting the two immediately find a level of communication to which Olga has no access. Ruth's visions, her later suicide attempt, and her treatment at a mental hospital have their parallel in Renate's fate. Ruth has an additional double in her mother, a paranoid, psychologically unstable woman who like her was married to a man who undermined her self-confidence and instilled guilt feelings in her, though she nevertheless defends him against others so as not to have to admit to herself that her dreams have come to nothing.

The negative mirroring of her characters in their mothers' existence is a constant element in Margarethe von Trotta's early films. These mothers are women of the war generation whose life revolved around the household and the children and who, because of a strong need for harmony, constantly try to cover up and repress their own conflicts and those of their family. However, now that the children are grown-up, they begin to question the direction their lives have taken. »She had such an irrepressible imagination«, says the mother in *Schwestern* (*Sisters*) about Anna, »but she probably tended to be depressed, just like me. Only, if you're married and have kids, you don't have time to notice you're depressed.« Disillusionment, but also resignation, determines these women's attitude. They have learned to make the best of circumstances and are trying to come to terms with them. And yet a subliminal rebellion keeps surfacing. »Sure, often wonder why I of all people have children who're so ... so different«, says Christa Klages's mother to Lena, adding, »I often rebel, too, you know, or life would be impossible.« And the mother of the sisters in *Die bleierne Zeit* (*Marianne and Juliane*), speaking about her husband, says: »You know what I've been calling him to myself lately? The egoist ... I don't say Dad, or our Dad, just the egoist.« In their confrontation with their mother, the women protagonists recognize how they do not want to live, and yet they see themselves being forced into the same role without wanting to. An example is *Paura e amore* (*Love and Fear*), where Maria becomes her mother's double, and the doppelgänger function of mother and daughter is most obvious.

The central question concealed in all the scenes where the mirror or doppelgänger motif is used is, Who am I? In *L'Africaine* (*The African Woman*) Ana engages in an active search for herself when she puts candles in front of a mirror, then places one of them in a bowl of water, kneels before it and looks into the water. This scene combines three elements that are all linked with the search for a deeper inner truth: the mirror as the traditional symbol of knowledge and self-knowledge, truth, and clarity; the candle as a symbol of light, the individual psyche, and the relation between animus and anima; and water as a purifying and renewing element, which in the Chinese yin and in psychoanalysis is also related to the feminine and the forces of the subconscious. A parallel to this ritual of healing is the Celtic holy well, and there is thus an association with the symbol of the well, which is connected in cultural history with concepts of purification, youth, and health, but also stands for the depth of the secret, and access to hidden sources of knowledge. The optic relationship between the mirror and the reflecting surface of the well water is taken up once more in *Paura e amore* (*Love and Fear*): Maria stands at the edge of the fountain in front of Massimo's country house and looks into the water, which returns her image, when suddenly Massimo comes and stands next to her like a menacing shadow, and his face is reflected next to hers. The contact through the mirror continues during the drive home, when Maria and Massimo exchange secret glances in the rearview mirror. Like Ana, Maria is in search of knowledge. »There's got to be something for me, too«, she says to her sister Velia, and she believes that in Massimo she has found her masculine counterpart and a kindred soul to whom she reveals her inmost heart as she never has to any other person, reading aloud excerpts from her journal to him and thus giving him a glimpse of her most intimate thoughts.

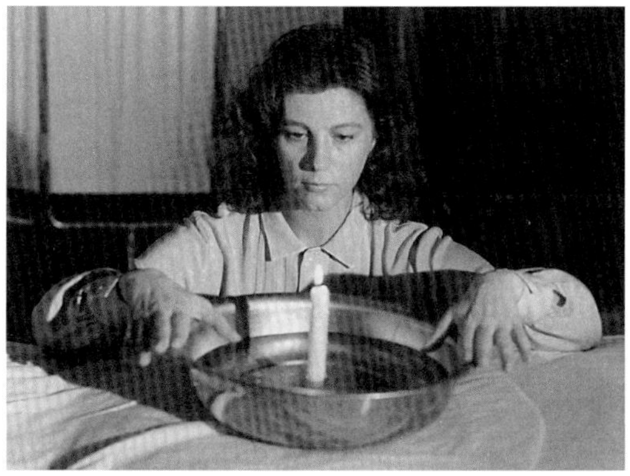

Used in this sense, a mirror reflection implies recognizing oneself in a more or less alienated likeness of one's own person. The doubling of one's own image creates distance and makes it possible to see oneself through the eyes of a stranger and to evaluate one's own existence in a new way. But the mirror motif also stands as a metaphor for the examination of the motives of the woman antagonist. In *Die bleierne Zei*t (*Marianne and Juliane*), after the argument with Marianne in prison, Juliane receives a conciliatory letter from her sister. She opens it while still in the entryway and reads it in front of a mirror recessed in the wall, thus creating the impression as though she were talking to herself. A similar motif is found in *Winterkind* (»Winter Child«): After she has brought her son to her place, Jelena stands deep in thought in front of the bathroom mirror gazing at her face while she talks about how Daniel will later accuse her of depriving him of his father and mother. Here the mirror motif is employed to put oneself in the situation of the other woman. Finally Jelena realizes that she is acting as egotistically as Michael once did, and is thus destroying the lives of three people.

This scene contains another important meaning of the mirror motif, that of switching roles, as preoccupation with the other woman at first leads to identification with her and in the end results in adopting her role completely. In *Die bleierne Zeit* (*Marianne and Juliane*) the reflection of the two sisters' faces in the glass partition of the prison's visitors' room begins the process of switching roles that is completed after Marianne's death. The frame where the sisters' features dissolve by overlapping and merge has frequently been compared with a motif from Bergman's *Persona*, but also has a parallel in Hitchcock's *The Wrong Man*, where he dissolves the features of a man who has been imprisoned although he is innocent into those of the actual murderer, then fuses them into a single face.

Switching roles

When two persons switch roles, the doppelgänger motif progresses to the point where one person completely identifies with the other. Behind it is Margarethe von Trotta's »wish that life would always hand you both sides of an issue, so that you can understand the other side as well«,[20] as she put it in a 1996 interview.

In *Das zweite Erwachen der Christa Klages* (*The Second Awakening of Christa Klages*) the strong, emancipated woman gives the weak, conformist one the courage to change, but at the same time they switch roles. With Werner's death Christa becomes the weak one, while her woman friend now displays unaccustomed resolution and takes the initiative. She hides Christa, whom her despair has made completely apathetic, and helps her escape. In the course of these events Christa's appearance is transformed as well, into the likeness of Ingrid: Christa modifies it to look like the photo in Ingrid's passport, which she will use to escape to Portugal. When Ingrid gets her ready, she is wearing the blouse Ingrid had on in the previous scene, and has the same hairstyle and makeup as her friend. These events are paralleled by a change in Ingrid that becomes noticeable in her appearance as well. When she visits Christa in Portugal behind her husband's back, Ingrid has exchanged her conservatively elegant clothing for jeans and wide-legged slacks in keeping with the type of clothes worn by Christa. Back in Germany, she finally completely adopts the role of her friend by leaving her marriage and moving to Christa's commune, while Christa for her part sits alone in the apartment of a housing development.

In *Schwestern* (*Sisters*), too, Anna's suicide turns Maria from the strong one into the weak one. As her younger sister did previously, she sees her only way out in a retreat to the solitude of

126, 127. In search of healing: Ana in *L'Africaine* (*The African Woman*).
128, 129. Image analogies: Maria with Anna, Maria with Miriam in *Schwestern* (*Sisters*).
130. Role reversal: Marianne and Juliane (*Die bleierne Zeit / Marianne and Juliane*).

the inn by the dike. There, her sister's shadow world overwhelms her. When she wanders ghostlike through the house at night, crouches in desperation on the floor next to her bed, or takes lonely walks by the river, Anna's character is reflected in her behavior. Only when Miriam meets up with her, a reflection of her actual persona – the successful executive secretary – shows through in her manner when, like a strict teacher, she dictates the texts of her friend Fritz for Miriam to type, and when Miriam moves in with her, Maria is completely back to her old self. A series of analogous frames and parallels clearly show how she tries to force her friend into Anna's role: When she comes home from work at night she goes over to where Miriam sits at the desk just as she once approached her sister in order to ask her if she has had supper or wants to go to the movies. She pressures both Anna and Miriam the same way to study for their exams. When Miriam refuses to take the position Maria got for her immediately after she graduates, she gets to hear the same accusations as Anna did when she expressed doubts about whether her studies made sense: She is told she must finally start making money since Maria does not intend to go on taking care of her. But the parallels also make it clear that Miriam is cast in a different mold than Anna. Both rebel by listening to music and dancing in Maria's absence instead of cramming for exams, but while Anna swayed to the music of Purcell, Miriam listens to Billie Holiday and dreams of stardom. Miriam fights against the role of Anna and again confronts Maria with her sister's accusations. Maria is left alone and realizes that she can recover her inner balance only by fusing Anna's wishes and dreams with her own rather rational ideas about life. The change in her appearance reflects the way her ideas move closer to those of her dead sister. Suddenly she is wearing her hair loose even at the office, and is dressed in a dark, flowered blouse in Anna's style, and when in the final scene, dressed in a flowing black dress with white dots, she goes to her sister's desk through the twilit apartment in order to continue writing in Anna's journal, she seems to be a reincarnation of her sister.

In contrast to *Das zweite Erwachen der Christa Klages* (*The Second Awakening of Christa Klages*), where switching roles causes Ingrid to break out of social conventions and promises a positive perspective, in *Schwestern* (*Sisters*) we have an inner, and therefore far more complex, process of discovery, whose outcome is uncertain. The switching of roles here serves to point out the inner contradictions, but also the personal limits placed on the development of a new female identity. In *Heller Wahn* (*Sheer Madness*) Margarethe von Trotta continues these reflections. She shows how the weak, depressed woman absorbs the other's strength, so that the other becomes the weak one at the end. Variations on a series of visual motifs and shots from the beginning scene, which shows Olga and Dieter's visit in the Provençal country house, recur during Ruth and Olga's visit at the end of the film: The car driving up through the vineyard and through the gate; being welcomed by Erika; supper on the terrace together, when the change in Ruth becomes apparent; and finally the argument between Franz and Olga, to which Ruth reacts exactly as she did to Olga's debate with Franz the first night, draw comparisons with the initial situation of the story and make it obvious that there hasn't been all that much change. In this scene, however, Ruth also manages – precisely because of her weakness, as she did before with her suicide attempt – to rise above her husband and to force him to give in, while on the other hand the episode sets off Olga's crisis. After returning to her apartment in Germany, Olga sees herself surrounded by the same silence as Ruth normally is at her home, and she moves through the rooms like a sleepwalker. The possibility that the differences between the two women could be canceled out seems very remote here. The only thing that becomes clear is that each has a different character, and that this is not going to change. Olga is frightened by the repercussions of her friendship with Ruth, but this will not shatter her, while Ruth's future development is indicated in a conversation with her therapist. »The people that are standing around me. They want something from me«, she says, and goes on, »I'm supposed to give a talk, but they already know everything I'm going to say. They've already got the manuscript of my talk ...« The therapist asks, »What's your talk about?« Ruth answers, »I'm not going to give it.« This dialogue raises questions: There is the pressure of other people's expectations to which Ruth feels exposed, and her refusal to live up to them. Will she find herself? And will she manage to push through her own ideas of life without once more becoming dependent on a stronger person? The film leaves the answers open, but this much is clear: Ruth's taking on the characteristics that the capable Olga possesses is no solution, and a synthesis of the characteristics of both women seems out of the question.

Rosa Luxemburg emphasizes the desperate attempts of the title character to reconcile the inner contradictions between reason and emotion, intrepidity and fears, the ability to carry out plans and weakness, faith in her political goals and self-doubt. She wants it all, and that is her downfall. Both this film, where the motif of switching roles is only hinted at – for example, when Rosa, after being released from prison, is lying in bed and Leo lovingly covers her, as she covered Leo in an earlier scene when he returned from Russia – and *Paura e amore* (*Love and Fear*) express the realization that it is impossible to reconcile opposing characteristics, for social pressures are too great, and personal limitations too insurmountable. The strong, emancipated Velia throws her ideas of women's solidarity to the winds and betrays Erika's interests by her affair with Massimo, but is then deceived herself when Massimo leaves her for Maria, who in turn finds him a disappointment. A key scene is the argument between Velia and Maria in which the former unexpectedly finds herself placed in Erika's role, whereupon she starts up a friendship with her. One series of analogies are mainly related to locales: Maria goes for a solitary walk along the river bank where Velia and Massimo make love in another scene. The two meet in the university library, the same place where Velia finally waits for him in vain. Their relationship begins at a café where Velia later sits having a lonely meal when she is invited by a nun to visit the convent. At the same café she celebrates her promotion alone when Massimo finds her and there is a reconciliation scene. The return to the same locales emphasizes the rigidity of external circumstances that is paralleled in the persons. Velia, Maria, and Erika go through a comparable situation, but none of them experiences growth in the process. The older sister, who temporarily toys with similar ideas of happiness as Maria, returns to her earlier ways and practices solidarity with Erika. Erika's change is initiated not so much by the fact that she has been betrayed – it is unclear whether she even knows about Massimo's infidelity – but by her friendship with Velia. Unburdened by a guilty conscience toward Erika or Velia, about whose relationship with Massimo she never finds out, Maria briefly comes to life again because of her love for Massimo, then relapses into her former depression. In the end nothing has changed for any of the women involved, except that Maria and Velia have become richer by one more disappointing experience and their original views have been reinforced, while Erika, after a short flare-up of a new self-confidence, falls back into her old emotional dependency on Massimo.

In *Die bleierne Zeit* (*Marianne and Juliane*) the motif of switching roles is used not in the sense of searching for an identity, but to discover what is the correct or the wrong conduct in the face of social injustice. The focus here is on shifting the conflict from one sister to the other. There is a twofold exchange of roles between the sisters. Marianne, who as a child was the good girl, the one who gave in and always wanted to please everybody, becomes a rebel when she grows up, while Juliane, who used to be recalcitrant, learns to conform. She, the older of the two, who was

131, 132. Anna and Maria in the final scene (*Schwestern / Sisters*).
133, 134. Marianne's and Juliane's last meeting (*Die bleierne Zeit / Marianne and Juliane*).

always Ismene, chooses the role of Antigone as an adult, but feels pressured by her younger sister to resume the role of Ismene again. She refuses as long as her sister is alive. The shock of Marianne's death brings about a new exchange of roles and cancels out the extremes the two sisters have embodied since childhood. Juliane feels she is a substitute for her sister, she takes on, though in a different form, Marianne's fight against the state and becomes more radical than she. This double switching of roles is represented in a series of frames and scenes, of which the above-mentioned fusing of the sisters' features as they are reflected in the glass of the partition most clearly indicates that one sister increasingly identifies with the other. In an earlier scene, Juliane with the help of her friend Sabine tries to reconstruct, by swallowing a tube, the force-feeding her sister underwent because of her hunger strike. This event foreshadows her later behavior, when her life is spent investigating her sister's death, and she performs all kinds of experiments in order to reconstruct what happened. The motif of switching clothes also occurs several times: In the prison's visitors' room, the two sisters have the apparently spontaneous idea of exchanging sweaters. Juliane at first interprets this as a childhood reminiscence until she realizes that her sister only gave her the pullover because there is a note hidden in it, and once more feels pressured into a role she does not want to take on. Yet this event has an additional significance: The sisters switch colors, for that day Juliane is wearing a white sweater while Marianne wears black, a color that used to be explicitly assigned to the young Juliane, the rebel who sports black jeans, reads Sartre, and defies bourgeois conventions to the indignation of her parents and teachers, while Marianne as an adolescent prefers good-girl dresses in light colors. Thus when the sisters switch sweaters Juliane gets back the color of her youth, which she at first rejects because of the circumstances. After her sister's death, however, she consistently wears only black, which, besides being a sign of mourning, here becomes an expression of rebellion.

The crucial scene when Juliane assumes her sister's identity is her breakdown after she has seen Marianne's body for a last time in the cemetery chapel: Juliane lies weeping on a gurney in an ambulance. Sabine and Wolfgang are with her, trying to comfort her. Sobbing, she gasps: »I'm absolutely certain I ..., she wanted ..., she wants .... I'm supposed to go on. I have to go on for her ... Remember the waists we wore?... Father said: ›Not her. She's not going to kill herself‹, ... maybe me. But not her.« While she speaks, music starts to play, and finally replaces the original soundtrack. Juliane falls asleep, is rolled into a hospital room on the gurney and lifted onto a bed. Finally the camera stops on her sleeping face. She has a dream: The two little girls are buttoning each other's waists. Wearing only their waists, they are fearfully looking at the painting of the crucifixion in their parents' home. It is replaced by the image of the father preaching in the pulpit. Juliane looks up at him and sees him bathed in red light staring down at her with an angry gesture. The buttoning of the waists thus becomes a symbol for the sisters' unswerving alliance. Complete identification with the other is here given a significance that was already inherent in the final scene of the film *Schwestern* (*Sisters*): the reincarnation of the dead woman in the living one.

Something similar happens at the funeral service in *Il lungo silenzio* (*The Long Silence*). Carla is standing between her mother and her friend Rosa accepting the condolences of the mourners. She pointedly refuses to shake hands with some of the men. After this she leaves the group and walks to her husband's coffin. The next frame shows a close-up of her face, the camera slowly pans around her figure as the zoom lens is very gradually raised and the camera shifts its position upward until it is centered above the action in a long shot that shows Carla's figure, which covers up her husband's coffin. The entire scene gets by without any dialogue, but is underscored with music, which changes from a sostenuto funeral melody to a variation on the leitmotif of Carla and Marco. Like Juliane, Carla, too, suddenly faces a decision now that her husband is dead. Of the conflict between her fear for his life and her loyalty toward him only the loyalty remains, and the wish that he did not die in vain. This is why she continues his struggle, even at the risk of suffering the same fate as he, while her mother is consumed with worry for her as Carla herself was once tortured with fear for Marco. Here, too, there is an exchange of roles, as Carla takes her husband's place while her mother takes Carla's previous position. This is underscored by a series of visual analogies and parallels in the plot: When Carla visits the courthouse after Marco's death she is seen in the same take as her husband was previously. She, too, walks down the long, glassed-in corridor, but with one difference – he was surrounded by his escort, while she is alone. Just as he once did, Carla now gets anonymous phone calls. On one occasion, her mother picks up the receiver, and now her face is also filled with fear and worry as Carla's was before. Another time Carla answers her mother's question as to who called by saying, as Marco did in an earlier scene, that somebody dialed the wrong number. In the scene

135. Friendship between women: Rosa Luxemburg (Barbara Sukowa) and Luise Kautsky (Adelheid Arndt).

shortly before Carla's death the mother is shown in the same take in the same armchair in which Carla used to sit waiting for her husband, and just as Carla found the grave candle that announced Marco's death, her mother has now found the second grave candle.

The motif of exchanging roles serves to examine different points of view. It is part of a process of knowing that results in a deeper understanding for the radically different other person, and, if possible, even reconciliation with that person. One slips into another's skin in order to be able to experience a conflict from the other's perspective. This does not mean giving up one's own personality. It means uncovering a hidden dimension that promises further possibilities of human growth. In this way it becomes clear that the differences between Christa Klages and a woman like Ingrid are not irreconcilable, that Juliane could just as well have taken the path of her sister Marianne, or in the case of Rosa Luxemburg a bourgeois existence with a husband and children might have been a conceivable lifestyle, a possibility that is suggested when Rosa, having returned to Berlin in 1906, greets her friend Luise Kautsky and the figures of the two women are doubled in the hallway mirror, a frame that establishes a connection with Rosa's broken mirror and emphasizes the contrast between Luise, the housewife with her apron, and Rosa, the revolutionary, as both are doubled. In *Il lungo silenzio* (*The Long Silence*) Rosa tells her friend Carla her love problems, and Carla responds: »You know, Rosa, sometimes I wish I could have an experience like that. A totally normal tragedy.« Whereupon Rosa says: »I often wonder: Would I want to switch places with Carla?«

In all these female characters, the most contrasting personality traits and possible ways of existing live side by side. This phenomenon reminds us of the filmmaker's affinity with Hitchcock, who believed that inside all people the exact opposite of what they appear to be is always concealed. The question as to what one's actual identity is can be settled only by mirroring one's self in the other person and discovering the antithesis of what one has decided to be. A new whole is created from the dialectical confrontation, a synthesis of convention and progress, conformity and rebellion, masculine and feminine world views, emotion and reason, strength and weakness, fighting spirit and fear, egotism and love that promises a rounding-out of the human personality, though often enough this is wishful thinking.

In *L'Africaine* (*The African Woman*) Margarethe von Trotta makes the switching of roles that was implicitly present in all her preceding films her central issue.The point of departure of the film is the wish to resolve a long-term conflict that has been weighing upon all three protagonists. There are conversations, a request for forgiveness, and magnanimous gestures, but these are not sufficient to bring about a reconciliation. Ana makes a futile attempt in this direction by inviting Martha and Victor to dance with each other, as though she wanted to cede a piece of him to her. But by doing so she merely opens an old wound, for the parallel reminds Martha once more of the day when she discovered the affair between Ana and Victor. By having Ana take her place during the dance, she indicates that as before she is willing to make way for Ana. But the hurt is still there and can be healed only by the exchange of roles between the two women. This happens when Victor and Martha become reconciled. Some elements of the scene refer to Ana: for example, when Victor hurls Martha to the ground after she attacks him, she falls on a spot that is lit by a blue streak of light, the color of Ana's nightmare in the opening credits. The same blue light illuminates the sofa on which Martha and Victor embrace shortly thereafter. Ana therefore makes a connection between her discovery that the two have become reconciled and her dream, and screams across the back yard telling Martha to get out of her bed. Once again bathed in blue light, Martha thereupon sits weeping in the apartment across the yard because she has realized that she would betray Ana just as Ana betrayed her before, while Ana recognizes that in spite of her vow to cede Victor to Martha if she is cured, she reacts just as violently, with just as much hurt and jealousy as Martha did earlier. Only after one woman has lived the role of the other can she come to understand the behavior of the other and can the two women forgive each other and risk a new beginning together. Unlike earlier Trotta films, *L'Africaine* (*The African Woman*) is obviously not concerned with searching for a new female identity by fusing the characteristics of two women, but with tolerance and acceptance of others with all their faults. Behind this tolerance and acceptance are Margarethe von Trotta's reflections on a new quality of interpersonal relationships as described in an Adorno quote placed as an epigraph at the beginning of the screenplay of *Heller Wahn* (*Sheer Madness*): »Der nur liebt dich, bei dem du schwach dich zeigen darfst, ohne Stärke zu provozieren.« (»How do you know someone loves you? Only if you are free to show your weakness in that person's presence without triggering power.«) The film is about leaving others as they are without approaching them with selfish expectations – about accepting every aspect of their personality.

The director sees this realized mainly among women. Women's friendships such as those between Christa and Ingrid in *Das zweite Erwachen der Christa Klages* (*The Second Awakening of Christa Klages*), Juliane and Sabine in *Die bleierne Zeit* (*Marianne and Juliane*), Carla and Rosa in *Il lungo silenzio* (*The Long Silence*), Jelena and Ana in *Winterkind* (»Winter Child«), Rosa Luxemburg's relationships with Luise Kautsky, Clara Zetkin, and Sonja Liebknecht in *Rosa Luxemburg*, or the relationship of the three sisters and of Velia with Erika in *Paura e amore* (*Love and Fear*) are based on fundamental solidarity, mutual help, and support in coping with life, and are stronger than ideological differences or disagreements. Thus in *Die bleierne Zeit* (*Marianne and Juliane*) Sabine supports Juliane's efforts to investigate the prison situation of her sister and the circumstances of her death, although she disapproves of her obsession. The friendship between Rosa Luxemburg and Luise Kautsky continues although there is a rupture between Rosa and the Social Democrat leadership. And in *Winterkind* (»Winter Child«) Ana, who believes it is a mistake for her friend to resume her affair with Michael, nevertheless sticks by her. The new quality of women's friendships expressed in these relationships provides a conciliatory and reassuring element, and at the same time serves as a model for a conciliation between the sexes. This idea appears in *Paura e amore* (*Love and Fear*), where shortly before the end of the film Massimo asks Velia, »Have you forgiven me?« And she answers candidly, »Yes.« It is formulated even more clearly in *L'Africaine* (*The African Woman*), where the two women potentially include Victor in their reconciliation.

The world inside versus the world outside

The house as a feminine living space

An analysis of the conditions of feminine existence necessarily brings us to an issue around which many discussions within the women's movement have revolved in the past and still revolve today: the way women have traditionally been confined to the restricted intimate sphere of the household and childrearing, and have been excluded from the public sphere. »All right, then I'll give you a little tour of the neighborhood while it's still light«, says Bruno to Dieter in *Heller Wahn* (*Sheer Madness*), only to go on, turning to Erika, »And you can show Olga round the house if she feels like it.« The remark sounds like a cliché, since it describes the traditional role allocation in society that still persists despite the women's movement: The world outside belongs to the

View from the window

136. Rosa Luxemburg (Barbara Sukowa) in the Wronke prison.
137. Maria after Miriam moves out (*Schwestern / Sisters*).

The house as a cave

138. Anna in Schwestern (*Sisters*).
139. Juliane after Marianne's death (*Die bleierne Zeit / Marianne and Juliane*).

man, while women are restricted to the house. The director translates the dialectics between the public, masculine sphere and the private, feminine sphere into images where she contrasts exterior and interior spaces, the intimacy of the house with the generally accessible public sphere.

As a specifically feminine living space, the house is given a metaphoric character. It is the traditional realm of women, their hereditary place in society. Sabrina in *Paura e amore* (*Love and Fear*) brings social prestige and power to the role of the lady of the house in charge of the bourgeois palazzo. She will not rest until she has driven Velia and Sandra out of the house. »I realize it's hard for you to leave the house. But after all, our children are here now. And so it goes on being the house of the Parini«, she later tells Velia as she shows her the new nursery. Children and motherhood cement a woman's social position, give meaning to her life, and drive away loneliness. »I haven't had a real friend since you. But I've had lots of acquaintances, only we haven't kept in touch since the move. But when the children are there ...«, Ingrid tells Christa Klages. Women associate love, happiness, and security with the house. Even a revolutionary like Rosa Luxemburg associates her dreams of a middle-class life with a house. »I'd like us to live together in a little apartment of our own with some of our own furniture ..., a library«, she says to Leo.

On the other hand the closeness of the house limits the space in which women can develop and excludes them from the public sphere. For Margarethe von Trotta the image of the woman at the window, which serves as a leitmotif in *Heller Wahn* (*Sheer Madness*), contains a fundamental definition of the social position of women: Limited to the house, she is condemned to observe the outside world from afar, from inside. The view from the window symbolizes the longing to be able to take part in life in all its abundance and all its diversity, an image Margarethe von Trotta found in one of Rosa Luxemburg's letters, where Rosa describes how she stands at the window and thinks that beyond these rooftops is real life, from which she is excluded. The director used this motif in *Paura e amore* (*Love and Fear*): Velia gives Sandra a good-night kiss in the latter's bedroom. Then she goes to the window, looks over the rooftops, and realizes, »There's a full moon.« But her sister is already asleep and didn't hear her. In this scene there is a condensation of Velia's situation: Trapped in traditional social structures and lonely, she feels her hopes have not been realized. The statement is given added significance when she later again stands by the window at the university and looks outside dejectedly while Marco tells her that a friend has been arrested. Variations of this motif are found in all of Trotta's films. In *Il lungo silenzio* (*The Long Silence*) Carla and Marco sit side by side inside the beach house to which the bodyguards have banished them, and look out the window at the sea as they speak of their longing for a normal life. In *Winterkind* (»Winter Child«), after Jelena has looked in vain in the telephone book for a clue to her son's adoptive family, she goes out on the roof terrace and looks longingly across the rooftops. The evening after the Christmas celebration with the others, she again sits on the roof terrace and gazes dreamily into the distance. In *Das Versprechen* (*The Promise*) the window is replaced by a pair of binoculars through which Konrad observes a young girl while he is on guard duty; the girl is looking over the Wall from the other side, and resembles Sophie. The same motif appears in *Das zweite Erwachen der Christa Klages* (*The Second Awakening of Christa Klages*), where Christa tries hard to catch a glimpse of her daughter with a pair of binoculars while Ingrid is attempting to hand over the stolen money at the child care center. Television as a window on the world is given a similar significance when Maria in *Paura e amore* (*Love and Fear*) watches a romantic movie and thinks of her unfulfilled dreams of great happiness. The two old gentlemen's curious glances into their neighbors' windows in *L'Africaine* (*The African Woman*) are in the long run also motivated by their longing to take part in life.

The scenes in which Rosa Luxemburg stands at the window of her prison cell and observes the sky or the tomtits on the windowsill express the same idea. Because Rosa Luxemburg is in prison, the visual motif of the window as a peephole to the outside world is here combined with bars that crisscross and intersect across the field of vision, but a similar visual motif is frequently applied to the representation of the house. Repeatedly, glazed doors and windows subdivided by muntins reproduce the pattern of the bars, for instance in the double doors in the parental house of the sisters and brother in *Paura e amore* (*Love and Fear*), in the living-room window of the mother in *Schwestern* (*Sisters*), in the glass walls of the greenhouse in *Winterkind* (»Winter Child«), and particularly in *Heller Wahn* (*Sheer Madness*), where the image of the window is used throughout as a symbol for prison, and is frequently combined with struts and grating. A similar symbolic content is conveyed in *Winterkind* (»Winter Child«) by a glimpse of Michael and Jelena through the barred rear window of the cab of his van when he drives away with her to keep her from finding out the truth about the adoption of her son. Especially noteworthy is the use of the prison bars motif in the death scene in *Rosa Luxemburg*: When Rosa is knocked down by a

Reichswehr soldier in front of the door of the Hotel Eden, she falls on a rectangular glass window mounted in the floor and lit from below, behind which looms a large grid pattern. Condensed in this image is the quintessence of her life – imprisonment. A variation of the barred window are the closed shutters that serve as a leitmotif in *Il lungo silenzio* (*The Long Silence*) and symbolize imprisonment. When Carla flings open the shutters after Marco's death, she performs an act of liberation. However, she pauses when she gets to the shutter through which she used to watch her husband leave with his escort, and then defiantly closes the shutters again. The motif of the closed shutter is already used in *Paura e amore* (*Love and Fear*), which leads one to conclude the meanings are connected: Here, too, looking out the window represents a longing for happiness. But while Massimo regards the sight of Maria as a promise, the couple by the fountain watched by Velia symbolizes her approaching frustration and resignation.

An additional meaning of the window motif is contained in the first frame of *Die bleierne Zeit* (*Marianne and Juliane*). It shows the cross of a closed window, creating an association with the painting of the crucifixion in the parents' house, and thus a symbolic connection between being imprisoned, patient suffering, and martyrdom, which reappears in substance in other Trotta films as well. Both images in combination are found in *Das Versprechen* (*The Promise*), where, at the protest campaign on the 20th anniversary of the building of the Wall, Harald ties himself to the mullion and crossbar of a window like the crucified Christ. The cross motif is picked up again in a later shot, where Barbara's figure is visible behind a cross as she conducts a church service after Harald's death, and her grief bursts forth.

The house as a cave: retreat and inner prison

But the house is also shown as a place of safety that promises protection from the dangers and hostility of the outside world. If the protagonists feel overtaxed or threatened, they feel compelled to retreat to interior spaces: At night, when her husband looks at her reproachfully because of her inability to communicate, Ruth leaves the rest of the company sitting around the table and withdraws inside the country house. Afraid of discovery, Christa Klages flees into the entrance of a house when she catches sight of a woman friend on the street. The same impulse compels Carla to run back inside the apartment when she feels observed on the street. During their vacation, she and her husband are restricted to the house by the bodyguards after she thoughtlessly flicks on a cigarette lighter during supper on the terrace, and in Rome they lock themselves into their apartment out of fear of the Mafia's threats. In moments of sadness, pain, and despair people also seek healing and comfort in the intimacy of interior spaces: When Martha sees a group of blacks in a café during one of her lonely excursions through Paris, she feels impelled to join them so that there will be a place where she can feel at home. Christa Klages is driven back into her friend's apartment by her horror at Werner's death. Later Ingrid hides her in a summer house until she gets over her initial shock. Maria in *Schwestern* (*Sisters*), grieving over Anna's death, flees to the seclusion of the vacation home of her childhood; after Marianne's death Juliane locks herself alone into her darkened hotel room; and Carla lies across the bed crying in her dark bedroom after her husband's funeral. Rosa Luxemburg mourns the victims of the war at night in the solitude of her prison cell. Maria in *Paura e amore* (*Love and Fear*) kneels next to the bed in the darkness in Massimo's country house and weeps for the loss of her dream of happiness, and in *Das Versprechen* (*The Promise*) the pain about her separation from Konrad breaks forth from Sophie in the dark, abandoned showroom of the fashion salon. Over and over, the retreat into the house is associated with the image of holing up somewhere: Christa Klages burrows into her sleeping bag on the floor of the empty apartment where she has sought refuge – she lies »on the floor motionless like a larva«, says the screenplay; in *Schwestern* (*Sisters*) Anna is hunkering in a corner one evening when Maria comes home; Ruth in *Heller Wahn* (*Sheer Madness*) hides in a cellar vault, where Olga finds her crouching in a hidden recess; in *L'Africaine* (*The African Woman*) Martha cowers slumped in the dark apartment and cries over her betrayal of her friend. In these scenes the house becomes a cave to which people flee as animals do seeking relief and healing, a motif that is incorporated in *Die bleierne Zeit* (*Marianne and Juliane*), where little Jan makes a cave in the woods into his refuge. The cave of all places almost becomes a death trap for him when he is the victim of an arson attack.

The security of the house proves to be just as deceptive and fragile. Not only does the apparent intimacy turn out to be an illusion because there are eyes secretly watching through the window from the outside: the sister (*Schwestern / Sisters*), husband (*Heller Wahn / Sheer Madness*),

Images of loneliness

140. Maria after the quarrel with Miriam (*Schwestern / Sisters*).
141. Foreigners by themselves: Martha with her African acquaintances (*L'Africaine / The African Woman*).

or neighbors (*L'Africaine / The African Woman*). Outside the protective walls, the external world is also lurking as a real danger in the form of police observation and persecution (*Die bleierne Zeit / Marianne and Juliane*, *Rosa Luxemburg*, *Das zweite Erwachen der Christa Klages / The Second Awakening of Christa Klages*), surveillance by the Stasi (*Das Versprechen / The Promise*), a Mafia murder threat (*Il lungo silenzio / The Long Silence*), a subjectively perceived threat coming from strangers, or pressure to perform at work. At moments like these the feeling of safety and the healing effects of seclusion suddenly turn into uneasiness, fear, and despair, and the house is transformed into a prison.

This becomes especially apparent in *Das zweite Erwachen der Christa Klages* (*The Second Awakening of Christa Klages*), where Christa seeks refuge in an empty apartment because she is wanted by the police, and withdraws deeper and deeper within herself until she decides to take her life. The fear of punishment causes her to go into captivity herself. »I had to first create my own prison in order to understand what had happened to me«, she comments on this prison situation in retrospect. Even the beginning frames of this first film which Margarethe von Trotta directed herself show that she is fascinated by prison images, one of the constant and most striking features of her work.

In the depiction of the house as a prison are incorporated motifs from real prisons, shaped by the director's own experiences visiting prisons and impressions formed during one day she spent in prison in the early 1970s because of a heckling remark during a trial: The feeling of being powerless and at the mercy of others, the realization that the door can be opened only from the outside and not from the inside, and the memory of a ray of light that fell into the cell when the door was finally opened. The prototype of a prison cell in all its monstrosity is shown when Rosa Luxemburg is first committed to prison in Berlin, in 1915: a narrow, dark room with gray walls, empty except for a bunk that folds down, a folding table, and a stool, with a tiny barred window, through which a diffuse gleam of light enters into the cell. As in this film, imprisonment is always associated with images of being locked up in dark, bare rooms, with loneliness, isolation, and silent despair. Margarethe von Trotta uses the motif of the ray of light in *Il lungo silenzio* (*The Long Silence*): Because the shutters are constantly closed, the apartment lies in semidarkness, illuminated only by the light that falls through the cracks and throws bright streaks on the dark walls. Rooms with closed curtains, venetian blinds, and shutters, or with small windows that let in hardly any light or are covered with net curtains that prevent one from looking outside – characteristic for the way Margarethe von Trotta depicts 1950s apartments – are part and parcel of the prison situation and are related to the world of shadows in which characters like Anna (*Schwestern / Sisters*) or Ruth (*Heller Wahn / Sheer Madness*) move, and in which darkness stands for the spiritual, the irrational, the occult, but mainly for fear, »this childlike fear of darkness, of night, or ghosts, ghosts of the mind«,[21] which, as the filmmaker confessed in a conversation with Dorothee Sölle, is still with her. Behind it is Anna's nightmare (*Schwestern / Sisters*), the story of the two little sisters who wander through a deep, dark forest in the dark night and must not rest because if they do, the wild beasts will attack them while they sleep. In this sense, imprisonment means: the fear of a child, alone and vulnerable in the darkness.

It is not by chance that in Margarethe von Trotta's work prisons are always associated with images of loneliness, like that of Christa Klages on her mattress in the empty apartment in front of a wall covered with scribbled texts; or those of Marianne and Rosa Luxemburg walking in the yard during their prison term; or that of Carla sitting reading the paper in her kitchen as she eats a lonely meal. These scenes are related to others that refer less obviously to a prison situation, like the scene where Anna (*Schwestern / Sisters*) sits lost in thought in front of her terrarium or at her desk; where Juliane, in her apartment, engages in hectic activities to clear up her sister's death; Ruth lies watching television on the floor of her dark living room; Rosa Luxemburg sits eating with only her cat for company; Velia eats at the restaurant with a book in front of her or drinks a glass of champagne alone to celebrate her promotion to a professorship. Let us also recall Konrad, who after being ostracized by society eats an indifferent meal in his cramped one-room apartment, or Martha (*L'Africaine / The African Woman*) and Maria (*Paura e amore / Love and Fear*) as they take their lonely walks. These scenes are not about an externally imposed prison situation, but about a self-created inner prison. As in the case of Christa Klages, it is always fear, resignation, or a combination of the two that drives individuals to create their own prison-anxiety before an examination (*Schwestern / Sisters*), strangers (*Heller Wahn / Sheer Madness*), death (*L'Africaine / The African Woman*), the fear that the circumstances of the sister's death will for ever be swept under the rug (*Die bleierne Zeit / Marianne and Juliane*), that the husband might have died in vain (*Il lungo silenzio / The Long Silence*), or resignation because of social conditions, and because happiness is impossible (*Rosa Luxemburg*, *Paura e amore / Love and Fear*, *Das Versprechen / The Promise*).

What is involved, always, is self-blame and self-punishment motivated by a sense of guilt because a sister, a brother, or a friend has committed suicide, as in *Schwestern* (*Sisters*) and in *Heller Wahn* (*Sheer Madness*); by remorse because a character has betrayed another woman or her own ideals, as in *Paura e amore* (*Love and Fear*) and *L'Africaine* (*The African Woman*); or by a feeling of failure, as in *Schwestern* (*Sisters*) or *Rosa Luxemburg*. Doesn't Juliane's excessive identification with her dead sister stem from her belief that she has wronged her and let her down? And in the end, by his rupture with the GDR government, doesn't Konrad atone for the privileged position he has been enjoying for years and thus admit that Sophie is right in her accusations that his career was the reason he did not follow her to the West? In *L'Africaine* (*The African Woman*) it is explicitly stated that Martha's departure is first and foremost an inner emigration, and implies self-punishment. The same is true of Christa Klages's flight to Portugal. She later tries to complete her work and to kill herself, another kind of departure. Both are ways of retreating from reality. And even the journey of the two friends to Egypt in *Heller Wahn* (*Sheer Madness*), after Ruth, too, makes a suicide attempt, signifies nothing other than a running away from problems. For when Ruth is again confronted with a conflict situation, it turns out that regardless of her miraculous change everything has basically remained the same, and she flees once again. Thus, even though foreign countries are colorful and full of life, though there are picturesque sunsets and drives through open country, though the people are friendly and the atmosphere casual and unconstrained – characteristics emphasized in the films that stress the contrast with the eternally cheerless, gray mood in Germany – the rest of the world appears to be a no-man's-land, a beautiful and pleasant prison, for it is impossible to escape oneself.

Imprisoned in the labyrinth of one's own self

Retreat from the world, whether voluntary or forced, throws individuals back upon themselves. They become prisoners of their own psyche, can no longer step outside themselves; they become unable to communicate and lapse into speechlessness. The confrontation with one's self forces one to press forward to the precipices and frontiers of one's own ego, producing a confusion of emotions, on the brink of obsession and delusion. It leads into an inner labyrinth in which people lose their way, an idea that, in *Winterkind* (»Winter Child«), the filmmaker associates with the legend of the Minotaur. The interiors in Trotta films also abound in corridors, staircases, nooks and crannies, and systems of frames and struts which make it impossible to see them at a glance and give them the appearance of a labyrinth. Again and again, narrow corridors move into the frame: In the initial sequence of *Das zweite Erwachen der Christa Klages* (*The Second Awakening of Christa Klages*) the camera slowly travels along the long, dim corridor toward the figure of Christa – who sits on the floor beyond the open door next to her carryall – and tells of a space from which there is no exit. The palazzo in *Paura e amore* (*Love and Fear*) with its hallways and interconnecting rooms also resembles a labyrinth. The evening after Sandra's birthday party Velia walks along the corridor. The camera covers the length of the passageway in central perspective, the walls occupy two-thirds of the frame and seem to close around the figure of Velia. The feeling of being confined intensifies as she approaches the mirror in the passageway, in which the lattice pattern of the glass doors leading to the living room is duplicated. In *Heller Wahn* (*Sheer Madness*) a look through one, sometimes even several doorways into a room beyond in Ruth and Franz's house gives the impression of encapsulated interiors, for instance, on Olga's first visit, when Franz opens the front door and his figure stands out against the light that spills through the doorway while Ruth is visible behind him in the doorframe of the adjoining room, or when in the next shot Franz takes Olga into the living room and at the same time Ruth is in the background preparing the meal in the kitchen. The frame in which little Jan crawls around between stacks of newspapers in the narrow, dark hallway of the editorial office where Juliane works (*Die bleierne Zeit / Marianne and Juliane*) represents a parallel to his cave in the forest. Later Juliane enters the same hallway at night after deciding to write an article about her sister, and the echo of her steps in the abandoned building creates a reference to Marianne's walk through the barred prison hallway to the visitors' room at the beginning of the preceding scene.

Stairs and stairwells are a frequently recurring visual motif. Here the film director echoes the Germans' predilection for staircases. By incorporating these in the action, she, too, expresses

142, 143. Locked away inside oneself: Anna (*Schwestern / Sisters*).
144. Descent into death: Rosa Luxemburg on the staircase of the Hotel Eden.

»the respect Germans have for harmony and balance that forces upon them the symmetry of a stairwell structure, a symbol of this desire so to speak«, as Lotte Eisner said of the directors of the classic German silent film.[22] The striving for balance and harmony is one of the central themes in Margarethe von Trotta's films. It can also be discerned in the structure of her frames. However, at the same time staircases in her films also have an element of menace reminiscent of the staircase in Hitchcock's *Psycho*, in which she sees a condensation of the ideas she associates with this motif.

When she shows someone climbing the stairs, the depiction conveys what is waiting at the other end. In most cases there is an unpleasant or alarming situation ahead. When Werner in *Die bleierne Zeit* (*Marianne and Juliane*) comes up the stairs with Jan asleep in his arms, it is apparent how difficult and unbearable his responsibility as a father has become for him, while Juliane's hesitant steps on the staircase in her parents' house are associated with the memory of the ghastly painting of the crucifixion past which she and Marianne crept hand in hand with fearful glances when they were little girls, and which, now that they are adults, still fills Juliane with uneasiness every time she visits. In *Das Versprechen* (*The Promise*) Sophie's mother's way to the office of the school principal who will forbid her to have any contact with her daughter takes her up a twisting staircase and gives her a foreboding of the conflict ahead of her. When Miriam in *Schwestern* (*Sisters*) runs hurriedly up the stairs as she returns from the club late at night, she knows that she must face Maria's remonstrations once she enters the apartment. Carla's slow, weary steps as she climbs the stairs to her apartment shortly before her death in *Il lungo silenzio* (*The Long Silence*) indicate that on the other side of the door her mother is waiting full of fear and worry. In *L'Africaine* (*The African Woman*) despair and hopelessness are expressed in the scene where Victor goes up the stairs to the neighbors' apartment from which Ana has been observing him and Martha, and after he is turned away, he slumps dejectedly on the steps, an image that synonymously appears in *Das Versprechen* (*The Promise*), where Harald, after his expulsion from the GDR, sits hunched on the stairs in front of Sophie's apartment.

Like the narrow corridors and dark hallways, the staircase motif is often associated with transition from the outside world to the inner world. There is such a transition as Maria laboriously climbs the stairs to her apartment in *Schwestern* (*Sisters*), and similarly in *Il lungo silenzio* (*The Long Silence*) on Carla and Marco's return from their vacation, when, surrounded by bodyguards, they are conducted upstairs like prisoners and must first wait on the landing, pressed to the wall, until one of the policemen has finished searching the apartment. In both cases the stairs lead to imprisonment: in the first case Anna's inner prison, and in the latter case a de facto house arrest – a security precaution in response to actual outside danger. In *Das zweite Erwachen der Christa Klages* (*The Second Awakening of Christa Klages*), the staircase motif is also connected in substance with the stations on the road to her self-created prison – for example, when she climbs the steep, narrow stairs at the parsonage with Hans, or races up the flights of stairs to Ingrid's apartment after Werner's death. In *Rosa Luxemburg* the staircase motif is linked with that of prison bars when Rosa, after being discharged from prison in 1918, walks with difficulty on Leo's arm up the stairs to his boardinghouse room, and they walk through a white latticed door on the mezzanine landing.

On the other hand, scenes where people are running down the stairs are related to fear, flight, and death. One of Juliane's early childhood memories in *Die bleierne Zeit* (*Marianne and Juliane*) is connected with a staircase down which she and her mother and little sister rush into the basement along with other panic-stricken people whenever there is an air raid. Martha in *L'Africaine* (*The African Woman*) is engaged in a different kind of flight when after a fight with Victor she runs crying down the stairs and seeks solace among her African friends. The association with a precipice is evoked in *Il lungo silenzio* (*The Long Silence*) by a vertical look down a steep flight ofstairs by which Ms. Fantoni runs away in a panic when Carla asks her to help with her investigations. Carla herself has a similar reaction when she discovers the grave candle on the landing, and seeks refuge with her friend Rosa. Again, after her mother finds the second grave candle, Carla runs downstairs and out on the street, driven by fear for the papers at her office, but this time she runs into the hands of her assassin. Rosa Luxemburg's last walk before she is murdered also takes her down a staircase to the door of the Hotel Eden, a scene that creates a connection to the staircase she walked down blindfolded in the Warsaw prison, to what was ostensibly her execution.

In *Die bleierne Zeit* (*Marianne and Juliane*) the image of the staircase in connection with death appears together with another important motif, that of the forest: After Werner drops off his son at Juliane's house, he hurries downstairs as though someone were after him, bumping into Wolf-

gang in his haste, and rushes out on the street. The next frame shows his white Renault, in which he has killed himself, in a forest clearing. In *Das Versprechen* (*The Promise*), too, Harald flees from Sophie's stairwell into the forest, where he climbs over the border fence and is shot in the no-man's-land zone.

The forest, in Margarethe von Trotta's films, always appears when people have no idea what to do next. In *Il lungo silenzio* (*The Long Silence*) Carla goes into the forest when tension and danger threaten to overwhelm her, and shouts her rage and despair out loud. Christa Klages has the same reaction after she realizes the senselessness of the bank robbery, and later she says goodbye to Hans and Mischa by a forest pond before leaving for Portugal. The car in which Ingrid and Christa drive away plunges into a shady road while the man and child stand in the background in the sunlight, and finally this image is replaced by a blowup of Christa's sad face. There is a similar structure in a scene from *Dunkle Tage* (»Dark Days«), where Felicitas picks up her mother at the clinic after the detox treatment. The two descend the stairs from the veranda, cross a sunny piece of garden, and then walk down a path into a dark forest. In both cases the play of light and shadow expresses the conflict between sadness at having to leave and the hope for a new beginning, while the plunge into the forest serves as a sinister omen for the future. The image of the forest contains the same ambivalence. The road into the forest has something liberating about it, but at the same time leads into a realm of darkness whose characteristics indicate that it is related to the labyrinth: There is no way out, and terrible things happen there. Werner and Harald are not the only people to die in the forest – the car accident in which Sandra's friend is killed in *Paura e amore* (*Love and Fear*) also takes place there; little Jan in *Die bleierne Zeit* (*Marianne and Juliane*) experiences it as a flaming inferno; and for Anna in *Schwestern* it becomes a symbol for her fear of life, the home of spirits and demons that haunt her subconscious, and an expression of her longing for death, which drives her to commit suicide. In this case, too, the forest represents departure and liberation – departure from the world and liberation from the trials and tribulations of life. This liberation is denied her by her sister's voice in her frightening vision. The road into the forest, which leads into the labyrinth of death, is the way of escape chosen by the weak.

Another, less threatening opportunity for refuge is offered by walks in the open air, on which Margarethe von Trotta sends her women protagonists in search of inner balance and comfort. Portraying the life of Rosa Luxemburg, she emphasizes this facet of the revolutionary and shows how it is connected with her »feminine«, emotional side. For Rosa escape into nature means distance from her public life and reflection upon her own self. A remark during a walk with Kostja Zetkin in a field of lupines is the only time she is critical of political work. She describes the struggle in the party as a »constant affront to all that is good in human beings«, and, hearing the song

Walks in the woods

145. Martha and Ana converse about death (*L'Africaine / The African Woman*).
146. Harbinger of war: Rosa Luxemburg and Clara Zetkin observe an army maneuver.
147. Water as a healing force: Ana drinks from the source in Bretagne (*L'Africaine / The African Woman*).

of a bird, says, »Listen, a titmouse. You haven't discovered yet how much animals can help a person.« During her prison term in Wronke she finds consolation in her little garden and experiences moments of rapturous joie de vivre that give her the strength to keep her optimism alive. Nature has a similar meaning in the other films as well. Almost always one more element is added – water. Since her excursions to the Rhine in her childhood, Margarethe von Trotta has associated water with the constant flowing of a river that carries away all that has been dammed up and that allows one to forget one's worries. This image is conveyed both by the lonely walks by the river or the sea in *Paura e amore* (*Love and Fear*) and *Il lungo silenzio* (*The Long Silence*) and by Ana's visits in *L'Africaine* (*The African Woman*), to the Celtic holy well from whose water she hopes for healing. The women protagonists in *Schwestern* (*Sisters*), too, seek the calming effects of water: Maria takes a boating trip on the river, first with Anna, and later with Miriam, and one of the few moments when Anna seems relaxed and almost happy shows her walking along an arcade by the river, then stopping to listen to a street musician playing the flute. The comforting aspect of water is here combined with music as an expression of harmony. On the other hand the scene where, after her sister's death, Maria stands up to her knees in water and Miriam asks her to come back to the bank is inherently ambivalent, for here the comforting effect of water is linked with the idea of drowning oneself. There is a similar ambivalence when in *Heller Wahn* (*Sheer Madness*) Olga sticks her head under the water in the bathtub during her great crisis after returning from Provence.

Trees are yet another positive natural motif. In contrast to the forest, a tree is a symbol that represents life. Sandra's tree in *Paura e amore* (*Love and Fear*) is a magic tree which she has climbed ever since childhood to seek refuge, and which, she says, fulfills all her wishes. In *Schwestern* (*Sisters*), during a drive to visit her mother, Anna passionately speaks of how the birch tree is the tree of beginning and of life, which has the power to exorcize evil spirits. And, in *L'Africaine* (*The African Woman*), Ana and Martha stand under an oak speaking about immortality and victory over death.

Nature and natural images like the forest, water, or trees refer to the characters' inner world both in the way they are used and in terms of their symbolic value, and are closely related to the house. They are symbols of an inwardly directed search for liberation which at best helps the protagonists to gather new strength in moments of weakness, and at worst leads to death; they are thus facets of inner captivity.

Into an unknown, menacing world

The borderline between the inner and outer world in Margarethe von Trotta's work runs between the private and the public sphere. No doubt there are women like Sabrina, Rosa Luxemburg's friends Luise Kautsky and Sonja Liebknecht, or the mothers of the women protagonists, whose aspirations do not go beyond the traditional women's role and the domestic sphere, or who long to find their happiness in traditional ways through relationship with a man, like Maria in *Paura e amore* (*Love and Fear*) or Ana in *L'Africaine* (*The African Woman*), but these play a subordinate role. For the filmmaker is interested in looking at the consequences that arise when people are not prepared to accept the limitations imposed on them, but rebel and want more.

Thus, for instance, in a previously mentioned scene from *Heller Wahn* (*Sheer Madness*), Erika initially acquiesces and goes on a tour of the house with Olga, but during the big confrontation at the end of the film she rebels just like Ingrid (*Das zweite Erwachen der Christa Klages / The Second Awakening of Christa Klages*) against her existence as a housewife. There are also women like Olga (*Heller Wahn / Sheer Madness*), *Rosa Luxemburg*, Maria (*Schwestern / Sisters*), Juliane and Marianne (*Die bleierne Zeit / Marianne and Juliane*), or Velia (*Paura e amore / Love and Fear*), who have already had the courage to break out and secured a place for themselves in the outside world, while Ruth (*Heller Wahn / Sheer Madness*), or Erika (*Paura e amore / Love and Fear*), and to a certain extent even Sandra (*Paura e amore / Love and Fear*) feel they are incapable of holding their own in the public sphere or are tortured by self-doubt, and Anna (*Schwestern / Sisters*) is not prepared to sacrifice her emotional life for a career, and refuses.

When women rebel, it is because they are fighting for a place in society that will meet their needs and does justice to their abilities and interests, and that does not reduce them to a socially determined role. That means they also want access to an equal-opportunity professional career and professional recognition, which is still denied to them, as Sandra laments in a conversation with Velia: »D'you know what Professor Mancini said to me yesterday? He said women can't become surgeons because according to him they can't manage to stay on their feet for four hours at a stretch holding their instruments.« And, about Velia's situation, she comments: »They didn't let you become a professor. They 're still not going to recognize you.« Her words imply criticism of a society that represents the interests of men and a masculine world view characterized by striving for power, unquestioning faith in progress and science, and unthinking destruction of the environment and of human lives. In *Schwestern* (*Sisters*) Anna explains her wish to break off her studies by saying: »You see, up till now nobody has renounced knowledge or inventions only because they might one day be put to the wrong use. I don't want to have any part in it.« Similarly, Sandra tells Massimo: »You've seen what can happen. And still you physicists go about your lives as though nothing had happened.« Massimo responds: »No catastrophe in the world will force science to turn back.« And on another occasion Sandra accuses him: »You can't just simply do something without asking yourself what you're going to unleash by doing it.« Behind these words is the conviction that the autocracy of men is driving the world toward a catastrophe, which is why the principle that governs women's lives is needed to provide alternatives.

Accordingly women's entry into the public, masculine sphere implies, on the one hand, breaking through social barriers, and on the other fighting to change society so that it will conform to a feminine view of life. In Margarethe von Trotta's films, giving up the traditional role is linked to leaving the house. We see this most clearly in *Paura e amore* (*Love and Fear*) when Sandra and Velia fight their dejection by running through the streets at night and spraying slogans on the walls. As they are passing Erika's house, it suddenly occurs to them to take Erika along. Erika joins them and thus takes a first step into independence. Soon after this we find the three women in a bar dancing boisterously, a scene that suggests they are celebrating their liberation from hearth and home. A similar cheerful mood pervades the spontaneous party organized by Ruth, Olga, and the gallery owner in *Heller Wahn* (*Sheer Madness*) after they have decided to have a show of Ruth's paintings. In this film, too, Ruth's liberation begins by her leaving the house. She, who is afraid of opening the door or making a phone call, and who feels uneasy when she is with other people, goes out in public voluntarily because of her interest in Olga, bringing about an apparently chance meeting between them; she learns to phone Olga and is finally even able to go back to work as a teacher again. Likewise Ingrid in *Das zweite Erwachen der Christa Klages* (*The Second Awakening of Christa Klages*) does not begin to move around outside her apartment until she goes against her husband's wishes and helps Christa after Werner's death. The step outside into public space thus represents an act of rebellion. A similar metaphor, though in a different context, is used in *Das Versprechen* (*The Promise*) when, after the Soviet invasion of Prague, Sophie fights her way out of the hotel lobby into the open. In *Il lungo silenzio* (*The Long Silence*) the same idea is behind Carla's decision to mobilize the wives of the victims of the Mafia so that they can come out into the open with their accusations.

Rebellion inevitably meets with resistance, and only too often it fails. It is true that there is something liberating about taking back the street, but a street is unsafe, often hostile, terrain. Sometimes the monumentality of public buildings seems to overpower people: Looked at from the foot of the wide flight of outdoor stairs (*Das Versprechen / The Promise*), the then Berlin Kongreßhalle (»Congress Hall«) towers ponderously above the GDR scientists as they move toward the entrance. Equally massive, the Cologne Cathedral rises above Jelena in *Winterkind* (»Winter Child«), making her appear small and vulnerable. Only rarely pleasant things happen on the street: for instance, in *Das Versprechen* (*The Promise*), the enthusiastic joy of Sophie and her friends after their successful flight, Sophie and Konrad's reunion on the Hradjin in Prague, or the euphoric moments after the opening of the Wall. Mostly the street appears strange and lonely. Martha's endless roaming through the streets of Paris in *L'Africaine* (*The African Woman*) or Jelena's road accross the square in front of the Cologne railway station bathed in bleak morning light and along gray rows of houses in *Winterkind* (»Winter Child«) speak of being uprooted and homeless. The streets around the West Berlin Bahnhof Zoo railway station in *Das Versprechen* (*The Promise*) feel oppressive and dark when Harald arrives there after his expulsion from the GDR. Homeless people are loitering on the dirty stairs, and the shadow of the Gedächtniskirche (»Memorial Church«) looms over him menacingly.

The street exposes people to secret glances and hostile behavior. In *Das Versprechen* (*The Promise*) state security agents observe Sophie's passage during her visit in East Berlin through a car window, while in *Die bleierne Zeit* (*Marianne and Juliane*) Juliane is confronted with police in a parked car every time she leaves the house. Subliminal aggression erupts, for example in *Schwestern* (*Sisters*) on the country road during the drive to visit the mother, or in *Paura e amore* (*Love and Fear*), where after an argument with Nicola at the university Sandra experiences a sim-

148, 149. Breaking out into the street: Sophie during the 1968 invasion of Prague (*Das Versprechen / The Promise*).

The street as an alien, menacing place

150. The evening of the opening of the Wall, a distraught Konrad looks out at the street (*Das Versprechen / The Promise*).
151. Roadblock in *Rosa Luxemburg*. (Margarethe von Trotta and Christiane Ensslin, *Rosa Luxemburg. Das Buch zum Film*, Nördlingen 1986.)

ilar situation as she rides her bicycle along a narrow street and Nicola pursues her in the car and trains his sights on her, so to speak.

For Rosa Luxemburg the street is not only a lonely place, but a dangerous one as well. When, in 1906, she walks through the door of the Warsaw prison and crosses the square in front of the prison alone carrying her suitcase, the shadow of a pursuer falls next to her own. In other ways as well, the streets she moves through feel eerie and frightening: the dark lane down which she is led at night on her arrival in Poland to meet Leo; the nocturnal drive through Berlin behind baskets and sacks on the back of a delivery cart when she and her companions encounter a roadblock; her parting from Leo on the unlit street in front of their last hiding place, the villa of a doctor. The street in *Il lungo silenzio* (*The Long Silence*) appears equally frightening: The hectic watchfulness of the escort, the sirens, the noise on the street, the camera gazing at the prosecuting attorney's convoy diagonally across the roadway or from a bird's-eye view surround the return from the vacation, the drives to the office, or the visit to the restaurant with a climate of fear and danger. A distanced focus from a place of concealment has an alarming effect and suggests that there are secret observers and pursuers, for instance, when Carla with Marco's papers in her purse hurries across the street into a bank, leaves the house to buy a newspaper, or runs panic-stricken toward a telephone booth after an anonymous phone call.

Christa Klages also experiences the street as a place of imminent danger when she avoids discovery by Lena by a hair's-breadth while waiting for Ingrid on the square in front of the child-care center, like Konrad in *Das Versprechen* (*The Promise*), whose flight to the West is prevented at the last minute by an army truck that suddenly appears before him out of the darkness like a dark monster. At a later attempt to escape, when he approaches the prearranged meeting place, he watches concealed by a streetcar as the members of the escape organization are taken into custody. In Trotta's films arrests generally take place on the street. Christa Klages is grabbed by two policemen and dragged into a car in front of her house as she comes back from shopping, and when, in *Das Versprechen* (*The Promise*), Barbara and her friends are arrested in front of the university because they have been protesting the invasion of Czechoslovakia, the caretaker first blocks their retreat into the building.

Elsewhere, too, the street proves to be the place where defeats overtake people. Thus Felicitas in *Dunkle Tage* (»Dark Days«) sees her worst fears confirmed and her of happiness vanish when she and Fabian find their mother drunk on the street. Frustration and despair are also written all over the faces of Rosa Luxemburg and Clara Zetkin as they walk down the street in 1914 at the beginning of World War I after saying goodbye to Kostja at the conscripts' gathering point, against the flood of a crowd of happy and exultant people. In *Winterkind* (»Winter Child«) Elke's world falls apart completely when, on the street in front of her house, Daniel and Jelena get into the ambulance that is taking old Jonathan away, and the boy pushes Elke away screaming, »Go away! I hate you!« Rosa Luxemburg and Karl Liebknecht, Werner (*Das zweite Erwachen der Christa Klages / The Second Awakening of Christa Klages*), Carla (*Il lungo silenzio / The Long Silence*), and Nicola (*Paura e amore / Love and Fear*) meet their death on the street.

People give the impression of being far more vulnerable outdoors whenever they enter a phone booth. For Carla it becomes a glass coffin, an image Margarethe von Trotta uses deliberately. In *Heller Wahn* (*Sheer Madness*) Ruth has anxiety attacks when she goes into a telephone booth, and in her distorted perception the adjacent booths at the post office seem like aquariums, against whose glass walls human faces press like grotesque fish, menacing her. Juliane in *Die bleierne Zeit* (*Marianne and Juliane*) finds her fear that her sister is dead confirmed by a phone call to her father that she makes in a cramped wooden phone booth with a tiny window in the door, all of which evoke associations with a coffin. In another phone booth she receives further shattering news. She tells a journalist of the result of her investigations, and he tells her bluntly that nobody is interested in her sister's death anymore. Christa Klages, too, experiences a moment of acute danger in a telephone booth: Trying to reach Ingrid, she is discovered by a woman acquaintance and fears the woman might betray her. After Konrad's abortive escape in *Das Versprechen* (*The Promise*), his father pushes him into a phone booth, in front of him like a prisoner – to quote the directions in the script – in order to report him to the police. Here the phone booth becomes a prison cell, a meaning that Margarethe von Trotta transfers to the motif of the elevator in *Dunkle Tage* (»Dark Days«), since there are characteristics it shares with a phone booth. She shows the mother being led into an elevator by two nurses upon her arrival at the clinic, and disappearing out of sight upstairs. In a later scene a connection is made between the image of the elevator and death when a neighbor tells Felicitas that when her mother made a suicide attempt she dragged herself there.

The public sphere as prison

In the long run the break-out from the house leads back into the interiors, the offices, banks, universities, hospitals, or government buildings, which give off an emphatically impersonal chill. The frame is characterized by cool gray-blue, white, or beige, and somber, dull brown, smoothly functional furniture, and the cold gleam of rows of windows and glass façades. Long shots across the room or across long corridors in central perspective, where the walls seem to close in around the people, underscore that they are at the mercy of unfamiliar surroundings, and stress the insignificance of the individual. In *Paura e amore* (*Love and Fear*) a scene that shows Roberto at work in the bank illustrates his professional position: He is sitting at his desk speaking with a client about investments. The camera slowly zooms out until the whole width of the central hall of the bank is included in the frame and we realize that Roberto's work space is limited to a corner partitioned off by file cabinets and potted plants where he is isolated yet exposed. At the same time his voice keeps receding into the distance and is finally drowned in the general babble of voices. The manager's condescending friendliness as he demands that Roberto work overtime resembles the calculating flattery Münzinger uses in *Schwestern* (*Sisters*) to get Maria to type his son's Ph. D. dissertation in her free time.

Thus women's entree into the public »masculine« sphere proves not to be liberation, but exposes them to an unfamiliar, cold world with new constraints and dependencies. It takes them into the functional ugliness of the bank in *Das zweite Erwachen der Christa Klages* or into the »glass box«, as Miriam in *Schwestern* (*Sisters*) calls the open-plan office where, in the cold fluorescent light, fifty closely packed desks with typing women stand side by side and a supervisor checks who takes bathroom breaks and how long. The executive floor where Maria works (*Schwestern / Sisters*) feels more tasteful and luxurious with its light-colored carpet, plants in front of the window, and prints on the walls; the light is more muted and the atmosphere more intimate. But the original concrete walls emit coldness, and especially at night, when Maria sits alone in the big office that opens into the hallway, her loneliness and isolation comes to the fore. The lowered venetian blinds in front of the large windows are reminiscent of Marco's office in *Il lungo silenzio* (*The Long Silence*) where the light that comes through the slits of the blinds traces a pattern of bright stripes on the wall, a visual reference to the closed shutters in his apartment. The prison situation to which he is subjected in his private life continues to exist at his place of work. And in the final analysis the office is a prison for Maria as well. Visual motifs associated with captivity occur repeatedly when people are portrayed in the public sphere, for example when, in *Die bleierne Zeit* (*Marianne and Juliane*), Juliane is shown behind the iron bars of a lattice fence along which she walks to meet her sister at the museum – a motif that reappears in *Dunkle Tage* (»Dark Days«) when the mother waits outside the school for her daughter – or when the two sisters are seen through the latticed glass door of the cafeteria before they come into the room. Again, in the depiction of the Prague hotel in *Das Versprechen* (*The Promise*), the repeated view of the street from the hotel lobby through the glass revolving door, by placing the struts of the door in the frame, draws attention to the limitations of space, and creates a mental association with the prison motif. After the military occupy the city, the hotel becomes an actual prison for those who live there, just as the Hotel Eden does for Rosa Luxemburg and Karl Liebknecht after they become the prisoners of the Reichswehr. Like the house, public spaces have something of the labyrinth about them, for instance, the institute for astrophysics in *Das Versprechen* (*The Promise*) with its maze of pipes, iron ladders, staircases, and the metal struts of the telescopes and other apparatus for observing the sky, or the editorial office of the *Rote Fahne* (*Red Flag*) in *Rosa Luxemburg*, where to see the outside one looks through several glass walls that partition the room. Frequently motifs related to the labyrinth such as columns and stairs appear. In *Paura e amore* (*Love and Fear*) particularly, the colonnades and walls of the old university constantly intrude in the frame, recalling omnipresent traditions and conventions. A scene in *Die bleierne Zeit* (*Marianne and Juliane*) conveys a similar message: 15-year-old Juliane hides behind a column while secretly smoking in the school corridor when she hears footsteps.

The self-contained world of hospitals represents prisons of a different kind. Individuals are subjected to an unfamiliar regimen and feel they have been taken back to the dependent situation of a child. Although Ana in *L'Africaine* (*The African Woman*) is perfectly capable of getting around all by herself, she is pushed around in a wheelchair when she is outside her room. To mail a letter she has to ask a nurse to help her. During physicals she lies motionless on a gurney, helpless as the machine rolls around her humming loudly, while nurses monitor the procedure on a screen next door. Attached to tubes and surrounded by medical gadgets, Ruth lies behind

Offices in *Schwestern* (*Sisters*)

152. Maria with her boss Münziger (Heinz Bennent).
153. Miriam in the open-plan office.

Prison motifs in public spaces

154. Marianne and Juliane at the museum (*Die bleierne Zeit / Marianne and Juliane*).
155. Martha and Juliane at the restaurant (*L'Africaine / The African Woman*). (Photo: Filmverlag der Autoren.)
156. Stairwell in the Africans' lodging house in Paris (*L'Africaine / The African Woman*).
157. Marianne in front of the sculptures in the museum arcade (*Die bleierne Zeit / Marianne and Juliane*).
158. Courtroom in *Rosa Luxemburg*.

glass walls after her suicide attempt and becomes part of the equipment. Particularly strong associations with a prison are evoked by the clinic in *Dunkle Tage* (»Dark Days«), where the glass walls and doors which, during the daughter's visits, repeatedly stand between her and the mother emphasize the boundaries between inner space and the outside world and are reminiscent of the partition in the visitors' room at the high-security prison in *Die bleierne Zeit* (*Marianne and Juliane*). There the relationship between hospital and prison appears in a different sense. After her breakdown, Juliane is admitted to a clinic, and in the cloistered space of a hospital room endures her inner crisis, as a result of which she assumes her sister's role and puts herself in a prison situation of her own.

Universities do occasionally appear as free spaces where women can establish themselves. Also, the quiet seclusion of libraries and museums makes possible moments of familiarity and intimacy – for example, in *Die bleierne Zeit* (*Marianne and Juliane*), *Heller Wahn* (*Sheer Madness*), *Paura e amore* (*Love and Fear*), and *Das Versprechen* (*The Promise*). But again and again it becomes obvious that they are an integral part of the »masculine« power complex of business and science that Margarethe von Trotta discussed when she was making *Schwestern* (*Sisters*). A police interrogation of Velia about her connection to the Red Guards in *Paura e amore* (*Love and Fear*) underscores male supremacy and the vulnerability of women in the world of men: Velia, visibly ill at ease, sits down on a chair near the door. Opposite her, at the back of the room, stand the rector and the policeman, while next to her a stone male bust rises on a pedestal. Thus she seems practically cornered and encircled by the presence of men. The motif of the stone sculpture as a symbol for the ubiquity of men in history, politics, and science appears at the very beginning in the opening sequence: A long shot shows a stairwell at the university and Velia descending the staircase. The next shot begins with a view of the covered walk in the inner courtyard, along which the camera slowly pans to linger on the stone statue of a man. In later scenes, the same motif recurs: After Velia waits in vain for Massimo at the university library, she crosses the inner courtyard in the dark, and behind her loom the statues of scholars. On another occasion Sandra drops leaflets into the inner courtyard over the second-floor balustrade as the camera focuses, from the level of the courtyard across a monumental male sculpture, on her figure and the pieces of paper fluttering down. A variation of this motif is the ancestors' gallery at the university, which Velia accidentally enters while looking for Massimo, and which once again makes her realize that the history of the university was written by men. The convent that the three sisters visit represents a counterpart to these monuments to male dominance. It, too, is a place rife with history in which the traditional historical role of women is consolidated: renunciation of the world by retreating behind walls that promise security and peace, though at the price of loneliness and exclusion from public life.

The first time Margarethe von Trotta uses the motif of sculptures as a metaphor for history as the domain of men is in *Die bleierne Zeit* (*Marianne and Juliane*), where the two sisters arrange to meet at a museum and Juliane walks down a long row of stone figures of men until she finally meets Marianne. The bust of Voltaire in Rosa Luxemburg's apartment refers to the same symbolic context, which is picked up once more and developed further when Karl Liebknecht gives a talk in front of a monument in the Tiergarten Park in Berlin: While he challenges them to revolutionary action with impassioned words, Rosa stands nearby looking sceptical. A look at the audience shows heads with black hats, caps, and umbrellas, above which waves a single red flag. At Liebknecht's last words the frame changes to a documentary shot of the top part of the Brandenburg Gate, on which workers are hoisting a red flag. This sequence defines Liebknecht as a violent man of action, but because of its gloominess and because the members of the audience are faceless it simultaneously suggests that he is courting disaster. The woman tries to stop him, but fails since she is denied participation in public decisions. The idea is emphasized when during the occupation of the newspaper offices at the end of 1918 Rosa goes behind the barricades and tries to convince the fighting men of the uselessness of this renewed bloodshed, but is told, »That's nothing for a woman.« In *Il lungo silenzio* (*The Long Silence*) Carla and Ms. Fantoni also meet at a museum, where an endless row of stone men's busts is exhibited in cabinets. This scene, too, is about the conflict between getting involved in public events and staying in the private sphere – the conflict between activity and passivity.

In *Das Versprechen* (*The Promise*) the monumental power of the figures at the entrance of Berlin's Olympiastadion, before which the figure of Konrad seems tiny, symbolizes the rise of fascism and its consequences, which Sophie is explaining to a group of tourists: World War II, the Soviet occupation, and the Berlin Wall. The broad, brown columns in the vestibule of the Reichstag building feel somber and oppressive in *Rosa Luxemburg* when Rosa receives news from Karl that the war credits have been approved. A long shot over the looming, tall marble columns and the wide, curving stairs of the entrance hall of the courthouse in *Die bleierne Zeit* (*Marianne and Juliane*) conveys the coldness and soullessness of the judiciary, while sober ugliness characterizes the youth welfare department in *Winterkind* (»Winter Child«) and the police station in *Das zweite Erwachen der Christa Klages* (*The Second Awakening of Christa Klages*). These images reflect a perception of the German state as the embodiment of despotic power, misanthropy, aggressiveness, and militarism, as Margarethe von Trotta presents it in *Die bleierne Zeit* (*Marianne and Juliane*), *Rosa Luxemburg*, and *Das Versprechen* (*The Promise*). The representatives of the state are the only people to whom she refuses to give the sympathy and understanding she usually has for her characters. They appear as simple policemen who set German shepherd dogs on an unarmed boy or shoot a fleeing man in the back (*Das zweite Erwachen der Christa Klages / The Second Awakening of Christa Klages*), who, unmoved by the relatives' grief, come accompanied by police dogs and heavily armed, denying freedom even to the dead (*Die bleierne Zeit / Marianne and Juliane*) or, unquestioningly doing their duty and in obedience to authoritarian ideology, put into practice the pettifogging and misanthropical regulations of their employers (*Die bleierne Zeit / Marianne and Juliane*, *Rosa Luxemburg,* or *Das Versprechen / The Promise*). The women prison guards in *Die bleierne Zeit* (*Marianne and Juliane*) and *Rosa Luxemburg* represent the same narrow-minded belief in authority – dour, elderly women who basically lead a life in captivity themselves and vent their aggressions about their situation on the prisoners. The upper ranks, like the police officer in Warsaw, the judge, and the Reichswehr officer in *Rosa Luxemburg*, the police official in *Paura e amore* (*Love and Fear*), or the Stasi officials, party secretaries, and police officers in *Das Versprechen* (*The Promise*), on the other hand, rarely behave aggressively, and occasionally even adopt an outwardly genial and patronizing attitude, behind which, however, their cold cynicism and inhuman sadism become apparent. In *Paura e amore* (*Love and Fear*) the policeman asks Velia about her former student's credibility and she confirms it, whereupon he answers with relish that consequently everything the student said about the others in his group can be believed. The police officer at the Warsaw prison considers the mock execution to which he subjects Rosa Luxemburg colossal fun, and is tickled pink about it. In *Das Versprechen* (*The Promise*) personnel officer Ruhländer feigns sympathy when Konrad's planned travel permit to Stockholm is cancelled, although he was already spying on him in Prague and the measure was obviously taken at his instigation. Stasi officer Müller uses the visits of Konrad's son to force Konrad to make more and more concessions, smiling amiably all the while, finally revoking the visitor's permit just the same. The Stasi people who stand in the way of Barbara's peace prize accuse her of having a disturbed relationship to democracy because she rejects their provocations.

An equally negative attitude appears in *Il lungo silenzio* (*The Long Silence*) toward the Italian state, which is said to be rotten to the core. To be sure, the focus here is on civil servants who become victims of the ruling regime themselves: a small group of prosecuting attorneys and police who try to swim against the stream of general corruption. Accordingly not only the attorneys but the police, too, are drawn as positive figures as the film shows that they endure the same human conflicts as the protagonists.

Occasionally there are also public spaces that resemble the intimacy of the house and serve Margarethe von Trotta's protagonists as a refuge in difficult times, but also as places of leisure and contemplation, like the club to which Miriam escapes to forget everyday life, Martha's café in *L'Africaine* (*The African Woman*), or the halls in which Rosa Luxemburg strolls through the crowd of workers when she appears at their meetings. This category includes particularly churches, simple, clearly structured interiors like those shown in *Das zweite Erwachen der Christa Klages* (*The Second Awakening of Christa Klages*), *Heller Wahn* (*Sheer Madness*), and *Das Versprechen* (*The Promise*), islands of quiet and peace: Long, centered shots across the length of the nave with a view of the altar or an organ gleaming gold and silver, and emphasis on magnificent details such as old paintings, elaborate wooden carvings and examples of the stone-cutter's art, or stained-glass windows with muted daylight falling through them convey symmetry, clarity, and harmony and create an atmosphere of intimacy. In *Das Versprechen* (*The Promise*) a close-up of burning candles, something that is actually characteristic of Catholicism, introduces the meeting of the peace group led by Barbara, and thus creates an association between the church and the image of inner knowledge and enlightenment.

Repeated thematic references to the church have less to do with religion or with the particular meaning that Protestant values have for Margarethe von Trotta, as Thomas Elsaesser argues[23], but rather are linked with the image of interior space as a place of refuge. For what takes place

The state as prison

159. Search during a visit to the prison (*Die bleierne Zeit / Marianne and Juliane*).
160. Waiting room at the border crossing to East Berlin (*Das Versprechen / The Promise*).
161. Juliane in front of the high-security prison (*Die bleierne Zeit / Marianne and Juliane*).

People in cages

162. Barbara and Harald in the Stasi prison (*Das Versprechen / The Promise*).
163. Rosa Luxemburg in prison.

in the church? In *Das zweite Erwachen der Christa Klages*, Hans emphasizes in his sermon that Christa's actions are not without moral justification. Immediately after the church service she succeeds in getting his help to continue her escape. The chance meeting between Olga and Ruth at the old village church in *Heller Wahn* (*Sheer Madness*) is the starting point of their friendship. And, finally, in *Das Versprechen* (*The Promise*) the church both as an institution and as a building is a refuge for opponents of the regime as it has been throughout GDR history, while it is also a place of grief and comfort for Barbara after her husband's death. The same idea is expressed by a scene from *Rosa Luxemburg*: In a moment of despair Rosa enters the prison church in Breslau in which a church service is just taking place, but leaves immediately afterward. There are two reasons for this. One is explained by her history, the other is told by visual motifs: She does not find the comfort she seeks in this place because as a communist she does not believe in God. Also, the church space lacks intimacy.

The figure of the father (*Die bleierne Zeit / Marianne and Juliane*) occurs in a different context. He is seen less in his function as a pastor than as a prototype of the authoritarian, punishing father, a man who does not care if a skin forms on the cocoa during prayers, who allows the gentle, feminine Marianne to twist him round her little finger while he punishes the rebellious Juliane – an egotist, as the mother calls him, representing the traditional masculine role. On the other hand younger pastors, like Hans in *Das zweite Erwachen der Christa Klages* and the small-town pastor in *Die bleierne Zeit* (*Marianne and Juliane*), are portrayed throughout as positive representatives of the church as an institution.

All in all, the road into the outside world does not imply liberation, it merely modifies the conditions of imprisonment and leads into new prisons, real prisons with iron cell doors, dark corridors, barred windows, or actual cages as shown in *Rosa Luxemburg*, *Die bleierne Zeit* (*Marianne and Juliane*), and *Das Versprechen* (*The Promise*), or voluntarily chosen ones like the office, bank, or university job. This supposed freedom turns out to be a subtle captivity in a net of personal and social restraints, in the ground plan of life, as Margarethe von Trotta calls it, and that means continued self-surrender, loneliness, and isolation that prevail even in self-created prisons.

Filmmaking as liberation

Memory: mourning and elixir of life

»I've never thought much about myself«, Christa Klages begins telling her story and starts to remember as she looks out the window of the departing train. Scenes like this one occur in Trotta's films surprisingly often. Watching the outside world from inside a train compartment, a car, or a bus, images of moving trains, roads, or railroad tracks that disappear on the horizon, a look at a station platform, landscapes, streets, the façades of houses, or walls going past the window testify to a departure from one place to another, but they are also moments of being detached from time and space when one's thoughts can set out on a journey. Whether the autumn colors of the idyllic landscape through which Juliane (*Die bleierne Zeit / Marianne and Juliane*) goes by taxi on a visit to the prison make her aware of the contradiction between the beauty of the journey and the unpleasantness of the destination, or whether at the sight of the almost endless prison wall that moves past the bus windows on her way to the new high-security prison worry and anxious expectation are written in her face; whether in *Schwestern* (*Sisters*) the road bordered with birches inspires Anna to rapturous reflections about the magic significance of trees, or in *Il lungo silenzio* (*The Long Silence*) the long vision of the white-bordered black ribbon of the nocturnal road that vanishes at the horizon suggests Carla's gloomy forebodings of the future on the drive home from the restaurant, car and bus rides always invite the protagonists to reflections about themselves and the world. Past events appear before their mind's eye, awakening longings, nostalgia, grief, and bitterness. The train ride through fields of rape gleaming in the sunshine, blooming yellow as Rosa Luxemburg travels from Warsaw to Berlin in 1906 brings back visions of the care-free days when the break with Leo, the disagreement with the Social Democrat leadership, and the horrors of war seemed to be far, far away. When Martha during her drives through Paris in *L'Africaine* (*The African Woman*) recognizes the streets of the city, and sees the new opera house that was built after she left, she becomes aware of the strangeness of what was once so familiar, and the feeling of bitterness that drove her into emigration intensifies. After her return she keeps encountering things that remind her of the past. The painting that was once her favorite, and in front of which she discovered Victor and Ana in an embrace, the tape of a TV interview

that Victor gave and that documents the fact that they agree on politics, a photograph of Ana he hides in his desk so as not to remind her of the past, the song Ana puts on at the party to celebrate her discharge from the hospital, meant to remind Martha of the days of their former friendship, recall the pain she suffered and force her to face up to it. Going away as flight into forgetting is in dialectical opposition to return as remembrance and confrontation with the past, a precondition for healing psychic wounds and for forgiveness.

In Margarethe von Trotta's work forgetting always means the conscious or unconscious repression of pain, guilt, loss, fears, an idea that in *Die bleierne Zeit* (*Marianne and Juliane*) she transfers to the attitude of the Germans toward their history. Flashbacks to Juliane's and Marianne's childhood and adolescence make it clear that the roots of their later behavior lie in the past. The enormity of the older generation's guilt and the fact that their elders refuse to learn from experience weighs heavily on the sisters and fills them with shame and horror. Acting on behalf of their parents they begin to process what happened by snatching the past from oblivion. Motifs that have to do with remembering are a central element of the film: Marianne's picture on the apartment wall preserves her memory and the shared ideals that motivate Juliane; dated files document Juliane's struggle to keep the circumstances of her sister's death from being forgotten, and the photographs spread out on the floor, part of an article about the situation of mothers in the Third Reich, are a reference to the German past. As Juliane is taking little Jan to his foster parents, the two of them at first sit silently in the train looking out the window. Suddenly she takes his hands and asks him, »Do you remember Marianne, Mama Amelie?« »No«, he answers, and as though trying to apologize, he adds, »I'm still a child, you know.« In the beginning scene he kneels on the back seat of his father's car and looks back through the rear window at the road behind him until he finally falls asleep. Looking back as a metaphor for remembering is here contrasted with forgetting. The contrast is reiterated in the final scene, when the boy tears up Marianne's photograph and thus also the memory of her, whereupon Juliane explains to him that he is wrong, and offers to tell him the story of his mother. In this scene remembering has a twofold significance. On the one hand, it is about healing, for the boy can deal with the trauma of losing his parents and the hostile actions of those around him – which almost cost him his life – if he comes to terms with them. On the other hand, remembering is about keeping alive the memory of the past in order to keep the past from repeating itself.

An additional aspect of the dialectical opposites forgetting and remembering appears in this scene. It is expressed even more clearly in *Paura e amore* (*Love and Fear*): The forgetting of wishes, ambitions, and dreams causes the kind of resignation and stagnation characteristic of the »leaden time« of the 1950s that Velia equates with the mood of the late eighties, while remembrance arouses longing for change, opposition, rebellion, it sets things in motion. If the

Symbols of reflexion and remembering

164. Martha takes a bus through the streets of Paris (*L'Africaine / The African Woman*).
165. Jan tears up his mother's photograph (*Die bleierne Zeit / Marianne and Juliane*).
166. Miriam gazes at the dead Anna's portrait (*Schwestern / Sisters*).

meaning of life is struggle, as Margarethe von Trotta once said, then stagnation means death, an inner numbing that condemns people to a shadowy existence. Memory is an elixir of life. In *Il lungo silenzio* (*The Long Silence*), the memory of her husband moves Carla to continue his struggle. The reading of the testament, when he seems to be speaking with her over the voice of the notary public, the unpacking of the box in which his personal efects from the office were handed over to her – a similar motif occurs in *Die bleierne Zeit* (*Marianne and Juliane*) –, the photographs in Francesco's office, the sight of the closed shutters, or a walk through Villa Adriana, where she often went with Marco, give her the strength to go on living and fighting. If the dead go on existing in the memory of the living, they become immortal. When, seeing her mother in an old home movie, Velia (*Paura e amore / Love and Fear*) tells Dr. Cecchini that her mother is now nothing but a segment of film, he answers: »For me she exists. As for me, I'm not so sure I exist, but she exists. Forever.«

Speech and feminine language

However, remembering also implies bringing up what is concealed from the hiding places of the subconscious. It is risky, for it tears down protective walls that people have created for themselves. That is what happens in nightmares in *L'Africaine* (*The African Woman*) and *Die bleierne Zeit* (*Marianne and Juliane*) or the terrifying and violent visions in *Schwestern* (*Sisters*) and *Heller Wahn* (*Sheer Madness*), where what is hidden in the subconscious breaks forth directly and ominously, throwing life off balance. If confrontation with the past is to bring deliverance and healing, it is necessary to put the thoughts in words and to voice them. For things to be destroyed, »cast out« of one, as Margarethe von Trotta wrote in her journal,[24] they must be written down, described, expressed. She sees writing as self-purification and as an essential part of a healing process, an idea she embodies in the character of Fritz (*Schwestern / Sisters*), based on the manic-depressive writer Wolfgang Bächler whose (*Traumprotokolle / Dream Transcripts*) she uses in the film. The subconscious becomes the source of the poetic, as the feminist literary historian Julia Kristeva[25] put it, while the linguist and psychoanalyst Luce Irigaray regards the subconscious, dreams, and poetry as the place of the feminine, where women, condemned to silence in patriarchal society, take refuge and live out their difference.[26] As a result, women's writing was traditionally restricted to intimate and poetic forms of expression like journals, letters, and poems. The examination of the traditions of women's communication is an important element in Trotta's films, starting with *Rosa Luxemburg*, where the private letters of the revolutionary to her women friends are placed in the center of the work and determine the course of the narrative. They not only represent a piece of female life experience, but also hold the key to the hidden part of the personality, which particularly interests Margarethe von Trotta. As well as being communication with another person, letters to the male friend (*Das zweite Erwachen der Christa Klages / The Second Awakening of Christa Klages*), the woman friend (*L'Africaine / The African Woman*), or the sister (*Die bleierne Zeit / Marianne and Juliane*) are always a coming to terms with oneself as well, a clarification of one's own positions, feelings, and views, which are rarely expressed in direct conversation. »I notice that it's important to speak«, writes Christa Klages from Portugal, anticipating a realization of whose full implications she does not become aware until later. And Marianne writes, after an argument with Juliane, »Please come and visit, dearest, don't be mad, you know what I meant.« Letters are messages from the inner world, from real or self-created prisons and from inner exile. They often contain calls for help, as does Ana's letter to Martha in *L'Africaine* (*The African Woman*), which does not reach the addressee.

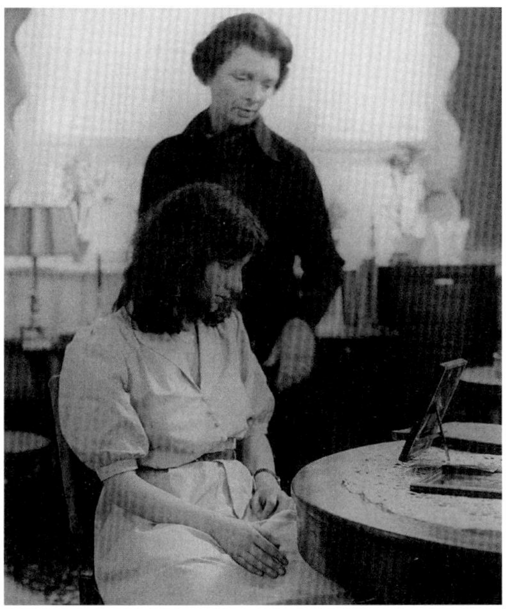

Even more personal and intimate is the journal, in which women try to give verbal form to emotions from an area on the borderline of their subconscious so as to make them real and tangible, and in the process write down words and sentences that approach the realm of dreams and poetry, like the fable of the bee and the meadow which Maria reads to Massimo in *Paura e amore* (*Love and Fear*). In *Schwestern* (*Sisters*) Anna fills her journal with images of fear: a stone statue with its mouth opened to scream, paintings by Goya or Munch, with comments like, »I am not disturbed, only my fear is growing.« Or, »The dream I've formed of my life will cost me my life.« And, interspersed among the comments, expressions of rebellion and protest: »They manipulate genes, but do not know how to deal with love.« Or the last entry before her suicide: »I'm tearing up one of the rules of nature.« This language reduces profound realizations to their minimum form. Like the sentence scraps Christa Klages writes on the walls in the solitude of her empty apartment, it is like an outcry in times of speechlessness. Indeed, language in Margarethe von Trotta's work never sounds spontaneous, is never taken for granted – rather, it is very deliberate. For through the act of speaking women, who in male-dominated society are traditionally excluded from conversation, enter unfamiliar terrain that forces them to feel their way forward carefully and with consideration. When they begin to speak, they do so in sentences that are the result of long reflection and stick in one's memory. Thus, while »Margarethe von Trotta's cinema is addicted to language«, »the language does not flow, it shows traces of a paralysis that comes out of silence«,[27] as Jutta Brückner aptly said in her tribute when the filmmaker was awarded the 1994 Konrad Wolf Award of the Akademie der Künste.

Filmmaking: conquest of public space and inner liberation

Like language, films as a whole are the product of intensive reflection. The reconstructing of the process of realization itself is left to the viewer. Moreover, the stories of the first five Trotta films up to and including *Rosa Luxemburg* are structured as the retrospective narratives of women – the director uses the same principle more single-mindedly than ever in *Dunkle Tage* (»Dark Days«). This narrative method links reflection about oneself and one's own life with the element of remembering and dealing with the past. The insights to which this process leads the women narrators are condensed and anticipated in the beginning sequences. This creates a distancing element that is reinforced by comments spoken offscreen, letters, and poems, and makes it possible to report events in reflected form, compressed to what seems essential in retrospect. In this way film serves as a public forum for women portraying themselves. Women who had been condemned to silence for thousands of years are allowed to speak. In this context speaking – writing, filmmaking – becomes a subversive act, for like all creative, public acts it breaks through the existing boundaries of patriarchal society, destroys myths, and disregards conventions. It com-

167. Remembering: Margarethe von Trotta looks at herself in one of her early films. (Photo: Ute Karen Seggelke.)

pels the viewer to take note of women publicly, no longer to reduce them to a mirror image of men's wishes and fears, but rather to give them a place in culture and history on the basis of who they are themselves.

For a generation that grew up in the »leaden« 1950s under a bell jar of silence, the two opposites speech and silence have far-reaching significance that includes not only opposing social standpoints but also the question of identity. Speech means breaking out of the dull masses of the silent majority, swimming against the stream, struggle, renewal, life beyond death, as exemplified by Rosa Luxemburg, for whom Margarethe von Trotta has created a cinematic monument, or Carla in *Il lungo silenzio* (*The Long Silence*), whose voice, recorded on a cassette, moves her friend Maria and many other women to continue their struggle against the wall of silence erected by the Mafia even after her death. Silence, on the other hand, stands for the hushing up of the past, for refusing to listen to reason, for inflexible social structures, isolation, stagnation, and death. Silence not only makes social injustice possible, it also relegates women to their traditional role, makes them into the appendages of men, and robs them of their identity.

Consequently, speaking as a metaphor for autonomous, public expression is synonymous with liberation as an act of social resistance and the conquest of public space. But apart from this, speaking, for Margarethe von Trotta, has another important aspect – that of inner liberation. For becoming silent is one of the characteristics of inner imprisonment in the labyrinthine, ominous shadow world of the subconscious inhabited by fear. Even if the immediate causes of silence in her films may be diverse, in the final analysis silence can always be traced back to the phenomenon of fear: fear of the police, of the judiciary and jail, the Mafia, losing one's job and social ostracism, violence, war, and death, or else the unrealistic fear of not being a match for the superior strength of male-dominated society, the fear of struggling for one's existence, of not being able to meet the expectations of others, of being hurt and disappointed by other people, or of darkness and loneliness. Often, reasons for fear may overlap.

The breaking of silence demands that a character overcome her fear by escaping the inner world in a real and figurative sense. Only when human beings manage to liberate themselves from their fear, the transition to the outside world no longer leads into a new prison, for no one can take away a person's inner freedom, not even behind bars and barbed wire. Why, despite all adversities and sacrifices, doesn't Rosa Luxemburg lapse into despair? Where does she get the strength to comfort her friends even in prison? Because she would rather die than give up her ideals, and therefore the fear cannot hurt her. Why, on the other hand, does Christa Klages lose the courage to face life? She, who was never afraid, as her friend Ingrid says, allows her fears to overwhelm her.

The dialectics of fear and courage is one of the central themes in Margarethe von Trotta's films, if not the central theme to which she keeps coming back. These concepts are the common denominator of the contradictions between weakness and strength, irrationality and rationality, figures of shadow and light, the private and the political, and the inner and outer world. They are also signposts on the road Margarethe von Trotta travels over and over again in her artistic work. Asked about her modus operandi as an auteur and film director, she has frequently pointed out that the first thing she needs to do is open her mind to the world in order to gather information. She questions people who have been involved in an event, reads countless books, and takes in images and impressions. Then, however, she needs to pull back in order to search for a connection between reality and dream, between conscious experience and the subconscious. She is lost to the world, as she once declared, quoting a song by Gustav Mahler, and plunges into a different, inner, world where she encounters imagination and poetry, but is also confronted with her own fears and unresolved conflicts. This is where she finds the shadow worlds she keeps recreating in her films. But in order to give them artistic form, she must cross the bridge from the subconscious to the conscious with them, must tear down the barrier of self-protection and expose her innermost self, a risk she keeps taking upon herself. Because for her, filmmaking means struggle and liberation – struggle against the fears and demons within her and against the constraints, limitations, resistance, and hostility to which she feels exposed as a woman in patriarchal society and as a woman filmmaker in a man's profession.

Notes

[1] Volker Schlöndorff quoted in Robert Fischer and Joe Hembus, »Der neue deutsche Film 1960–1980«, in: *Citadel Filmbücher bei Goldmann*, Munich 1981, p. 111.
[2] Wolfram Schütte, »An editing Room of one's own«, in: *Artforum,* 24, Nov. 1985, pp. 66–72.
[3] Stig Björkman, *Torsten Manns and Jonas Sima, Bergman über Bergman. Interviews mit Ingmar Bergman über das Filmemachen*, Frankfurt/M, Berlin, Vienna 1978, p. 23.
[4] Edwin Elliker, »Erinnern und Vergessen«, in: *Film und Ton Magazin*, 12/27/1981, pp. 51/52.
[5] See Barton Byg, »German History and Cinematic Conventions Harmonized in Margarethe von Trotta's ›Marianne and Juliane‹«, in: S. Frieden, R. Mc Cormick et al. (eds.), *Gender and German Cinema*, vol. II, Oxford 1993.
[6] See Charlotte Delorme, »Zum Film Die bleierne Zeit von Margarethe von Trotta«, in: *Frauen und Film*, no. 31, 1982, and: Charlotte Delorme, »On the film ›Juliane and Marianne‹ by Margarethe von Trotta«, in: University Film and Video Association, Department of Communication, Arts and Sciences, Rosary College (ed.), *Journal of Film and Video*, no. 2, 1985, pp. 47–51.
[7] See Thomas Elsaesser, *Der neue deutsche Film*, Munich 1994.
[8] See Ernst Schumacher, »Zwei Schritte vorwärts, ein Schritt zurück«, in: *Film & Fernsehen*, no. 10, 1986, 12–17. Klaus Hannuschka, »Porträt einer einzigartigen Frau«, in: *Märkische Volksstimme*, 11/27/1986.
[9] See also J. Hoberman, »Film. La vie en Rosa«, in: *Village Voice,* 32, 5/12/1987, New York, p. 61.
[10] See also Erwin Schaar, »Ein Film für höhere Söhne?«, in: *Medien und Erziehung 30*, no. 3, 1986, Munich, pp. 167–169.
[11] See also Peter Boris, »Der arme Büffel und der Klassenfeind«, in: *Die Welt,* 4/15/1986.
[12] See Sonia Dayan-Herzbrun, »Rosa la Rouge avec les ›Verts‹«?, in: *Cinema 86*, no. 372, Oct. 1986, Paris, pp. 15–21.
[13] See Richard Porton, »Rosa Luxemburg«, in: University of California Press (ed.), *Film Quarterly*, 4, no. 2, 1989, Berkeley, California, pp. 39–42.
[14] Margret Köhler, »Lernprozesse. Gespräch mit Margarethe von Trotta«, in: *Film-Dienst*, no. 6, 1993, p. 5.
[15] Protokoll über die 415. Sitzung des Programmbeirats DFS (16/17, December 1997, Cologne), p. 19.
[16] Interview with Agnes Fink in: Margarethe von Trotta, *Heller Wahn*, Fischer Taschenbuch, Frankfurt 1983, p. 138.
[17] *Der Spiegel*, no. 49, 12/1/1997, Hamburg, p. 251.
[18] See »Die Neugier immer weiter treiben: Die filmische Befreiung der Margarethe von Trotta«: Film essay by Peter Buchka, Kick-Film, Munich 1996.
[19] Lotte Eisner, *Die dämonische Leinwand*, Frankfurt/M 1975, p. 104.
[20] See »Die Neugier immer weiter treiben, loc.cit.
[21] *Als Frau ist es wohl leichter Mensch zu sein: Gespräche mit Dorothee Sölle, Margarethe von Trotta u. a.*, Reinbek bei Hamburg 1984.
[22] Lotte Eisner, *Die dämonische Leinwand*, Frankfurt/M 1975, p. 116.
[23] Thomas Elsaesser, »Mother Courage and the divided daughter«, in: The British Film Institute (ed.), *Monthly Film Bulletin 50*, July 1983, London/England, p. 177.
[24] »Tagebuch, 1.4.80«, in: Margarethe von Trotta, *Heller Wahn*, Fischer Taschenbuch, Frankfurt 1983, p. 95.
[25] *La révolution du langage poétique*, Paris 1974. German edition: *Die Revolution der poetischen Sprache*, Frankfurt/M 1978.
[26] Luce, Waren Irigaray, *Körper, Sprache. Der verrückte Diskurs der Frauen*, Berlin 1976.
[27] Jutta Brückner, *Für Margarethe von Trotta,* in: Peter Schneider, Margarethe von Trotta, *Das Versprechen oder Der lange Atem der Liebe*, Berlin 1994, pp. 154/155.

List of works

Starred in the following films

1968
Schräge Vögel/Spielst du mit schrägen Vögeln
Direction: Gustav Ehmck
Cast: Jürgen Draeger, Horst Janson, Margarethe von Trotta
Production: Gustav Ehmck Film Gräfelfing
Premiere: 17 April 1969, Munich

1969
Brandstifter
TV film
Direction: Klaus Lemke
Cast: Margarethe von Trotta, Iris Berben, Veith von Fürstenberg
Production: Westdeutscher Rundfunk, Cologne
First aired: 13 May 1969

1969
Baal
TV film
Direction: Volker Schlöndorff
Cast: Rainer Werner Fassbinder, Sigi Graue, Margarethe von Trotta
Production: Hallelujah-Film GmbH, Munich/Hessischer Rundfunk, Frankfurt/Bayerischer Rundfunk, Munich
First aired: 7 January 1970

1969
Drücker
TV film
Direction: Franz Josef Spieker
Cast: Frithjof Vierock, Carola Rabe, Brigitte Wenzel, Margarethe von Trotta
Production: Westdeutscher Rundfunk, Cologne
First aired: 16 April 1970

1969
Götter der Pest (*Gods of the Plague*)
Direction: Rainer Werner Fassbinder. Direction assistant: Michael Fengler
Cast: Harry Baer, Hanna Schygulla, Margarethe von Trotta
Production: Antiteater-X-Film, Munich
Premiere: 4. April 1970, Vienna (Viennale)
German premiere: 30 June 1970, Berlin

1970
Inspektor a. D. Kaminski und das hinderliche Kind (in the series *Hauptbahnhof München*)
TV film
Direction: Peter Schubert
Cast: Alfred Balthoff, Robert Klupp, Margarethe von Trotta
Production: Eikon gemeinnützige Gesellschaft für Fernsehen und Film mbH, Munich, for ZDF, Mainz
First aired: 13 October 1970

1970
Die kleine Schubelik
TV film (series *Der Kommissar*)
Direction: Georg Tressler
Cast: Erik Ode, Günther Schramm, Reinhard Glemnitz, Fritz Wepper, Margarethe von Trotta
Production: Neue Münchner Fernsehproduktion GmbH, Geiselgasteig for ZDF, Mainz
First aired: 30 September 1970, ZDF

1970
Der amerikanische Soldat (*The American Soldier*)
Direction: Rainer Werner Fassbinder
Cast: Karl Scheydt, Elga Sorbas, Jan George, Margarethe von Trotta
Production: Antiteater-X-Film, Munich
Premiere: 9 October 1970, Mannheim (IFF)
First commercial screening: 27 November 1970

1970
Warnung vor einer heiligen Nutte (*Beware of a Holy Whore*)
Direction: Rainer Werner Fassbinder
Cast: Lou Castel, Eddie Constantine, Hanna Schygulla, Margarethe von Trotta
Production: Antiteater-X-Film, Munich in collaboration with Nova International, Rome
Premiere: 28 August 1971, Venice (IFF).
German premiere: 1 September 1971, Hamburg

1970/71
Paul Esbeck
TV film
Direction: Erich Neureuther
Cast: Henning Gissel, Robert Klupp, Helma Seitz, Margarethe von Trotta
Production: Südwestfunk, Baden-Baden
First aired: 8 April 1971, ARD

1971
Tod eines Ladenbesitzers
TV film (series *Der Kommissar*)
Direction: Wolfgang Staudte
Cast: Erik Ode, Günther Schramm, Reinhard Glemnitz, Fritz Wepper, Margarethe von Trotta
Production: Neue Münchner Fernsehproduktion GmbH, Geiselgasteig for ZDF, Mainz
First aired: 18 June 1971, ZDF

1971/72
Alkoholiker
TV film (series *Der Fall von nebenan*)
Direction: Tom Toelle
Cast: Ruth Maria Kubitschek, Gerd Baltus, Witta Pohl, Margarethe von Trotta
Production: Studio Hamburg Atelierbetriebs GmbH, Hamburg for Norddeutsches Werbefernsehen GmbH, Hamburg
First aired: 2 November 1972, BR

1972/73
Desaster
TV film
Direction: Reinhard Hauff
Cast: Klaus Löwitsch, Dieter Laser, Ruth Maria Kubitschek, Margarethe von Trotta
Production: Bavaria-Atelier GmbH, Munich for Westdeutscher Rundfunk, Cologne
Premiere: May 1973, Cannes (IFF – Quinzaine)
First aired: 6 September 1973, ARD

1973
Die Verrückte
TV film (series *Ein Fall für Männdli*)
Direction: Wolf Dietrich
Cast: Ruedi Walter, Margit Reiner, Inigo Gallo, Margarethe von Trotta
Production: Intertel AG, Basel for DRS, Zurich/Bayerische Rundfunkwerbung GmbH, Munich
First aired: 27 August 1973, BR

1973
Sonderbare Vorfälle im Hause von Professor S.
TV film (series *Der Kommissar*)
Direction: Wolfgang Becker
Cast: Erik Ode, Günther Schramm, Reinhard Glemnitz, Fritz Wepper, Margarethe von Trotta
Production: Neue Münchner Fernsehproduktion GmbH, Geiselgasteig for ZDF, Mainz
First aired: 21 September 1973, ZDF

1973
Wochenende mit Waltraut
TV film (series *Motiv Liebe*)
Direction: Roger Fritz
Cast: Friedrich Schütter, Claudia Buthenuth, Peter Chatel, Margarethe von Trotta
Production: Studio Hamburg Atelierbetriebs GmbH, Hamburg for Norddeutsches Werbefernsehen GmbH, Hamburg
First aired: 7 May 1974, ARD

1973
Übernachtung in Tirol
TV film
Direction: Volker Schlöndorff
Cast: Margarethe von Trotta, Reinhard Hauff, Rita Scherrer
Production: Hallelujah-Film GmbH, Munich/Hessischer Rundfunk, Frankfurt
First aired: 8 October 1974, ARD

1974
Une invitation à la chasse (*Einladung zur Jagd*)
TV film (series *Histoires insolites* [*Phantastische Novellen*])
Direction: Claude Chabrol
Cast: Jean-Louis Maury, Margarethe von Trotta, Henri Attal
Production: Technisonor, Paris/Cosmovision Paris for ORTF, Paris.
First aired: 2 November 1974, ORTF I
German premiere: 20 September 1976, HR 3

1974
Georginas Gründe/Les raisons de Georgina
TV film
Direction: Volker Schlöndorff
Cast: Edith Clever, Joachim Bissmeier, Margarethe von Trotta
Production: Bavaria-Atelier GmbH, Munich/Technisonor, Paris/Cosmovision, Paris; for Westdeutscher Rundfunk, Cologne/ORTF, Paris
First aired: 27 April 1975, ARD

1974
Das Andechser Gefühl
Direction: Herbert Achternbusch
Cast: Herbert Achternbusch, Margarethe von Trotta, Barbara Gass
Production: Bioskop-Film GmbH, Munich
Premiere: 19 April 1975, Gauting

1975
Die Atlantikschwimmer
Direction: Herbert Achternbusch
Cast: Herbert Achternbusch, Heinz Braun, Alois Hitzenbichler, Margarethe von Trotta
Production: Herbert Achternbusch Filmproduktion, Buchendorf
Premiere: 27 February 1976, Gauting

1976
Bierkampf
TV film
Direction: Herbert Achternbusch
Cast: Herbert Achternbusch, Annamirl Bierbichler, Sepp Bierbichler, Margarethe von Trotta
Production: Herbert Achternbusch Filmproduktion, Buchendorf/Zweites Deutsches Fernsehen
Mainz premiere: 4 March 1977, Munich
First aired: 29 September 1977, ZDF

1983/84
Blaubart (*Bluebeard*)
TV film
Direction: Krzysztof Zanussi
Cast: Vadim Glowna, Karin Baal, Vera Tschechowa, Margarethe von Trotta
Production: Westdeutscher Rundfunk, Cologne/Fernsehen der deutschen und rätoromanischen Schweiz, Zurich
First aired: 28 October 1984, ARD

Starred in and acted as assistant director in the following films

1971
Die Moral der Ruth Halbfass
Direction: Volker Schlöndorff. Assistant Directors: Klaus-Oliver Keil, Margarethe von Trotta
Cast: Senta Berger, Helmut Griem, Peter Ehrlich, Margarethe von Trotta
Production: Hallelujah-Film GmbH, Munich/Hessischer Rundfunk, Frankfurt
Premiere: 13 April 1972, Bonn

Starred in, acted as assistant director, and wrote the screenplay for the following films

1970
Der plötzliche Reichtum der armen Leute von Kombach (*The Sudden Wealth of the Poor People of Kombach*)
TV film
Direction: Volker Schlöndorff
Screenplay: Volker Schlöndorff, Margarethe von Trotta
Cast: Reinhard Hauff, Georg Lehn, Karl-Josef Cramer, Margarethe von Trotta
Production: Hallelujah-Film GmbH, Munich/Hessischer Rundfunk, Frankfurt
First aired: 26 January 1971, ARD
First commercial screening: 29 January 1971, Frankfurt

1972
Strohfeuer (*Summer Lightning*)
Direction: Volker Schlöndorff
Screenplay: Volker Schlöndorff, Margarethe von Trotta
Cast: Margarethe von Trotta, Friedhelm Ptock, Martin Lüttge
Production: Hallelujah-Film GmbH, Munich/Hessischer Rundfunk, Frankfurt/Main
Premiere: September 1972, Venice (IFF)
German premiere: 1 November 1972, Munich
First aired: 2 November 1972, ARD
German Critics' Award (Deutscher Kritikerpreis) 1972 to Margarethe von Trotta
IFF Brussels 1973: Prix Femina to Margarethe von Trotta
Workers' Award of Czechoslovakia 1974 to Margarethe von Trotta.

1976
Der Fangschuß (*Coup de Grâce*)
Direction: Volker Schlöndorff
Screenplay: Geneviève Dormann, Margarethe von Trotta, Jutta Brückner; based on the novel *Coup de Grâce* by Marguerite Yourcenar
Cast: Margarethe von Trotta, Matthias Habich, Rüdiger Kirschstein
Production: Bioskop-Film GmbH, Munich/Argos Films, Neuilly/Hessischer Rundfunk, Frankfurt
Premiere: 22 October 1976, Hamburg

Co-authored screenplays for the following films

1981
Die Fälschung (*Le faussaire*; *Circle of Deceit*; *False Witness*)
Direction: Volker Schlöndorff
Screenplay: Volker Schlöndorff, Jean Claude Carrière, Margarethe von Trotta, Kai Hermann; based on the novel by Nicolas Born
Production: Bioskop-Film GmbH, Munich/Artemis-Film GmbH, West Berlin/Argos Films, Neuilly/Hessischer Rundfunk, Frankfurt
Premiere: 15 October 1981, Wiesbaden
Trotta collaborated on the screenplay in its very first stages.

1983/84
Unerreichbare Nähe
Direction: Dagmar Hirtz
Screenplay: Margarethe von Trotta, Dagmar Hirtz
Production: MfG Film GmbH, Munich/Roxy Film GmbH, Munich/Westdeutscher Rundfunk, Cologne
Premiere: 20 August 1984, Montreal (IFF)
German premiere: 27 October 1984, Hof
First commercial screening: 23 November 1984, ARD

Directed synchronization in the following films

1978
The Unmarried Woman (*Eine entheiratete Frau*)
Direction: Paul Mazursky

1986
Anne Trister
Direction: Léa Pool

Directed the following films

1975
Die verlorene Ehre der Katharina Blum (*The Lost Honor of Katharina Blum*; *L'honneur perdu de Katharina Blum*)
Direction: Volker Schlöndorff, Margarethe von Trotta
Screenplay: Margarethe von Trotta, Volker Schlöndorff; based on the story by Heinrich Böll
Camera: Jost Vacano (Dieter Lohmann)
Music: Hans Werner Henze
Sound: Klaus Eckelt
Costumes: Annette Schaad
Editing: Peter Przygodda
Production design: Günther Naumann
Assistant directors: Alexander Ebermeier von Richthofen, Gerhard von Halem
Cast: Angela Winkler (Katharina Blum), Mario Adorf (Inspector Beizmenne), Dieter Laser (Journalist Werner Tötges), Jürgen Prochnow (Ludwig Göttgen), Heinz Bennent (Attorney Blorna), Hannelore Hoger (Trude Blorna), et al.
Production: Bioskop-Film GmbH, Munich/Paramount-Orion Film Produktion GmbH, Munich/Westdeutscher Rundfunk, Cologne
Producer: Eberhard Junkersdorf
Location: Cologne and surrounding area, Hochgurgl im Oetztal
Length: 106 min.
Premiere: September 1975, San Sebastian (IFF)
German premiere: 9 October 1975, Berlin
Dietrich Lohmann shot the carnival scenes; he was replaced after four days of shooting.
IFF San Sebastian 1975: OCIC Prize, CEC Prize
German Critics' Award (Deutscher Kritikerpreis) 1975 to Angela Winkler
German Film Award (Deutscher Filmpreis) 1976:
Filmband in Gold (Best Actress) to Angela Winkler,
Filmband in Gold (Camera) to Jost Vacano

1978
Das zweite Erwachen der Christa Klages (*The Second Awakening of Christa Klages*; *Le second éveil de Christa Klages*)
Direction: Margarethe von Trotta
Screenplay: Margarethe von Trotta, Luisa Francia
Camera: Franz Rath
Music: Klaus Doldinger
Sound: Vladimir Vizner
Costumes: Gerlind Gies
Editing: Anette Dorn
Production design: Toni Lüdi
Assistant directors: Alexander von Eschwege, Christa Ritter.
Cast: Tina Engel (Christa Klages), Silvia Reize (Ingrid Häkele), Katharina Thalbach (Lena Seidlhofer), Marius Müller-Westernhagen (Werner Wiedemann), Peter Schneider (Hans Grawe), et al.
Production: Bioskop-Film GmbH, Munich/Westdeutscher Rundfunk, Cologne
Producer: Eberhard Junkersdorf
Location: Munich and environs, Kirchheim-Unterteck, Portugal
Length: 93 min.
Premiere: 24 February 1978, Berlin (IFF–Forum)
First commercial screening: 14 April 1978
IFF Berlin 1978: »Otto-Dibelius-Filmpreis« of the Interfilm

German Film Award 1978: Filmband in Silver (Production), Filmband in Gold (Best Actress) to Tina Engel

1979
Schwestern oder Die Balance des Glücks (*Sisters or The Balance of Happiness*; *Les sœurs*)
Direction: Margarethe von Trotta
Screenplay: Margarethe von Trotta; co-authors: Luisa Francia, Martje Grohmann
Dreams based on Wolfgang Bächler's »Traumprotokolle«
Camera: Franz Rath
Music: Konstantin Wecker, Henry Purcell
Sound: Vladimir Vizner
Costumes: Ingrid Zoré
Editing: Annette Dorn
Production design: Winfried Hennig
Assistant director: Helenka Hummel
Cast: Jutta Lampe (Maria), Gudrun Gabriel (Anna), Jessica Früh (Miriam), Konstantin Wecker (Robert), Rainer Delventhal (Maurice), Agnes Fink (Mother), Heinz Bennent (Münzinger), et al.
Production: Bioskop-Film GmbH, Munich/Westdeutscher Rundfunk, Cologne
Producer: Eberhard Junkersdorf
Location: Hamburg, West Berlin
Length: 95 min.
Premiere: 18 September 1979, Hamburg (film festival)
First commercial screening: 21 September 1979
German Film Award 1980: Filmband in Gold (Best Actress) to Jutta Lampe
IFF Sceaux 1981: first prize
IFF Hyères 1981: grand prize

1977–79
Die Patriotin
Direction: Alexander Kluge
Production: Kairos-Film, Munich/Zweites Deutsches Fernsehen, Mainz
Premiere: 20 September 1979, Hamburg (Film Festival)
First commercial screening: 7 December 1979
In his film, Kluge montaged a sequence (»Bundeswehrlied« with Marius Müller-Westernhagen) that Margarethe von Trotta had shot for *Das zweite Erwachen der Christa Klages*, but had not used in the completed film

1981
Die bleierne Zeit (*The German Sisters*; *Marianne and Juliane*; *Les années de plomb*)
Direction: Margarethe von Trotta
Screenplay: Margarethe von Trotta, Christiane Ensslin
Camera: Franz Rath
Music: Nicolas Ecomonou
Sound: Vladimir Vizne
Costumes: Monika Hasse, Jorge Jara
Editing: Dagmar Hirtz
Production Design: Georg von Kieseritzky
Assistant Director: Helenka Hummel
Cast: Jutta Lampe (Juliane), Barbara Sukowa (Marianne), Rüdiger Vogler (Wolfgang). Verenice (Verena) Rudolph (Sabine), Luc Bondy (Werner), Doris Schade (Mother), Franz Rudnick (Father), et al.
Production: Bioskop-Film GmbH, Munich/Sender Freies Berlin, West Berlin
Producer: Eberhard Junkersdorf
Location: West Berlin, Stuttgart-Stammheim, Beirut and environs, Catania/Sicily and Etna region
Length: 107 min.
Premiere: 4 September 1981, Venice (IFF)
German premiere: 25 September 1981 (first commercial screening)
IFF Venice 1981: Leone d'oro, FIPRESCI Prize, OCIC Prize of the journal »Cinema Nuovo«, Prize of the Italian National Bank; Award for Best Director to Margarethe von Trotta; Golden Phoenix (Best Actress) to Jutta Lampe, Barbara Sukowa
IFF Valladolid 1981: Critics' Award
IFF Chicago 1981: Golden Hugo
David di Donatello (Best Foreign Director) 1982 to Margarethe von Trotta
German Film Award 1982: Filmband in Gold (Production), Filmband in Gold (Best Actress) to Barbara Sukowa
GDR Critics' Award 1984 (Best Film for 1983)

1982
Heller Wahn (*Friends and Husbands*; *Sheer Madness*; *L'amie*)
Direction: Margarethe von Trotta
Screenplay: Margarethe von Trotta
Camera: Michael Ballhaus
Music: Nicolas Economou
Sound: Vladimir Vizner
Costumes: Monika Hasse
Editing: Dagmar Hirtz
Production design: Jürgen Henze, Werner Mink
Assistant director: Helenka Hummel
Cast: Hanna Schygulla (Olga), Angela Winkler (Ruth), Peter Striebeck (Franz), Christine Fersen (Erika), Franz Buchrieser (Dieter), Agnes Fink (Mother), Wladimir Yordanoff (Alexej), Felix Moeller (Christof), et al.
Production: Bioskop-Film GmbH, Munich/Les Films du Losange, Paris /Westdeutscher Rundfunk, Cologne
Producer: Eberhard Junkersdorf, Margret Menegoz
Location: Berlin, Southern France, Cairo
Length: 105 min.
Premiere: 24 February 1983, Berlin (IFF competition)
First commercial screening: 25 February 1983

1986
Rosa Luxemburg
Direction: Margarethe von Trotta
Screenplay: Margarethe von Trotta
Coaches for the Polish dialogues: Jan Biczicky, Henrik Baranowkski
Historical and scientific consultants: Annelies Laschitza, Bernhard von Mutius, Helmut Hirsch
Camera: Franz Rath
Music: Nicolas Economou
Sound: Christian Moldt
Costumes: Monika Hasse
Editing: Dagmar Hirtz
Production design: Bernd Lepel
Assistant directors: Eva Ebner, Helenka Hummel-
Cast: Barbara Sukowa (Rosa Luxemburg), Daniel Olbrychski (Leo Jogiches), Otto Sander (Karl Liebknecht), Adelheid Arndt (Luise Kautsky), Jürgen Holtz (Karl Kautsky), Doris Schade (Clara Zetkin), Hannes Jaenicke (Kostja Zetkin), Jan Paul Biczycki (August Bebel), Karin Baal (Mathilde Jacob), Winfried Glatzeder (Paul Levi), Eva Jaboubkov (Sonja Liebknecht) et al.
Production: Bioskop-Film GmbH, Munich/Project im Filmverlag der Autoren, Munich/Regina Ziegler Film Produktion, West Berlin/Bären-Film, West Berlin /Westdeutscher Rundfunk, Cologne; in collaboration with Studio Barrandov, Prague/ C. S. Filmexport, Prague
Producer: Eberhard Junkersdorf
Location: West Berlin (Studio: Havelchaussee), Prague, Kudna Hora, Karlovy Vary (Czechoslovakia), Lazise (Lake Garda)
Length: 123 min.
Premiere: 4 October 1986 (first commercial screening)
IFF Cannes 1986: Award (Best Actress) to Barbara Sukowa
IFF Karlovy Vary 1986: Honorary Award
German Film Award 1986: Filmband in Gold (Production); Filmband in Gold (Best Actress) to Barbara Sukowa
Guild Award of German Art Film Theaters (Gildepreis deutscher Filmkunsttheater) 1986
GDR Critics' Award 1987 of the Association of Film and TV Artists (Verband der Film- und Fernsehschaffenden) (Best Film for 1986)

1988
Felix. Episode 3: Eva
Direction: Margarethe von Trotta
Screenplay: Margarethe von Trotta
Camera: Franz Rath
Sound: Ernst-Hermann Marell
Editing: Jane Seitz
Production design and costumes: Heidrun Brandt
Assistant director: Uschi Pflügler
Cast: Ulrich Tukur (Felix), Eva Mattes (Eva), Annette Uhlen (Susanne), Nadine Rensing (Child), Brigitte Obermaier (Woman Doppelgänger), Ulrich Mayer (Man at the Bar)
Production: Futura Film GmbH, West Berlin
Producer: Theo Hinz
Location: Hamburg
Length: 18 min.
Premiere: 13 January 1988, Hamburg
The other episodes are by Christel Buschmann, Helke Sander, and Helma Sanders-Brahms; total length of the film: 95 min.

1988
Paura e amore (*Love and Fear*; *Three Sisters*; *Fürchten und Lieben*)
Direction: Margarethe von Trotta
Screenplay: Margarethe von Trotta, Dacia Maraini; based on the stage play *Tri Sestry* (*Three Sisters*) by Anton Chekhov
Camera: Giuseppe Lanci
Music: Franco Piersanti
Sound: Bruno Charrier
Costumes: Nicoletta Ercole
Editing: Enzo Meniconi
Scenery: Giatito Burchiellaro
Production design: Sabina Segatori
Assistant director: Beatrice Banf
Cast: Fanny Ardant (Velia), Greta Scacchi (Maria), Valeria Golino (Sandra), Peter Simonischek (Mas-

simo), Sergio Castellitto (Roberto), Jan Biczicky (Cecchini), et al.
Production: Erre Produzioni S.r.l., Rome/Bioskop-Film GmbH, Munich/Cinemax-Génerale d'Images, Paris
Produced by: Angelo Rizzoli, Eberhard Junkersdorf, André Djaoui
Location: Pavia
Length: 112 min.
Premiere: IFF Cannes 1988
Italian entry for the 1988 Cannes Festival
Nominated for the Federal German Film Award (Bundesfilmpreis) 1989

1990
L'Africaine (*The African Woman*; *The Woman from Africa*; *Die Rückkehr*; *Trois sœurs*)
Direction: Margarethe von Trotta
Screenplay: Margarethe von Trotta
Camera: Tonino Delli Colli
Music: Eleni Karaindrou
Sound: Remo Ugolinelli
Costumes: Nicoletta Ercole
Editing: Nino Baragli
Production design: Antonello Geleng
Assistant director: Beatrice Banfi.
Cast: Barbara Sukowa (Martha), Stefania Sandrelli (Ana), Sami Frey (Victor), Jan Biczicky (Jan), Alexandre Mnouchkine (Andrej), et al.
Production: Scena-Group, Rome/Bioskop-Film, Munich/Rachel Productions, Paris
Producer Camenito, Eberhard Junkersdorf
Location: Rome (Studio), Paris
Length: 105 min.
Premiere: 4 September 1990 (IFF Venice)
Opening film at the Venice Biennale 1990

1993
Il lungo silenzio (*The long silence*; *Zeit des Zorns*; *Le long silence*)
Direction: Margarethe von Trotta
Production and screenplay: Felice Laudadio
Camera: Marco Sperduti
Music: Ennio Morricone
Sound: Remo Ugolinelli
Costumes: Carlo Poggioli
Editing: Ugo de Rossi, Nino Baragli
Production design: Antonello Geleng
Production: Samantha Antonnicola
Assistant director: Béatrice Banfi
Cast: Carla Gravina (Carla Aldrovandi), Jacques Perrin (Marco Canova), Alida Valli (Carla's Mother), Ottavia Piccolo (Rosa), Giuliano Montaldo (Tommasco), Paolo Graziosi (Francesco Manzini), Agnese Nano (Maria Mancini), Ivano Marescotti (Fantoni), Antonella Attili (Fantoni's Wife), Italy/France/FRG
Production: Evento Spettacolo Union P. N./K.G., Rome/Bioskop-Film, Munich
Length: 93 min.
Location: Rome, Ostia
Premiere: Palermo, April 1993
Audience Award IFF Montreal
Best Actress Award of the IFF Montreal to Carla Gravina.
Nomination for the Federal Film Award 1994
Golden Globes in Rome for Carla Gravina, Felice Laudadio, and Ennio Morricone

1994
Das Versprechen (*The Promise*; *Les années du mur*; *La Promesse*)
Direction: Margarethe von Trotta
Screenplay: Margarethe von Trotta, Peter Schneider
Camera: Franz Rath
Music: Jürgen Knieper
Sound: Christian Moldt
Costumes: Petra Kray
Editing: Suzanne Baron
Production design: Benedikt Herforth
Assistant directors: Doris Borkmann, Helenka Hummel
Cast: Meret Becker (Sophie I), Corinna Harfouch (Sophie II), Anian Zollner (Konrad I), August Zirner (Konrad II), Susann Ugé (Barbara I), Eva Mattes (Barbara II), Pierre Besson (Harald I), Hans Kremer (Harald II) et al.
Production: Bioskop-Film, Munich/Odessa-Film, Paris/J. M. H. Productions, Lausanne, Westdeutscher Rundfunk; in collaboration with the Studio Babelsberg, Canal Plus Paris, and CNC Paris
Funded by Eurimages of the Council of Europe
Producer: Eberhard Junkersdorf
Location: Berlin, Potsdam, and Prague
Length: 119 min.
Festival premiere: Competition of the International Film Biennale of Venice (Sept. 1–12, 1994)
First commercial screening: February 1995
Opening film of the IFF Berlin 1995
Bavarian Film Award 1995
German nomination for the Oscar 1995

1997
Winterkind
TV film
Direction: Margarethe von Trotta
Screenplay: Nicole Houwer
Camera: Jörg Widmer
Music: Norbert Schneider
Sound: Udo Steinke
Editing: Inez Regnier
Costumes: Barbara Grupp
Assistant director: Michael Kreindl
Cast: Lena Stolze (Elke Berger), August Zirner (Michael Berger), Susanna Simon (Jelena Uschakowa), Benjamin Kaatz (Boris/Daniel Berger), Joachim Kemmer (Georg Berger), Rolf Ludwig (Jonathan Frey), Lucia Stefanel (Ana), et al.
Production: Colonia Media Film-Produktion GmbH/Cologne, commissioned by Westdeutscher Rundfunk
Producer: Sonja Goslicki
Editing (WDR): Helga Poche
Length: 87 min.
Location: Cologne and environs
First aired: 3 December 1997

1999
Mit fünfzig küssen Männer anders
TV film (series *Lauter tolle Frauen*)
Direction: Margarethe von Trotta
Screenplay: Alistair Beaton und Martin Hennig, based on the novel with the same title by Dorit Zinn
Camera: Stefan Spreer
Music: Konstantin Wecker
Sound: Simon Buchner
Editing: Gaby Grausam
Costumes: Claudia Bobsin
Production design: Barbara Becker
Cast: Senta Berger (Marie), Ulrich Pleitgen (Dietrich), Konstantin Wecker (Gerd), Hans Peter Hallwachs (Eugen), Gerd Warmeling (Udo), Eleonore Weisgerber (Anna), Heinrich Schafmeister (Bernhard), Tina Ruland (Petra), Martin Feifel (Kevin), Edgar Selge (Dr. Heinrich), Daniela Ziegler (Gallery owner), et al.
Production: Regina Ziegler Filmproduktion, Berlin/DEGETO FILM GmbH, commissioned by ARD
Producer: Josef Göhlen
Edited by: Renate Michel
Length: 87 min.
Location: Munich and environs
First aired: 9 April 1999

1999
Dunkle Tage
TV film
Direction: Margarethe von Trotta
Screenplay: Margarethe von Trotta
Camera: Franz Rath
Music: Tom Dokoupol
Sound: Arno Wilms
Editing: Corinna Dietz
Costumes: Marion Boegel
Production design: Naomi Schenck
Cast: Suzanne von Borsody (Angela Rinser), Stefanie Stappenbeck (Felicitas, 17), Siggi Kautz (Max, 15), Steffen Groth (Fabian Groll), Marie-Helen Denhorn (Felicitas, 12), Cornelius Lehmann (Max, 10), Konstantin Wecker (Frieder Rinser), et al.
Production: Colonia Media Film-Produktion GmbH/Cologne, commissioned by Westdeutscher Rundfunk
Producer: Sonja Goslicki
Editing (WDR): Helga Poche
Length: 87 min.
Location: Cologne and environs
First aired: 5 May 1999

Films about Margarethe von Trotta and her work

1979
Margarethe von Trotta. Porträt einer Filmregisseurin
TV portrait
Direction, screenplay: Katja Raganelli
Camera: Konrad Wickler
Film editing: Renate Metzner-Wilde
Sound: Carl H. Aussen
Production: Diorama-Film GmbH, Munich, for WDR, Cologne
Producers: Katja Raganelli, Konrad Wickler
Edited by: Lisa Kraemer
Length: 43 min.
First aired: 15 November 1979, ARD
Excerpts from the films *Der Fangschuß* (*Coup de Grâce*) and *Das zweite Erwachen der Christa Klages* (*The Second Awakening of Christa Klages*); stills from the shooting of *Schwestern oder die Balance des Glücks* (*Sisters or The Balance of Happiness*)

1986
Die Lust zu kämpfen, die Kraft zu lieben. Margarethe von Trotta verfilmt Rosa L.
TV documentary (series: *Deutschlandbilder*)
Direction, screenplay: Heide Mundzeck
Camera, film editing: Wolfgang Fischer
Production: Fischer Film Team, Hamburg, for Westdeutscher Rundfunk, Cologne
Producer: Wolfgang Fischer
Edited by: Helga Märtesheimer
Length: 29 min.
First aired: 18 March 1986, WDR 3

1995
Maria Heiderscheidt im Gespräch mit Margarethe von Trotta
TV portrait (series *Frauenprofile*)
Production: SFB Berlin
Length: 30 min

1995
Die Neugier immer weitertreiben: Die filmische Befreiung der Margarethe von Trotta
Film essay with interviews
Direction, screenplay: Peter Buchka
Camera: Claus Gottschall
Narrator: Hans-Jürgen Stockerl
Edited by: Hubert von Spreti
Production: Kick-Film, Munich
Length: 60. min.
Excerpts from the films *Das zweite Erwachen der Christa Klages* (*The Second Awakening of Christa Klages*), *Schwestern oder Die Balance des Glücks* (*Sisters or The Balance of Happiness*), *Die bleierne Zeit* (*Marianne und Juliane*), *Heller Wahn* (*Sheer Madness*), *Rosa Luxemburg*, *Paura e amore* (*Love and Fear*), *L'Africaine* (*The African Woman*), *Das Versprechen* (*The Promise*)

Bibliogaphy (selection)

Screenplays and material

Volker Schlöndorff and Margarethe von Trotta, *Die verlorene Ehre der Katharina Blum*, transcript by Andrea Park, Tübingen 1981.
Peter Schneider and Margarethe von Trotta, *Das Versprechen oder Der lange Atem der Liebe*, Berlin 1994.
»Margarethe von Trotta, *Schwestern oder Die Balance des Glücks*«, ed. by Willi Bär and Hans Jürgen Weber, Frankfurt am Main 1979.
Margarethe von Trotta, *Die bleierne Zeit*, ed. by Hans Jürgen Weber, Frankfurt am Main 1981.
Margarethe von Trotta, *Heller Wahn*, Frankfurt 1983.
Margarethe von Trotta, *Die bleierne Zeit und andere Filmtexte*, ed. by Günter Agde, Berlin 1988.
Margarethe von Trotta, Christiane Ensslin, *Rosa Luxemburg. Das Buch zum Film*, Nördlingen 1986.
Margarethe von Trotta, Luisa Francia, *Das zweite Erwachen der Christa Klages*, Frankfurt 1980.

Interviews and conversations

»Natürlich will ich verführen«, in: *Stern*, no 7, 7 Feb. 1995, Hamburg.
Als Frau ist es wohl leichter Mensch zu sein: Gespräche mit Dorothee Sölle, Margarethe von Trotta u. a., Reinbek near Hamburg 1984.
»Rote Augen im Kino«, in: *Der Spiegel*, no. 4, 24 Jan. 1994, Hamburg, pp. 180–82.
»Entretien avec Margarethe von Trotta«, in: *Jeune Cinéma*, no. 138, Nov. 1981, Paris, pp. 21–23.
Edwin Elliker, »Erinnern und Vergessen«, in: *Film & Ton Magazin*, no. 12, 27 Dec. 1981, Munich, pp. 51–53.
Marli Feldvoß, »Dieses spiegelverkehrte Leben«, in: *EPD-Film*, no. 1, Jan. 1991, Frankfurt/Main, pp. 24–29.
Renate Fischetti, »Großes Erzählkino mit neuen Inhalten«, in: *Das neue Kino – Acht Porträts von deutschen Regisseurinnen*, Dülmen-Hiddingsel 1992, pp. 151–174.
Reiner Frey, Christian Göldenberg, »Rebellinnen wider eine bleierne Zeit«, in: *Filmfaust*, no. 24, Oct./ Nov. 1981, Frankfurt/Main, pp. 30–36.
Margret Köhler, »Lernprozesse. Gespräch mit Margarethe von Trotta«, in: *Film-Dienst*, no. 16, 1993, Cologne, pp. 4–7.
Christa Maerker, »Was ich sagen möchte, kann ich so billig sagen. Gespräch mit Margarethe von Trotta und Helke Sander«, in: Hans Günther Pflaum, *Jahrbuch Film* 78/79, Munich/Vienna 1978.
Renate Möhrmann, »Margarethe von Trotta. Gespräch«, in: Renate Möhrmann, *Die Frau mit der Kamera*, Munich/Vienna 1980.
André Müller, »Ich weiß nicht, wo es mich hintreibt«, in: *Die Zeit*, 11 July 1986, Hamburg; republished in: Sam T. Cohen et al., *André Müller im Gespräch mit Rosa von Praunheim*, Hamburg 1989, pp. 106–116.
Ulla Schirmeyer-Klein, »Die Kraft der Utopie und der Frauenfilm: ein Gespräch mit Margarethe von Trotta und Luisa Francia zu ihrem neuen Film ›Das zweite Erwachen der Christa Klages‹«, in: *Film & Ton Magazin*, June 1978, Munich, pp. 68/69.
Bion Steinborn, »Heller Wahn«, in: *Filmfaust*, no. 32, Feb./March 1983, Frankfurt/Main, 35/39.
Joseph Treen, »The Lady Behind the Lens«, in: *Newsweek*, May 5, 1982, New York.
Margarethe von Trotta, Christel Buschmann, »Gespräch zwischen Margarethe von Trotta und Christel Buschmann«, in: *Frauen und Film*, no. 8, Berlin 1976.

General articles in books, journals and newspapers

Jutta Brückner, »Für Margarethe von Trotta«, in: Peter Schneider / Margarethe von Trotta, *Das Versprechen oder Der lange Atem der Liebe*, Berlin 1994, pp. 150–159.
Wolf Donner, »Blick für Frauen«, in: *Zeit-Magazin*, no. 17, 13 Nov. 1981, Hamburg.
Martin Donougho, Margarethe von Trotta, »Gynemaguery and the Dilemmas of a Filmmaker«, in: *Literature, Film Quarterly*, vol. 17, no. 3, 1989, Salesbury/Maryland, pp. 149–160.
Thomas Elsaesser, »Mother Courage and the Divided Daughter«, in: *The British Film Institute, Monthly Film Bulletin*, July 1983, London, pp. 176 to 178.
Thomas Elsaesser, *Der neue deutsche Film*, Munich 1994, pp. 312–320.
Christian Gollup, »Volker Schlöndorff and Margarethe von Trotta. Transcending the Genres«, in: Klaus Phillips, *New German Filmmakers*, New York 1984, pp. 266–302.
Claudia Hoff, »Margarethe von Trotta, Schauspielerin, Regisseurin«, in: *CineGraph*, no. 10, mit einer Filmo- und Bibliographie von Gerke Dunkhase, Munich 1988.
Raimund Hoghe, »Balanceversuch einer Rebellin«, in: *Die Zeit*, 8 May 1981, Hamburg.
Barbara Koenig Quart, *Women Directors. The Emergence of a New Cinema*, New York 1988, pp. 93–128.
Hans Bernhard Moeller, »The Films of Margarethe von Trotta: Domination, Violence, Solidarity and Social Criticism«, in: *Women in German Yearbook*, 2, London 1986, pp. 129–149.
Hans-Bernhard Moeller, »West German Women's Cinema: The Case of Margarethe von Trotta«, in: *Film Criticism*, no. 1/2, 1984, Meadville/Pennsylvania, pp. 11–26.
Alfred Nemeczek, »Die Blonde mit dem festen Blick«, in: *Der Stern*, no. 45, 28 Oct. 1976, Hamburg.
Maria Ratschewa, (ed.), »Margarethe von Trotta«, in: *Kulturreferat der Landeshauptstadt München*, Munich 1985.
Wolfram Schütte, »An Editing Room of One's Own«, in: *Artforum*, Nov. 1985, New York, pp. 66–72 .
Hans-Dieter Seidel, *Film als Ausdruck eines anderen Ichs: Margarethe von Trotta*, in: *FAZ-Magazin*, no. 71, 10 July 1981, Frankfurt/Main, pp. 7 to 9.

Reviews of individual films

»Tschechow in Pavia«, in: *Frankfurter Allgemeine Zeitung*, 18 May 1988, Frankfurt/Main.
Peter Boris, »Der arme Büffel und der Klassenfeind«, in: *Die Welt*, 15 Apr. 1986, Berlin.
Peter Buchka, »Die Balance des Unglücks«, in: *Süddeutsche Zeitung*, 7 Sept. 1990, Munich.
Peter Buchka, »Die Mauer im Kopf«, in: *Süddeutsche Zeitung*, 9 Feb. 1995, Munich.
Barton Byg, »German History and Cinematic Convention Harmonizes in Margarethe von Trotta's ›Marianne and Juliane‹«, in: S. Frieden, R. Mc Cormick et al., *Gender and German Cinema*, vol. II, Oxford, England 1993, pp. 259–271.
Daniel Cetinich, »Who's the Terrorist in West Germany?: ›The Lost Honor of Katharina Blum‹«, in: *Jump Cut*, no. 19, Dec. 1978, Berkeley, California, pp. 4–5.
John Coleman, »Films: Dead Ends«, in: *New Statesman*, 13 May 1977, London, p. 650.
John Coleman, »Films: Under the Skin«, in: *New Statesman*, 14 May 1982, London, pp. 29–30.
Sonia Dayan-Herzbrun, »Rosa la Rouge avec les ›Verts‹?«, in: *Cinéma 86*, no. 372, 15–21 Oct. 1986, Paris, p. 3.
Charlotte Delorme, »On the film ›Juliane and Marianne‹ by Margarethe von Trotta«, in: *Journal of Film and Video*, no. 2, 1985, River Forest/Illinois, pp. 47–51.
Lisa di Caprio, »›Marianne and Juliane/The German Sisters‹«, in: *Jump Cut*, no. 29, Feb. 1984, Berkeley, California, pp. 56–59.
Wolf Donner, »Der lüsterne Meinungsterror«, in: *Die Zeit*, 10 Oct. 1975, Hamburg, p. 44.
Wolf Egger, »Reinventing Rosa«, in: *The Nation*, 25 Apr. 1987, New York, pp. 546–549.
Thomas Elsaesser, »Schwestern oder Die Balance des Glücks« (Sisters or The Balance of Happiess), in: *Monthly Film Bulletin*, July 1983, London, pp. 175–176.
Lucy Fischer, *Shot/Countershot: Film Tradition and Women's Cinema*, Princeton, New Jersey 1984, pp. 205–215.
Jill Forbes, »Heller Wahn« (Friends and Husbands), in: Monthly Film Bulletin, Aug. 1983, London, pp. 214–215.
Lester D. Friedman, »Cinematic Techniques in ›The Lost Honour of Katharina Blum‹«, in: *Literature, Film Quarterly*, no. 3, 1979, Salisbury, Maryland, pp. 244–252.
Rainer Gansera, »Zeit des Zorns«, in: *EPD-Film*, no. 2, Frankfurt/Main 1991, pp. 32/33.
Molly Haskell, »Arts/Media: Women's Friendships«, in: *MS*, no. 12, Dec. 1983, Marion, Ohio, p. 23+(2p).
Annette Insdorf, »Film: von Trotta: By Sisters Obsessed«, in: *New York Times*, 31 Jan. 1982, New York, Sec. 2, p. 19+(2p).
Annette Insdorf, »Rosa Luxemburg: More than a Revolutionary«, in: *New York Times*, 31 May 1987, New York, Sec. 2, p. 17.
Sheila Johnston, »The German Sisters«, in: *Film & Filming*, no. 334, July 1982, London, pp. 25–26.
E. Ann Kaplan, »Film Review: ›Marianne and Juliane‹: Politics and the Family«, in: *Social Policy*, summer 1982, New York, pp. 54–56.
E. Ann Kaplan, »Discourses on Terrorism, Feminism, and the Family in von Trotta's ›Marianne and Juliane‹«, in: *Persistence of Vision*, no. 2, Autumn 1985, Maspeth, New York, pp. 61–68. Republished in: Janet Todd, *Women and Film, Women & Literature*, vol. 4, New York 1988, pp. 258–270.
E. Ann Kaplan, »Female Politics in the Symbolic Realm: Von Trotta's ›Marianne and Juliane‹«, in: E. Ann Kaplan, *Women and Film. Both Sides of the Camera*, New York 1983.
Stanley Kauffmann, »Stanley Kauffmann On Films: A Large Life«, in: *New Republic*, 18 May 1987, Washington D.C., pp. 24–25 .
Stanley Kauffmann, »Seen Twice«, in: *New Republic*, 30 May 1994, Washington D.C., pp. 28 to 29.
Stanley Kauffmann, »A German Gem«, in: *New Republic*, 10 Feb. 1982, Washington D. C., pp. 24–25.
Stanley Kauffmann, »Stanley Kauffmann On Films: Strictures and Stresses«, in: *New Republic*, 21 Sept. 1985, Washington D. C., pp. 24–26.
Philip Kemp, »Season of Mists«, in: *Sight & Sound*, no. 1, Jan. 1991, London, p. 67.
Andreas Kilb, »Zahme Herzen«, in: *Die Zeit*, 17 Feb. 1995, Hamburg.
Eva Kissin, »Rosa Luxemburg«, in: *Films in Review*, Nov. 1987, New York, pp. 549–550.
Margret Köhler, Erwin Schaar, »Deutsche Trennung und individuelles Schicksal«, in: *Medien und Erziehung*, no. 1, 1995, Munich, pp. 30–33.
Horst Peter Koll, »Das Versprechen/Filmkritik«, in: *Film-Dienst*, no. 3, 1995, Cologne, pp. 26 to 27.
Anna Kuhn, »Margarethe von Trotta's Sisters: Interiority or Engagement?«, in: *Women in German Yearbook*, 1, London 1985, pp. 77–84.
Anna Kuhn, »A Heroine for Our Time: Margarethe von Trotta's ›Rosa Luxemburg‹«, in: S. Frieden, R. Mc Cormick et al., *Gender and German Cinema*, vol. II, Oxford 1993, pp. 163–184.
Elke Kummer, »Diskussion«, in: *EPD-Film*, no. 5, Nov. 1989, Frankfurt/Main, p. 41.
Jörg Magenau, »Poesiealbum der Geschichte«, in: *Berlinale 95*, no. 7, 10 Feb. 1995, Berlin.
Renate Möhrmann, »The Second Awakening of Christa Klages«, in: S. Frieden, R. Mc Cormick, et al., *Gender and German Cinema*, vol. I, Oxford/England 1993, pp. 73–83.
Barbara Möller, »Mafia ohne Paten und Killer«, in: *Rheinischer Merkur*, 21 Jan. 1994, Bonn.
Roswitha Müller, »Images in Balance (The Cat Has Nine Lives, Sisters)«, in: S. Frieden, R. Mc Cormick et al., *Gender and German Cinema*, vol.I, Oxford/England 1993, pp. 59 to 72.
Hans-Günther Pflaum, »Noch mehr Schwestern«, in: *Süddeutsche Zeitung*, 29 Sept. 1988, Munich.
A. Philippon, »Heller Wahn«, in: *Cahiers du Cinéma*, no. 353, Nov. 1983, Paris, pp. 62/63.
Dietmar Polaczek, »Die stille Grausamkeit«, in: *Frankfurter Allgemeine Zeitung*, 28 Jan. 1994, Frankfurt/Main.
Richard Porton, »Rosa Luxemburg«, in: *Film Quarterly*, no. 2, 1989, Berkeley, California, pp. 39– 42.
Manuela Reichart, »Bilder? Beweise?«, in: *Die Zeit*, 2 Oct. 1981, Hamburg.
Carrie Rickey, »The Sisters Grimm: Women and Power Relations«, in: *Village Voice*, 3/9 Feb. 1982, New York, p. 44.
Andrew Sarris, »Films In Focus: What Do Women Want?«, in: *Village Voice*, 24 Sept. 1985, New York, p. 59.
Daniel Sauvaget, »Les années de plomb«, in: *Revue du Cinéma*, no. 372, (May 1982), Paris, pp. 29 to 31.
Ulla Schirmeyer-Klein, »Von der Kraft zum Widerstand«, in: *Film & Ton Magazin*, no. 24, June 1978, Munich, 67.
Ernst Schumacher, »Zwei Schritte vorwärts, ein Schritt zurück«, in: *Film & Fernsehen*, no. 10, 1986, Berlin (GDR), pp. 12–17.
Georg Seeßlen, »Fürchten und Lieben«, in: *EPD-Film*, no. 9, 1988, Frankfurt/Main, pp. 30/31.
Hans-Dieter Seidel, »Spiegelungen der Seele«, in: *Frankfurter Allgemeine Zeitung*, 5 Sept. 1990, Frankfurt/Main.
Hans-Dieter Seidel, »Die heikle Balance des Glücks«, in: *Frankfurter Allgemeine Zeitung*, 29 Sept. 1988, Frankfurt/Main.
Hans-Dieter Seidel, »Die Illusion der Mauer«, in: *Frankfurter Allgemeine Zeitung*, 11 Feb. 1995, Frankfurt/Main.
Stefan Seifert, »Mafia im Film«, in: *Filmwärts*, no. 30, June 1994, Hannover, pp. 45–48.
Ellen Seiter, »The Political Is Personal: Margarethe von Trotta's ›Marianne and Juliane‹«, in: *Journal of Film and Video*, no. 2, 1985, River Forest, Illinois, pp. 41–46 .
Daniel Serceau, Jean-Louis Cros, Daniel Sauvaget, Danièle Parra, »Margarethe von Trotta«, in: *Revue du Cinéma*, no. 388, Nov. 1983, Paris, pp. 34–40.
Robert Sklar, Adrienne Harris, »Marianne and Juliane«, in: *Cineaste*, no. 3, 1983, New York, pp. 41–44.
Karl Heinz Vosgerau, »Die verlorene Ehre der Katharina Blum«, in: Robert Fischer, Joe Hembus, *Der neue deutsche Film 1960–1980*, Munich 1981, pp. 109–112.
Martha Wallach, »Ideal and Idealized Victims: The Lost Honor of the Marquise von O., Effi Briest and Katharina Blum in Prose and Film«, in: *Women in Germany, Yearbook* 1, London 1985, pp. 61–75.
David Wilson, »Paura e amore (Three sisters)«, in: *Monthly Film Bulletin*, Feb. 1991, London, pp. 53/54.
Karsten Witte, »Preis der Ohnmacht«, in: *Die Zeit*, no. 5, 28 Jan. 1994, Hamburg.

General literature

Thomas Elsaesser, *New German Cinema: A History*, London 1983.
Julia Knight, *Women and the German Cinema*, London/New York 1990.
Anette Kuhn and Susannah Radstone, *Women in Film. An International Guide*, New York 1991.
Claudia Lenssen, »Women's Cinema in Germany«, in: *Jump Cut*, no. 29, Feb. 1994, Berkeley, Cal. 1984.